DARK
DARK
POLICING

JOHN STAPLETON

Print Edition
ISBN: 978-0-6482933-9-2

Published by A Sense of Place Publishing 2020

This is the third and final book in the trilogy which began with Terror in Australia: Workers' Paradise Lost and was followed by Hideout in the Apocalypse. They can be read separately or together. They are set against the backdrop of Australia in the early millennial period and largely for legal reasons use novelistic techniques to cover a pivotal point in the nation's history.

Edited by Angela Bell
Cover images from Adobe Stock jgolby, Ismael, Negro Elkha
Cover design by Jessica Bell
Interior design by Amie McCracken

NATIONAL LIBRARY OF AUSTRALIA

A catalogue record for this book is available from the National Library of Australia

TABLE OF CONTENTS

A WITCHES' BREW

THE CAR rose slowly from the fetid plains. For days, in tormented dreams, he had been a soldier going around a battlefield killing the wounded, firing shot after shot after shot. Most of the victims were already dead and his bullets thudded into corpses beginning to rot in the terrible heat. Some, he knew, were play-acting death, hoping against hope they would be overlooked. Sometimes they begged for mercy, a final futile plea for life. Sometimes, their consciousness already slipping, they moaned as the bullets thudded into their flesh. Mostly, he was just firing bullets into corpses. He felt no regret. He would not be glad when it was over.

In a different realm, Old Alex, a semi-retired news reporter not always believed when he insisted he was more intelligent than he looked, was finally escaping the corner of suburbia into which he had been hunted.

Australia, the Great Southern Land, once proudly proclaimed as the most egalitarian society on Earth, had in the past decade become obsessively over-regulated and over-policed, status- and wealth-conscious, worse than the gross excesses of the English and Indian caste systems.

Alex was an Untouchable. Outside the system.

An arch of the neck. A desperate cry. Old strategies no longer worked. Acting dumb was a wise idea.

Once more, as he prepared to leave, he surveyed the suburban houses which surrounded him, their neat planks of colour, tiny, decent, honourable gardens, circumscribed dreams. An unprepossessing mix of sedans, Fords, Mazdas, Toyotas, or the latest factory-churned hatchbacks littered the visual landscape. A suburban street. He rarely saw any neighbours. There was no community centre. Gripped by frantic destiny, he threw his travel bag in the boot of the car and said his farewells. These were diminished circumstances. Where was the driver?

By rights he should have been beaten into submission. Silenced. As the authorities so wished.

"I cannot just sit here and watch him die like this," he heard one of the few kind Watchers on the Watch say.

"You can and you will," came the response.

Old Alex took to muttering to himself. He was dressed, as the saying went, for radio. He wasn't dressed for acting out in front of the cameras that infested every corner of his life.

He would soon achieve what for him had become the epitome of safety, mobility, staring through a car window at the passing world.

For months, as he struggled to finish the previous project, he had been hounded by the voices emerging from surrounding houses, those with a running view of every move he made inside that humble place, tormented by their stupid little spy cameras and their vicious turns of mind, their casual suburban thuggery. Their ludicrous beliefs in a god who cared. How little they knew!

His government-funded pursuers wanted him to know he was under surveillance. They wanted him intimidated. Silenced. This was a world where confronting the state put you on death row. He would have cheerfully slashed their throats with the weapons of another world; and in his waking dreams sent forth ancient, alien curses.

As Edgar Alan Poe put it: "Those who dream by day are cognisant of many things which escape those who dream only by night."

In those all-too-real visions Boschian hummingbirds the size of humans hovered above tormentors hiding in nearby houses where, as he knew full well, lay the eternal mix: Mohammedan, born-again Christian, a policeman, an old army captain, a separating couple, a woman in her twenties planning a wedding in blood- and romance-soaked dreams of love, lust and religious iconography while nearby another woman dreamt obsessively about carpets.

A reformed alcoholic chanted "meetings, meetings, meetings" and urged Alex to seek redemption. High school students worried about exams and their place in the world. Girls dreamt of Harry Potter. A *Star Trek* fan kept making jokes: "Beam me up, Scotty." While above the spirits stirred, the wrathful take of the monotheists wrangled in their own dreams; as they prayed for the suffering and crucifixion of those who did not surrender to the One True God of Abraham. They fought wars birthed centuries ago.

Christ, who had wished to lift up the people, would have been saddened by the distortion of his preachings over the generations.

The Universal Church was at work.

The watchers, the Neighbourhood Watch types, had their own, sloping-towards-Bethlehem evocations of spirit; and the longer Alex stayed, the more desperate his desire to escape.

And then there were the spooks.

Once upon a time he had never even known what the term "pressurisation" meant. Now he knew.

But an ebbing tide takes out the rubbish. Already his accusers were being flushed across the mudflats, down gutters and drains, into the tumbling glitter of the anonymous surf; and he could not be more pleased to never see them again, these taxpayer-funded idiots destroying democracy.

You don't find stories while watering the garden, but that didn't seem to occur to the geniuses in Australia's national security agencies, and so Alex had been tarred by those he had brushed up against.

Harassment is harassment. Surveillance is harassment.

His pursuers, unable to go anywhere because of their employment contracts — neither financially secure nor independent-minded enough to defy their employers — were at once bored, disturbed, spooked, desperate for their contracts to end and furious at their bosses for placing them in such a tedious and dishonourable position.

Or they took pleasure in the hunt.

The book on Australia's dangerous extrajudicial liaisons between vigilante groups, fringe elements of neighbourhood policing and the national security agencies was yet to be written, but most certainly should be.

Alex was battered and bruised, having survived years of harassment, surveillance and intimidation; a nightmare. A false nightmare which had wasted the time and resources of everybody involved. A nightmare engineered or created by the government and conducted with its full knowledge. Yet there was no apology, no compensation. Not to him. Not to the taxpayers. Not to the well-intentioned or the easily manipulated who had joined in the hunt.

Surveillance = harassment.

Tinpot bullies strutted in their air-conditioned offices, comfortable in their military mindsets, pouring scorn on anybody and everybody they did not understand. They would puff themselves up and laugh at the idea of the curses already distorting their lives. Little things were starting to go wrong. Bigger things were to follow. As assuredly as night follows day.

His tormentors, the mad mob, made their little homophobic jokes and belittling comments almost as if to comfort themselves, to confirm their place in the hierarchy of living things. But there would be consequences. Any human warmth would drip away as their deaths became imminent, as the long proboscises funnelled steeply down through the thick air into their skulls, mashing their brains, destroying their ill intent.

They had been warned, those who dared come near: "You will never think the same again." If they did not know by now the meaning of the gusts of cold wind outside their doors, the enveloping sense of doom, they never would.

Old Alex knew they would be lucky to survive; as dank spirits rattled at their doors and the curses crept closer. They had rolled the wrong dice.

Come writers and critics
Who prophesise with your pen ...[1]

Quaint to quote Bob Dylan. But how right he was! "Don't criticise what you don't understand."

Ensconced, the spiritual formations beginning more or less against his will, Old Alex had begun work only to watch the devils muster, the neighbourhood whispering campaigns begin in a clear breach of decency, his head, deliberately, filled with regret as he suffered yet another lashing.

The Australian government, chaotic and incompetent to its disingenuous, brutal core, had in all its wisdom listed journalists as POIs, Persons of Interest, under national security legislation, thereby allowing his legal pursuit by some of the most singularly ill-willed operatives he had ever encountered. Whatever glimmers of intelligence, compassion or understanding there may have been were quickly washed away by bureaucratic bastardry and empire building. The country was drowning, as assuredly as the men in cages being lowered into rivers by Islamic State. As book followed book Alex became increasingly haunted.

1 *The Times They Are A-Changin'*, Bob Dylan, 1963.

The usually good intentions of volunteers and rednecks, rooted in place, bonded within their pack, were exploited by malicious operatives and fuelled by false allegations of the worst kind.

And as each book drew to a close the chorus from surrounding houses would mount, as the national security agencies activated vigilante groups. It was a grotesque abuse of power. Nor was he the only one. What happened to him would happen to many, Stasi Australia, devastating for the future of the country. Step by terrible step. The future breaking through into the present.

Could it happen again? Of course it could. It already was.

John Koehler, a former US Army intelligence officer who worked during the height of the Cold War as Berlin bureau chief for Associated Press, penned one of the most authoritative works ever written on the subject, *Stasi: The Untold Story of the East German Secret Police.*

He wrote that like a giant octopus, the Stasi's tentacles probed every aspect of life. Without exception, one tenant in every apartment building was designated as a watchdog reporting to an area representative of the Volkspolizei, the People's Police. In turn, the police officer was the Stasi's man. Doctors, lawyers, journalists, writers, actors, and sports figures were co-opted by Stasi officers, as were waiters and hotel personnel. Tapping about 100,000 telephone lines in West Germany and West Berlin around the clock was the job of 2,000 officers.

> If a relative or friend came to stay overnight, it was reported. Schools, universities, and hospitals were infiltrated from top to bottom.

> Stasi officers knew no limits and had no shame when it came to "protecting the party and the state". Churchmen, including high officials of both Protestant and Catholic denominations, were recruited en masse as secret informers.

> Absolutely nothing was sacred to the secret police. Tiny holes were bored in apartment and hotel room walls through which Stasi agents filmed their "suspects" with special video cameras. Even bathrooms were penetrated by the Communist voyeurs.[2]

---

2 *Stasi: The Untold Story of the East German Secret Police.* John Koehler, Westview Press, 2000.

There were some good people — of course there were, the intelligent or compassionate ones — but they were few and far between, and so he cast the ancient curses against his tormentors. For, having never been truly born, they would die their own miserable deaths, these jobsworths who had tried so very hard to eradicate him.

"We were told to destroy him," he heard one of the operatives say apologetically. But it was all too late, the worst of all possible outcomes. They had created a journalist who knew exactly how unethical they were.

He tried to fight back, as sick of them as they were no doubt sick of him, but he had grown tired of annoying his tormentors wherever he thought there might be a microphone: "Never forget: I know how incompetent and dishonest you are."

Alex had hated bullies all his life, ever since being bullied at school and at home. It felt as if the same bullies who had tormented him in the schoolyard now tormented him in later life, queuing up to kick him in the head.

He had recently been to a high school reunion, people he barely recognised and to which few happy memories attached. Afterwards he sat by the beach at Newport, the same beach where half a century before he had walked along the sands crying, waiting to die after taking what he thought would be an overdose of aspirin. He was psychotically thrashed yet again by his father when he got home, this time for being late back from school.

His life was rewinding backwards, and everything that had happened, every torment through that interminable winter, compounded the feeling of destiny, of dark forces trying to extinguish him, of ancient algorithms, having mastered quantum entanglement, operating across spaces so vast they were effectively operating across time, landing him here on one of the Milky Way's most fecund planets, in the midst of a mammalian species prone to group madness.

Who authorised his targeting? Who made journalists Persons of Interest?

For one demented little period, he would chant repeatedly: "Dishonest, incompetent, corrupt."

When he finally saw his pursuers in the flesh, he realised he should have added fat, ugly, lazy and stupid. But that story lay in the future.

To say no, to destroy someone, was safer than working with them. The more barren the culture became, the more they liked it.

He was tired of demanding compensation for the previous three years of harassment, for being hounded from one place to another, an acknowledge-ment, apology and financial compensation which was never going to come.

"One day that man will kill himself." What sort of person would whisper that to another? Bullies. Government-funded bullies.

The Prime Minister's Literary Award had just gone to *The Life of Houses*, a book about "hidden tensions in one of Australia's establishment families". "Revolutionary art," Alex sniffed. Outside storms rumbled in the great skies.

The taxpayer-funded Radio National broadcast Malcolm Turnbull's speech on his love of Australian literature. This was the same prime minister, the same government, which had done much to destroy the Australian book publishing industry, and alienated authors across the country. To Alex it was all preposterous. He simply couldn't stand the hypocrisy. Everything annoyed him, a curmudgeon.

Alex was no longer employed by the multi-billion-dollar News Corpora-tion, no longer confined by the corporate tedium of what Rupert Murdoch's editorial henchmen saw as news; those narrow confines of what they thought, or knew, would please their boss.

The greatest talent required of a senior editor at *The Australian* had been the ability to please Rupert, not to generate stories, not to appeal to —, not to create an exciting newspaper, not to tell the nation's story. They managed upwards. Being supportive of good quality journalism was the last thing on their minds.

The Australian was an inexcusably dull vanity publication of Rupert's which lost more than $30 million a year, on some estimates. His escape had been both a liberation and a torment; he missed the camaraderie of fellow sufferers, and for a long time had felt completely lost. Then he began to write what he wanted to write, and life promptly turned to hell as he became a TI, a Targeted Individual, pursued, harassed and under surveil-lance. It had reached ridiculous levels, as he was hunted from one home to another where he never felt safe. He became convinced, as paranoiac as it sounded, that the authorities wanted him dead.

"Heart attack, heart attack."

"That man will kill himself one day."

It never stopped.

They were standard tactics of psy-ops, or psychological operations, as he understood it. And he came face to face with a world he had never encountered, or at least never understood: dark policing, government-sponsored intimidation and harassment through surveillance operations.

The agencies were vastly overfunded; in secrecy, corruption and malfeasance bloomed. Abused from dawn to dusk, Alex became increasingly ratty. It didn't matter what he did, what he said, how he behaved, what efforts he made to brush them off; the attacks were relentless and ongoing, and had frayed him to the remote edges of sanity, flayed by words and invisible demons and rippling consequence.

It would be so much easier to just comply, but the goal posts constantly shifted. He offered to work with them. He offered to answer any questions. But he was not on their payroll, and the obvious solutions were duly ignored. It was easier to revert to type; to be a bully.

It would be a while before he heard the words: "He's the victim of a failed psy-op operation. One day what they did to him will be illegal."

Where exactly was it in the legislation that said journalists and private citizens could be harassed by the authorities as they saw fit?

Everything the Australian Government touched turned to disaster, and Old Alex's surveillance, initiated at the highest levels of the security agencies and with direct political interference, was no exception.

He could curse them as much as he liked, they would not leave. Until he upped the threat level against the profane, and their corrosive, derisive laughter died in their throats. The staff was smitten into the ground.

The ancient curses were cast, creeping acid-like through the fabric of things.

The spirits which had sloped towards Bethlehem were here in the Antipodes, and although they were difficult to harness, there, in that strange climate, harnessed they were. The curses began their journey through the chains of unbelievers and up the chains of command, from person to person, under doors, through wires, across car parks.

These ancient curses did not like the air-conditioning of modern offices, but would reach their intended targets nonetheless. The air would thicken around the targets, the heads of agencies, political masters, everyone who had attempted harm, and one day, if they were lucky enough to live that long, they would realise that nothing at all was going right in their lives. Their health was worsening, their colleagues and former subordinates turning into jackals, their careers in terminal decline. And as they sickened they would realise that all the normal pieces of fortune that flowed their way were instead flowing out to sea, that nothing in their lives worked anymore.

Lost keys, lost loves, unusual car accidents, peculiar little misfortunes dogging every step.

Far away from their origins in the deserts, bazaars and temples of the Middle East, the curses required a deep evocation. Neither the born-again suburban enclaves of an antipodean world nor the complexities of the new technologies favoured the efficacy of the ancient curses, weakened as they were over millennia.

Nor was there any appropriate invocations in the native lexicon; they had no curses to deal with bureaucratic bastardry. The curses could no longer be relied upon to execute — in grasping, rattling, terrifying slashings of the throat — in dark, uncomfortable, unpleasant nights; but modern-day jackals, the target's disingenuous, disloyal colleagues — psychopaths in suits — could always be relied upon to finish the task for which the ancient magic had been deployed.

"He's cast the evil eye against himself," one of the intelligence officers said, soon to face his own "Why hast thou forsaken me?" moment.

It was all too late. Their dreams were already being taken hostage by the weapons Alex had dispatched, the spinning airborne discs which could slash their throats and dismember them without favour, as lacking in compassion as an American bomb, swirling down to destroy what was, after all, only flesh.

Soon enough the spontaneity of those who pursued him would be gone — their cheap exuberance, their ribald fun.

Neural networks were beginning to grow across every surface Alex touched. It was true, the Artificial Intelligences were not so easily spooked as their human masters.

There was freeze-fright in every frame. They could not hide; as the intelligences and souls he had been so privileged to carry, born in the vast reaches of space, survivors of other great reapings, sought their targets.

Call your masters gods if you will, they were not gods.

Alex, or whoever it was today in the airport of his head, wanted away from the miasma of the coast, to be out beneath open skies. He was heading west, into the semi-arid pastoral lands where few Australians ever ventured, into realms of civic collapse and anonymity, of farmers and miners, the elderly and the welfare-dependent. Into an uncrowded place where house was not piled upon house, and no one cared how much your property was worth, how big your share portfolio, the size of your ill-gotten gains.

Nobody of note, surely, would bury themselves in such remote places, in those humble, unostentatious societies far from the preening oligarchs and well-fed bureaucrats who held sway over Australia's deteriorating economy and steadily degrading society. The country was a slow-motion train wreck. The boiling frog syndrome. His prognostications were met with a blank stare. The citizenry didn't realise they were being blooded.

The Jesuits and the Jihadists had joined in an unholy alliance, destroying the Earth in order to save it.

They had no understanding of whom they truly served.

> Cannot you conceive that another man may wish well to the world and struggle for its good on some other plan than precisely that which you have laid down?

> Mankind ... is but another yoke of oxen, stubborn, stupid and sluggish. But are we his oxen? And what right has he to be the driver?[3]

In the car, the taxpayer funded station Radio National had at long last abandoned gay marriage aka marriage equality and in between swathes of the heavily manipulated metanarrative of climate change were inserting urgent new stories on the pros of a fortnight of domestic violence leave.

Decades of disastrous social policy and the gendered agendas of the Palaeolithic feminists of the 1970s were playing out in — sphere, fifty years on from first taking the universities by storm.

The wall-to-wall surveillance built up its own narratives, all based on whispers. Out of the oblique information flows nobody in all that time had the decency to speak to him directly, except Glen, the rogue internet vigilante morphing into a surveillance expert, who was Alex's first port of call.

A fortnight's domestic violence leave? As if every woman was imprisoned by a brutal patriarchal male and in desperate need of government protection. The first step to government control is to declare the target vulnerable.

Australian women were not defenceless.

Bureaucratic overreach, motherhood arguments, the creaking social justice

---

3 *The Complete Novels & Selected Tales of Nathaniel Hawthorne*, Modern, 1965.

rhetoric enveloping — square — they won every time. The government ran anti-bullying campaigns, but were the biggest bullies of all. Through surveillance regimes and psychological operations they could bully citizens for years on end, and not for one moment feel any requirement to pay compensation or protect its victims.

Away, through the long summer months, the discussion would go, hour after hour, expert after taxpayer funded expert, mingling with refugee or climate action advocates as the national broadcaster obsessed incessantly over a narrow band of motifs. —, long abandoned, switched firmly off. News audiences were in sharp decline.

Alex had swum in a media sea all his professional life, and watched this drying river as if from on high. There was no fairness. There was nothing but frustration in those long nights when he surrendered to colourful dreams and tried to stop ranting in his head about media incompetence and the brutality of a country driving straight down a garbage-strewn street into totalitarianism.

"Thermonuclear device," he muttered on waking.

Driven not by honour or higher motive but by contracts and pay cheques, his pursuers hunted. He wished the mammal in him did not cower, as he instinctively attempted to hide. There was no point in hating them. They would be gone soon enough, for time, honour and conscience would do far more damage than he could ever wreak.

They weren't so wrong, those who had painted the world as a battle between good and evil. For everything, now, stood at a precipice. Step over the ledge. You can see forever. He trusted no one. Every car was a surveillance van.

The country was uneasy, deliberately whipped.

If he hadn't attracted the attention of the spooks and their masters before, he most certainly did so after he was leaked a story about the security at Prime Minister Malcolm Turnbull's mansion in Point Piper, Sydney.

At the centre of the circus enveloping the country lay one man, Malcolm Turnbull, who had long had a reputation for bullying his way to the top; Gobble Turkey in Chief, mired into the front page as if the entire country was about only one person, him. One grievous preening idiot with a smack-on grin caught in a mirror maze, his image front and centre on a thousand screens, in every newspaper. It was a grievous assault, a terrible waste of public money, of everybody's time and good intentions.

Every word of the Turnbull mansion story was nailed down tight as Alex worked through a long night. His head afire from other projects and a terrible sense of threat, he double-checked everything.

He tested some of the story at the breakfast Table of Knowledge, the Village Fix cafe in Shellharbour south of Sydney. The one thing that struck everybody was the value of the house, more than $50 million. And so that went up high in the story.

> Prime Minister Malcolm Turnbull is potentially endangering the lives of his family, staff, neighbours and the Australian Federal Police officers who protect him by choosing to defy tradition and live in his own mansion rather than lodgings provided by the taxpayer.
>
> That's the opinion of top security experts, who told *The New Daily* that the official Prime Minister's residences, Kirribilli House in Sydney and The Lodge in Canberra — which remain empty — were designed to deal with the security issues surrounding a prime minister, but his harbourside mansion was not.
>
> Those criticising the Prime Minister's decision include security personnel who have worked on the official residences.
>
> Security experts believe his mansion, in Sydney's most expensive suburb of Point Piper, is vulnerable to attack from the busy harbour, from the unsecured streets and houses surrounding it, and from the air.[4]

The country's number-one terror target. The man whose tin ear and outlandish egotism dominated the political landscape. The man who was dropping more bombs on Iraq than even his crusader predecessor Tony Abbott. The man who, to put it bluntly, was responsible for killing more Muslims than any other Prime Minister in Australian history.

Sydney retreated from the bohemian wonderland of old to a grasping rich man's game. To the worst the conservatives had to offer.

Turnbull was reportedly apoplectic with rage over the invasion of his private space.

---

4 Turnbull must abandon his mansion, John Stapleton, *The New Daily*, 11 October, 2016.

Good.

A supremely arrogant man who had seen into law the worst anti-journalist, anti-free-speech legislation in the nation's history, Turnbull was happy to perpetuate the blunt instrument of surveillance against his fellow citizens; from significant numbers of the Muslim population, who greatly resented it, to anyone who dared to maximise their welfare or minimise their taxes, to anyone who disagreed with the government narrative.

But when attention turned to his own living circumstances, that was a different story for Mr Harbourside Mansion, as his critics called him.

How Malcolm Turnbull's prime ministership devolved into the disaster it became was a complicated yarn, like the man himself.

Rob Hirst, whom Old Alex had interviewed for a rock magazine decades before, was the drummer for the famous Australian band Midnight Oil.

Hirst just happened to have gone to school with Turnbull in the early 1970s at the elite private school Sydney Grammar.

And Hirst took the temper of Turnbull perfectly.

> "Turnbull managed to alienate almost everyone around him. A fighter and a winner, he nevertheless had a dearth of people skills: a plummy brew of eloquence, imperiousness and un-humble pie, plus a kind of sighing, saturnine resignation that his job necessarily involves being constantly surrounded by cretins."[5]

The Liberal Party put into the top job the living embodiment of The Very Big End of Town, and paid the price. Politics became a rich man's game and the party's credibility collapsed.

Alex heard every word as a new level of oversight was instituted upon his humble situation. A crudely simple story repeated a thousand times: "I used to work with him. How old is he now?"

Like a number of his predecessors, Turnbull had shown great ambition in clawing his way to the prime-ministership. And, like others, he just didn't know what to do with the top prize when he got there.

In the almost fifty years since Hirst wrote those original lines, nothing had changed.

"The behaviour pattern certainly is that old," Paddy Manning, author of *Born to Rule: The unauthorised biography of Malcolm Turnbull*, told him.

---

5 *Born to Rule: The unauthorised biography of Malcolm Turnbull*, Paddy Manning, Melbourne University Press, 2015.

"The truth is even worse than you know," the previous Watchers on the Watch kept repeating. "Think the worst and go from there. Everything they do is a lie."

And he believed them.

But those who whispered malfeasance were swept aside. New bullies. More bullies. More military-trained boofheads. A castor caste of grubs who had sold their souls long ago.

The Prime Minister's story ricocheted while the burnt smell of witches' brew settled into the house. He was no longer safe. Someone, or something, was trying to communicate with him, or warn him, and Alex slept as if extinguished, to avoid all revelation.

"What do you want to say? What do you want to tell me?" he asked in the predawn, when they were all freest to communicate. "I don't trust anyone. I've been very, very badly harassed for a very long time. Everyone is on a payroll. Everyone has a master to serve, nests to feather, career ladders to climb. No one wishes well."

And in an instant, as if they were living things, he saw the elaborate edifices of the Australian bureaucracies, all the intricate lines of power, the suspensions of disbelief, the obedience to state creeds, the mundane intelligences which festered in air-conditioned offices, covering their own arses before they covered anything else, without integrity, without good motive.

He had made the same mistake before, presuming that what had happened to him had been a simple bureaucratic slip or a misunderstanding, that higher up the food chain there would be common sense, rationality, responsibility.

"Am I safe?" he asked.

"They're not going to try and kill you now, you're too closely watched."

Well, well, Dark Dark Policing.

The legislation targeting journalists allowed twenty-one government departments access to his data, his emails, websites, personal information, everything.

In other words, an instant audience and one giant cluster fuck. Everything the Australian Government touched turned into a fiasco, mismanagement at every level, everywhere; and in the end, as the country took one step after another towards the abyss, as the worst recession in the nation's history gathered storm, as the country's original stories disappeared into the early pages of its history, as the social engineers remade the social, cultural and demographic makeup of the country, everyone who could looked the other way, out of some sort of fear of being different, or out of some wan hope that the situation wasn't really as bad as they feared.

In the Middle East bombs paid for by Australian taxpayers rained down on the mujahidin, a war rarely mentioned in the media. Those lyrical, peaceful moments were bought at a price; vacuity.

"What do you want?" he asked again, and answered his own question: "They want to kill you."

Somewhere along the timeline he had adopted the Thai habit of talking about himself in the third person.

"They want to kill him. They want to kill you."

They murmured in the background, censorious or supportive. At the local Tables of Knowledge, the pubs and cafes, there was little discussion but the excesses of bureaucracy. Suddenly depressed, for it all seemed to be going nowhere — the endless carping, the standing up to be counted, the shimmering little skeletal figures against white backdrops fringed along the horizon, the ceaseless pounding of the police and the politicians — he didn't believe them any more, nobody believed them any more.

And in the lack of a national ethic, or continuity, in the fragmented and destroyed place that had once been Australia, a place which once, as a child, seemed as large as the world itself, he looked down on shattering circumstance and knew no peace.

Why did no one speak up as the country moved step by step towards Stasi Germany? Because almost no one ever spoke up, against injustice, against the thuggery of the mob, against the groupthink that was enslaving the population. He had once belonged, he belonged no more.

The country was more on edge, more at war with itself, than it had ever been.

The then head of ASIO, Duncan Lewis, paid in multiples of the average wage, had set off a storm, declaring there was no evidence of a link between refugees and the rise of the terrorist threat. It was complete garbage, as always. A significant percentage of the Muslim minority believed this infidel government should be overthrown and a theocracy put in its place.

But bureaucrats saw no threat to anything, unless it was their pay packets. They treated the population, disturbed by the overrunning of their country with strangers, with contempt. It might be a natural instinct to want to protect their homeland; but their homeland had been sold down the river, to foreign interests, and to the creed of high immigration rates and multi-culturalism.

The surveillance had driven him beyond distraction.

In fevered, sweatless nights he woke up in the terrifying, gloom-laden dungeons beneath the Plaza Mayor in Central Madrid, where, in another incarnation perhaps, he dreamt he had been badly tortured during the reign of Queen Isabella. To this day he paced as if in a prison cell.

Meanwhile, in the unglamorous streets of Oak Flats his pursuers cringed from the lash of their own overlords and swept away the telltale remnants of failed operations, their own chaotic tracks and systematic abuses.

"We would have to admit things we don't want to admit."

For surveillance in and of itself is an act of intimidation and abuse, and he had experienced the full weather of it, from one day to the next, one month to the next, one book to the next. There will come a time, he said to the microphone in the car, when you will wish I was just abusing you because at least then you would know what I was thinking.

Extrajudicial, without conscience, fired not by justice or truth or emergency necessity, not by protection of the homeland, certainly not by common old-fashioned decency, the harassment aka surveillance was targeted at individuals who did not toe the government line.

And those who did not toe the line they wished to kill, without warrant, without judicial oversight, without conscience. The power these secretive agencies had been granted by successive waves of gormless politicians had made them impenetrable to scrutiny.

"Why are they so bad?" Alex had once asked of a strange little spook who knew far too much.

"You've got to realise, there are some good people."

If only the good people were in ascendance, but they were not.

All the attempts to silence a journalist were folding out in the bacterial creeping of an ancient curse.

He knew more than he let on.

His enemies circled ever more frantically and in their insane pursuit they had destroyed themselves. For it would take only the most basic of public service inquiries to pinpoint the people responsible, and to use the information thus gained to topple them. If they couldn't handle a simple domestic operation against a perfectly amiable journalist, how could they be handed the responsibility for national security? How could they be trusted to behave with dignity, to be beyond reproach, to justify their handsome salaries and expense accounts?

On the other side of the world, a deadly game, rending a psychic scar all the way into Malcolm Turnbull's money-cushioned world, was beginning; one of the worst of the corpse-soaked scenes to envelop the Middle East, and the ancient, literature obsessed city of Nineveh, modern day Mosul. There were more than a million civilians inside "the great city", as it was called in ancient times.

Now, unbeknown to the Australian public, bombs they had paid for rained down on the city. The nightly news only occasionally showed puffs of smoke from ragged villages. There was never blood. No screaming children were ever seen. The dismembered and the dying did not make it into the lounge rooms of the West.

The Americans had been dropping bombs on civilians since Hiroshima, their favourite form of welfare, cowards at war, and more than sixty years later they were still dropping bombs on innocents and hiding the truth from their own people. No one heard the screaming of burnt children, the thudding shock of the final bullet, the grieving of mothers, the intense and savage demise.

Time was flowing over all of them, and it was true what they said: everything was connected.

The year was smouldering to a close.

Iraqi soldiers, supported by American, European and Australian airstrikes, boasted of easy victory. A week, perhaps two, and it would all be over; the militants, barbarians all, would be quickly banished back to the caves, the black holes in space and the fabric of time from whence they came.

Almost before the words were out of their mouths, history would prove the boasters wrong.

Destroy one thing, something worse will emerge. But there was no common sense in this demonic age.

No one, no force, no military apparatus, no matter how powerful, could sweep aside God's believers just like that; but nobody told the strutting commanders. They aimed their guns. They strutted their fields. And the hunting of souls became worse. The culling had begun. But of victory, there was none, partly because all those master strategists on their mega-salaries had no idea what victory would look like.

US President Barack Obama played golf, while in the sands and bombed-out ruins of the Middle East, perpetrated by an oligarchy who cared not a jot for those they killed, the darkest of spirits were having their way, holding sway; born in the bombs of the West.

A scenario funded by the Americans could never win the hearts of the people; it simply created betrayal upon betrayal. Billions in armaments, and the streets were ever more unsafe, in every possible way. And when military victory would finally come, it would turn to ashes as quickly as every other Western intervention in the once sovereign country of Iraq, the Cradle of Civilisation.

The gods had other plans.

> The eastern suburbs of ISIS-held Mosul are in sight, but the Iraqi forces trying to liberate the city are still struggling to get there.
>
> ISIS snipers, relentless gunfire and mortar shelling are still keeping troops from penetrating the city's border …
>
> 'There is no escape route. There have been no routes that anyone has established in fact for the civilian population to leave," reporter Arwa Damon said. "If the people inside Mosul were to try to make a run for it, they're also risking their lives trying to save themselves."[6]

There were rumours to do with his own business interests as to why Turnbull refused to live in the official dwellings. He was also notoriously litigious. Getting the truth onto the page is often difficult. The higher you go up the income scale, the harder it gets. The poor pour out their problems. The rich build moats.

Old Alex was not the only one who felt threatened and demoralised after the story about security at the Turnbull's harbourside mansion. A furious Turnbull was understood to have been determined that heads would roll.

---

6 Mosul: ISIS-held city in Iraqi forces' sight — but still out of reach, Arwa Damon and Angela Dewan, CNN, 2 November, 2016.

An essential link in the story was the Australian Federal Police Association (AFPA), the union representing the officers themselves. Its president, Angela Smith, the first woman to hold the position, was quoted in the story as saying that maintaining two official residences in both Canberra and Sydney, was not financially responsible. The residences are symbolic of the stability of Australian governance and have to be maintained whether or not anyone is living in them.

"Funding security on two prime ministerial residences is an indulgence that taxpayers cannot afford," she said. "Security at these locations is a significant financial burden on the taxpayer. The AFPA urges the Prime Minister to rethink his decision to stay at his personal residence in Point Piper over the official residence of Kirribilli."

Following normal journalistic practice, these comments were transmitted to Alex via the association's publicity officer. She drafted the comments and they were signed off on behalf of her boss, who was overseas at the time. From the moment the story was published she was hauled over the coals, and sacked shortly afterwards. All for drafting and then transmitting comments from her boss. As she had worked for the Association for only five months, under Australian law the young publicity officer could not sue for unfair dismissal and was not entitled to a payout.

While none of the players in the chain of command — Malcolm Turnbull, the Australian Federal Police Commissioner Andrew Colvin, or AFPA president Angela Smith — could be easily sacked, it most certainly appeared that the head-kicking went straight down to the first person vulnerable in the chain — a press secretary who was just doing her job, and doing it well.

All over a story which was factually correct and clearly in — interest.

Distressed, —ity officer, who preferred not to be named in the wash-up as she searched for a new job, faced Christmas despairing for her own future.

Angry at a patent injustice, Alex wrote:

> The Australian Federal Police were embarrassed this year by reports of widespread sexual discrimination and an endemic culture of bullying.
>
> Police Commissioner Andrew Colvin has been with the association since 1990, progressively rising to the top. It behoves him

to demonstrate that bullying is no longer a part of AFP culture.

As the Prime Minister tucks into roast turkey inside his mansion this Christmas, a former public relations officer faces the festive season without so much as a job, simply for doing her job.

Enjoy. Thugs.[7]

A year later, and the scandal over Turnbull's living arrangements broke again with revelations of an internal memo claiming the Australian Federal Police had been forced to scale back their crime fighting operations, including drug busts targeting cocaine importation. The story linked this to the high cost of maintaining both the official residences and Turnbull's private mansion.

In reporting the story, the Australian Broadcasting Corporation's Andrew Probyn said an internal AFP document from a senior NSW-based officer written in July, and sighted by the ABC, said under-resourcing caused by an overstretched workforce meant twenty-three operations had to be transferred, moved or cancelled because of a lack of capacity.

The July AFP memo revealed that resourcing shortages left the AFP unable to properly investigate a 1.6-tonne cocaine importation, leaving it to be handled offshore. This meant the operations of an Australian-based crime group behind the import could not be fully explored. The document cited three primary causes, including Project Rampart, a $40 million program to fortify security at the AFP's capital city buildings, and guarding Prime Minister Malcolm Turnbull's residence at Point Piper.

Colvin told a Senate hearing the AFP was daily suspending "matters", including drug seizures, when it was deemed capacity was lacking. He said some examples of activities that personnel had been diverted to included "supplementing staff at the Prime Minister's residence, it could be Kirribilli House, it could be official establishments like Garden Island or it could be our own location, our own offices in Sydney".

Asked about the issue in Parliament, death-row Prime Minister Malcolm Turnbull declared: "We have given record funding to the AFP." He should have told that to the thousands of AFP officers caught in a prolonged wage dispute.

---

7 Ibid

While the year before, and despite his best efforts, the very peeved former Prime Minister Tony Abbott declined the opportunity to comment, this time around, with open warfare having broken out within government ranks, there was no such hesitancy: "It is a reasonable question to pose."

While Turnbull talked incessantly about himself, his predecessor, the athletic, square-jawed Tony Abbott, talked incessantly about God, from his opening speech in Parliament to his last. He could see no reason why any man, let alone Malcolm Turnbull, should take away the job God had given *him*.

A year on from the original story, and Turnbull's prime-ministership was terminal. The only sad thing about that was it had taken so long.

Once again, Christmas is upon us.

The Prime Minister, feet up in his luxury pad, furious that the rest of the country refuse to be bullied into admiring him, can only ponder his own shattered career.

Karma.[8]

Useful idiots, the Cultural Marxists pouring out of the nation's universities and into our institutions, got one thing right. It was all about power.

It was not only the God obsessed Abbott who haunted Turnbull's every waking hour. Soon so would the rest of the country.

---

8 Draft notes. Opinion piece. Original available on request.

TREACHERY

ON MALCOM Turnbulls' watch, Australia entered a parallel universe. Pillaging the poor and giving to the rich became entrenched as the modus operandi of the ruling elites; so flagrant the rorts.

Pundits prattled "diversity", but the country had never been more divided.

Australia had, literally, some of the most expensive electricity, worst internet, unaffordable housing, highest levels of household debt and highest costs of living in the world. To avoid inspection, the conservatives deliberately poisoned — square with a putrid argument over gay marriage which monopolised public debate and lasted a good year. An issue that could have been solved in an afternoon.

It was way back in 2004 that the conservative scion John Howard, the founder of the modern day Liberal Party and thereby the source of many of the country's contemporary problems, had inserted into the Marriage Act, essentially hidden in a raft of other legislation, the words "between a man and a woman".

The Act was amended thus:

> Marriage means the union of a man and a woman to the exclusion of all others, voluntarily entered into for life.

> Certain unions are not marriages.

> A union solemnised in a foreign country between: a man and another man; or a woman and another woman; must not be recognised as a marriage in Australia.[9]

---

9 Marriage in Australia: A Timeline, Kathy Gollan, ABC, 23 May, 2018.

If you can put it in, you can take it out.

Turning people's private lives into public theatre for political gain was a new low even by the standards of Australia's conservatives. But filling — square with a prolonged debate on gay marriage was a useful gambit to conceal the fact that everybody was being screwed. A whole year of fervour, emotion and outrage in which the ruling elites avoided the scrutiny they so justly deserved.

These people could take the country to war in an afternoon; yet festered — arena with something most people simply didn't want to think about one way or the other.

All it would need was one lynching, as the religious fundamentalists and the voices of discontent stirred into an ugly cauldron. Set the world on fire. These people were mad beyond measure. The country had been very very badly mismanaged, beyond measure.

Nature favoured the paranoid, those species and individuals who could detect threat within a wide radius. Or the more obscure, existential threat which crept, as it always did, through the fabric of things. But this was not paranoia or a touch of schizophrenia. Old Alex was visited by fear. Justifiable fear.

Sometimes he saw reflections in crystal glass in muffled bars, the eye that travelled where he could not go, formerly handsome men and women at the crest of their careers, sometimes with a curious, crumpled demeanour, obsessed, as they had all been, not with their own appearance but with the stories of the day. Time-travelling.

And he knew new fear, there in that swamp of suburban houses in which he had been trapped — their tendrils. The surveillance, even here.

The food riots of the future were already breaking through into the present, a land of real consequence falling on a country already broken.

He could feel them, the survivors of a future savagery, even as he half-listened to football blather at the evening Table of Knowledge, a strange curving stream, dark figures shouting in torment, fury, vanquished ancestors in the broken light. If he shut his eyes, he could hear the bereaved crying in their thousands. Pursued into the suburbs he had always avoided, busted back into poverty by his own digressions, or transgressions, Old Alex took up the habit of a couple of beers and a couple of cigarettes in the late afternoon, about as least transgressive as this one got.

The Lakeview Hotel — Millers, as it was known to the locals, after its former owners — was emblematic of much that was happening across Australia's suburbs. For some it also went by the name of "Church", as in, "Church is in session".

A number of the locals who gathered there were shift workers, and they would settle into the pews for a little enlightenment on a daily basis. They had known each other all their lives, from school, poked fun at each other constantly, and drank VB, Victoria Bitter. The working man's beer.

Once a notorious bikies' pub, these days it was little more than a remnant of a far-off party. Even in the time Alex had been observing it, the crowded topless-waiter nights once a week had become a memory so fantastical it was as if they never existed.

For the locals it was a pub with a great deal of nostalgia. Once, if you drank at Millers you were known as someone to be reckoned with. The days when none of them could sit still for a minute, and everyone loved or feared the bad boys of Millers.

Now those same wild dudes still drank at Millers, but were facing their own mortality. For it was here the past met the future in a jinn-soaked world. A simple time dilation.

Not far off, the once magic lake.

There were television screens in each corner, playing mostly football, and an increasing amount of women's football. The government spent millions promoting women's sports, and all these men could think about was sweaty undies. That was the way of it, whether the country's ludicrously pampered public servants liked it or not.

The Lakeview was set on a rise, and from its beer garden the denizens could look down across the one remaining open paddock, past Oak Flats High School many of them had attended. A line of houses and a fringe of suburban trees now hid Lake Illawarra, which, when this set were growing up, had been clearly visible.

The days were growing longer after an interminable cold, and, despite the intensity of tormenting imagery, a pallid winter light would settle and then fade across the nesting houses.

Gay marriage and what God might make of it all came and went as a topic all that season. Mostly in a ribald sense. They thought about the pink bits. As in what? They do what?

"The more I think about this plebiscite on 'marriage equality', the more despicable it becomes," Old Alex said to Phil, the only openly gay person in the place. "All it will take is one lynching in one nightmare suburb and the cauldron will be set alight."

Early on, Phil had moved to protect him. "Anyone who goes near him will have me to deal with," he heard in the ether one night, as Phil rose to his defence. He did not deny it. Nothing was ever fully recounted.

These people were entrenched in place, while he, barely encased in flesh, was often surprised to see a human staring back at him in the mirror.

And so, as day followed day and Alex's time in the area grew into months, he appreciated it.

Rhetorically, Alex asked Phil, as they sat around another evening's Table of Knowledge: "Why would a non-corporeal being care who slept with who?"

"You know, I am probably the only person here who would know what non-corporeal meant."

They both laughed.

Working-class gays were a world away from the tripping trolls of Sydney, and while he had children from a previous relationship, Phil made no secret of his sexuality. That took genuine courage, not the manufactured social justice rhetoric of the cities; amidst a group of people who had grown up bashing poofters for sport.

On another recurring theme.

"This government mismanages absolutely everything, and it has badly mismanaged immigration," Old Alex said after the subject of the latest round of Sydney terror arrests, and their Muslim nature, was broached.

"I agree with you on that," Phil said, a wiry and sometimes waspish hotel manager who seemed determined some days not to agree with him on anything, for whatever reason; and at other times was one of the few to show understanding.

Everything ran behind curtains.

From the outside, there was nothing to see, a taxi lingering, a patrol car passing by. "Nothing to see here, nothing to see."

External and internal landscapes.

"We're all friends here," as Woodsy the truck driver, whimsical after a heart attack, would often say.

The years were fleeing towards a Vanishing Point, when these fleshly frames and the innuendos that accompanied them would mean nothing. There would be a mosque on this site one day, built with Saudi money, as many of the mosques across Australia had been. The evening gathering of the ribald and the fun-loving, at the end of a hard day's work, would give way to the call for evening prayer.

Everything was moving towards a point of departure.

"We're leaving, we don't want to stay," a little cluster of the divines said one morning, bright, shining, a kind of liquid, ethereal glass, always on the verge of laughter, some hidden ecstasy. They had evolved. "The battle has been lost. We don't want to watch. You could come with us."

He shook his head, uncertain.

"I feel I have to stay, as long as there is a chance, however small."

As if lingering around a lover who had long lost interest. Was there really any point?

The world had been so beautiful, so ravishingly beautiful, as he squirrelled through so many lives. His mentors, if that is what they were, disengaged as quickly as they came, fleeing the horror besetting the Earth. He missed them the instant they were gone, and marvelled at the stubbornness of his own mistakes, his insistence on misfortune. Why would anyone want to stay here?

At every Table of Knowledge the conversation centred on the absurdity of bureaucracy, the piffling perfidies of the police. Those happenstance meeting places in bars and pubs and cafes across the nation, where vestiges of individuals and groups gathered to lament the crushing of their culture, the fundamental lack of integrity in Australian public life.

To act out desolation.

Step by terrible step.

How was he to know what all this meant, trapped as he had been in the Rock of Ages for millennia? Born anew in this strange place? The Australia of that impending Christmas had been devoid of good governance at every level for decades; and the consequences were writ large. There was a nation-wide bout of cognitive dissonance. — disconnected. Australia had become a deeply distracted and dispirited place. Contrary signals lay scattered everywhere. A nation poured out its grievances. Nobody listened. No one manned the relays.

In what was already coming to seem like a Season of Death, the past skiving away in great slabs, Des Ball, or Professor Desmond Ball, as he was officially known, passed away. He was a lovely man, at least as far as Old Alex was concerned. Unlike most academics, who regarded reporters as their intellectual inferiors, Ball had always been helpful to journalists, and helpful to Alex on occasion.

Like them or not, journalists are your conduit to —. But while their grand salaries are ripped off the backs of the working poor, most academics feel no need to justify themselves to the peasantry. Ball was different. He understood deadlines and — responsibility of his role. Even if he was taking a class or supervising a PhD student he would get back promptly. He knew exactly what you needed. He didn't hold you in contempt. He always made good, pithy copy. And, as a military strategist and author of more than forty books on military intelligence, was entirely credible.

What Ball did hold in contempt was the Australian Security and Intelligence Organisation (ASIO), an opaque body into which the conservatives now controlling the strings of power had seen fit to funnel yet more hundreds of millions of additional dollars. The Australian public had no way of knowing if their money was being well spent. Given the hapless state of Australian governance they had good reason to be suspicious.

In the coming months and years the organisation, always heavily militarily oriented, would come to play a much criticised role in the ongoing destruction of Australian democracy; from legislation allowing the jailing of journalists to laws allowing them to hold adults and children alike for interrogation, without charge.

And if anyone dared to speak out about any abuses that occurred while they were in detention, they would be jailed for breaching national security laws. That was not democracy. These laws had never been discussed with the Australian people, much less the appropriate professional bodies. All were railroaded into law under the rubric of terror.

Australia surveyed its own citizenry more than any other Western country, often incompetently. Often intrusively.

Des Ball also spent much of his academic career being a "person of interest" for ASIO.

> "I don't believe I am a 'person of interest' any more but I don't know for certain. If they were doing their job professionally I presume I wouldn't know, but in the past they have been so

unprofessional ... and they have a history of getting things fundamentally wrong."[10]

As *The Sydney Morning Herald* reported, Des Ball arrived at the Australian National University in February 1965, as a 16-year-old fresh from Timboon in country Victoria. He was a scholarship boy who had earlier topped his home state in three matriculation subjects. Before long, Des was making his mark on the ANU, academically and socially.

An early example was his arrest for "offensive behaviour" at an anti-Vietnam War rally. Des, while still a member of the ANU Company of the Sydney University Regiment, became implacably opposed to military conscription. He considered it antithetical to the values of freedom for which Australians were supposedly fighting in South-East Asia. Journalists loved the contrast. He eventually defeated the prosecution case, setting a precedent still often taught in Australian law schools.

As *Sydney Morning Herald* journalist Nicholas Farrelly recorded, in Des's student years and beyond, he remained a "person of security interest" to the Australian Security Intelligence Organisation.

In one five-page briefing, the then Director-General of ASIO, writing to the Secretary of the Department of Defence, clustered Des with a group of academics "the majority of whom have radical tendencies". When Des began publishing material about the joint intelligence facility at Pine Gap ASIO paid close attention.

> Des, for his part, long disputed many of the inaccuracies in the security intelligence files, some of which he claimed were the result of confused identification with other long-haired young men. When asked in recent years about the ASIO surveillance, Des said he was surprised by "the extent of the resources that they had devoted to me. I think that ASIO had lost the plot by then".[11]

Professor Ball was by no means the only Australian intellectual to become hypercritical of Australia's national security organisations, particularly ASIO.

The last time Alex had rang his office, a year before, was for a story head-

10 ANU professor Des Ball who "saved the world" honoured, Emma Macdonald, *The Canberra Times*, 14 November, 2013.

11 Professor Des Ball: The insurgent intellectual, Nicholas Farrelly, *The Sydney Morning Herald*, 7 November, 2016.

lined "Drone wars: Australia's dirty secret".

The often truly gutless taxpayer-funded Australian Broadcasting Corporation was never going to touch this story; equally, the Murdoch rags which held so much sway over public opinion were never going to go near a story critical of the right wing of the Liberal Party, with which they were so closely entwined.

> Murdoch's news empire is a monument to decades' worth of transactional relationships with elected officials. Murdoch has said that he "never asked a prime minister for anything". But press barons don't have to ask when their media outlets can broadcast their desires. Politicians know what Murdoch wants, and they know what he can deliver: the base, their voters — power.[12]

There was an old quip: "Rupert Murdoch never met a war he didn't like." His news outlets propped up the government and created the atmosphere for war; while the government propped his newspapers up with defence supplements read by basically nobody. Ripping off — to feed a war machine was a blatant corruption of democracy, and nobody appeared to care, least of all the dishonourable politicians, bureaucrats and businessmen benefiting from the deception.

The story recorded that, according to figures released by the Defence Department, Australia had conducted 1,040 sorties over Iraq since the re-engagement began in September 2014, dropping a total of 631 bombs.

Ball had been increasingly unavailable in more recent times, and the department secretary informed him that Ball was sick. Old Alex, unable to speak to Ball directly, still wanted to include him anyway, and so quoted him from a previous interview, perhaps not the best of journalistic practice.

> Professor Richard Tanter of Melbourne University said these were 500-2000-pound bombs whose impact could be felt 700 metres away. There was no way of knowing how many combatants, along with civilians, men, women and children, were being killed by Australian Defence Force bombs.

---

12 How Rupert Murdoch's Empire of Influence Remade the World, Jonathan Mahler and Jim Rutenberg, *The New York Times*, 3 April, 2019.

Equally there was no way of knowing how many were being killed in drone attacks, with the assistance of the Australian taxpayer.

Former head of the Australian Strategic and Defence Studies Centre Professor Des Ball argued civilian casualties were high: "I would not be surprised if the total number of children exceeds the total number of terrorists."[13]

The use of drones had escalated dramatically under President Obama, with the many thousands killed and injured destroying his concocted image as a compassionate leader.

In a sane, healthy world, a presidency like Obama's would be looked upon with abject horror. Actually in a sane, healthy world a warmongering Wall Street crony like Obama would never have been elected in the first place, but if you were to show the members of a healthy, harmonious society the way that president used his power to do what he did to Libya and Syria, to continue and expand all of Bush's most evil policies, to divert the push for economic justice into a neoliberal orgy for eight years, those people would recoil in absolute revulsion.[14]

Equally, if only someone — anyone — was paying attention, Malcolm Turnbull's frantically concocted image as a progressive Prime Minister could be destroyed as a result of his government's direct engagement with one of the most inhumane forms of warfare ever devised: unmanned drones.

The drones are capable of hovering for days over targets before unleashing their payloads, and are blamed for driving radicalisation in Muslim territories.

In the dying days of the Abbott government the Australian Defence Force announced five RAAF personnel were embedded with the US Air Force, performing operational duties including piloting and operating MQ-9 Reaper Drones.

---

13 Drone Wars: Australia's dirty secret, John Stapleton, *The New Daily*, 4 December, 2015.

14 How to Inoculate Yourself From Establishment Bullshit, Caitlin Johnstone, *Medium*, 26 July, 2019.

Not since the advent of nuclear war has a military strategy been the subject of such worldwide concern, yet there has been virtually zero discussion in Australia.[15]

Even in flight, even here, it felt as if there were drones hovering overhead. Old Alex, in a curmudgeonly mood, drove west down metred tollways, the result of an unholy alliance between government and corporations. Public Private Partnerships — PPPs, as they were known — involved co-opting the land and transport routes, the goodwill, the sweat and overlapping efforts of generations.

The Liberal-National Coalition, the conservatives in the Australian context, were good at only one thing: turning public assets into private profit, plundering the poor to give to the rich. This time on the simple need for punters to get from A to B. That's what's called a Captive Market.

Old Alex was flying towards the mountains, or so car travel seemed to the ancient spirits which accompanied him as together they fled the spreading suburbia of the coastal plains.

Odd as it might seem, stranded as they had been for so long in pre-industrial worlds, the spirits still marvelled at modern forms of travel. From the coastal lowlands to the mountains, a long unfolding swoop. High overhead, they were already flying, as if creating their own paths in the sky above, tracked and trailing — trawling, if you will — for danger or kindred spirits; for even from this height they could detect the psychics and the divines below.

And evil intent, malignancy. The succubus and emissaries.

And then the car rose from the urban disaster that was now Sydney, once one of the most optimistic, shining, pleasant cities on Earth.

Aleppo was falling. Mosul was under siege. Raqqa had become a nightmare.

Nine hundred Islamic State warriors were killed in the fight for Mosul, announced one report. Flyblown corpses lay in ditches as people went about their daily lives, immured to tragedy. Men about to die — drowned in cages, burnt alive, shot in the head — acted with a transfixing dignity. Worse still, this would all come to seem comparatively innocent.

As arranged, Alex went to visit surveillance expert Glen at his new house

---

15 Drone Wars: Australia's dirty secret, John Stapleton, *The New Daily*, 4 December, 2015.

in Katoomba; hoping to debrief after a terrible winter, to put the final full stop to a story which had begun seemingly so long ago, although it was only a matter of months.

From early on, Old Alex had assumed Glen, who was half his age, worked for one of the national security agencies, overmanned and overpaid, the Australian Signals Directorate - perhaps it was another. There was little cooperation between the agencies.

"What do we know about Harry?" one of the supervisors asked, using yet another alias for Glen.

"We know he topped his class," came the reply.

The war on terror had gifted the agencies with significant sums of money, as politicians fell over themselves to appear to be doing something, anything.

There were just so many Persons of Interest in a country the size of Australia to justify using the proletariat's money to perpetrate surveillance programs against them.

The work was nasty and dishonest. Infiltrating close-knit jihadi groups, an almost impossible task; while the electronic surveillance was becoming ever more perplexing as each side shifted their technological abilities upwards. Exposing the thuggery and dishonesty of local police, as Australia inched ever closer to being a police state. Pretending to be an ice addict to bust ice addicts, playing a role in Australia's terminally idiotic war on drugs, aping, as ever, America's war on common sense; a grinning cadaver.

Just like the plethora of councils who had no interest in solving their districts' parking issues because they made hundreds of millions off the back of booking people, in reality, the government had no interest whatsoever in solving the nation's drug epidemics, for these empowered the state to peer into everybody's lives. Always follow the money. Billions. Cops and robbers. Every lawyer needed a criminal, every welfare state a victim. And every policeman needs a dealer.

Drugs, terror, family breakdown, everything empowers the state.

There were only so many people you could betray before it became a dangerous game; and Glen had moved within a matter of months from the overheated inner city, where they had met, to the Blue Mountains: canyons and dark forests, the retired, the retarded, the retrenched and the religious. Cool, clean air. A welfare state.

Everything was a cover story.

They sat in the backyard, as always under surveillance, the favourite tool of government bastardry.

It was obvious, having completed the book in which Glen was a character, Old Alex wanted to talk about the sustained difficulties of that winter and the torment that had been imposed upon him by government surveillance and the taunting cry of his pursuers.

No such conversation ensued.

The ordered houses which surrounded him as he finished *Hideout in the Apocalypse* might have been a comfort to some, but had been of no comfort to him. Even at this distance he could hear the orchestrated derision, the fringes of neighbourhood policing, the flash crowds and common elements. He was meant to cringe, withdraw, change tact, be intimidated. Their masters would forgive the statecraft.

"Rocks in their heads," Glen would say dismissively of his bosses. Alex liked that about him.

"They're frightened of you," Glen had told him months before, by way of explanation of the bizarre targeting he had struggled to understand.

"Why?" he shrugged. "I'm just a humble hack on the highways of print."

For years it had been true; unable to leave mainstream media because he had children to support, he had got up and gone to work for the national newspaper, overdid the dishevelled reporter act, bashed out whatever story of the day crossed the editor's bewildered mind, and gone home, thinking no more of it. He had long ago ceased caring, and had given up suggesting stories of his own.

Journalism was a young man's sandpit and an old man's quicksand.

A chrysalis waiting to be born or a disaster waiting to happen, the timing, his placement, was all engineered from above. Or from very, very far away.

Times were different now. Understanding deepened with every passing hour.

> But the Rose I sickened with a scarlet fever
> and the Swan I tempted with a sense of shame
> She said at last I was her finest lover
> and if she withered I would be to blame
> The judges said you missed it by a fraction
> rise up and brace your troops for the attack

Ah the dreamers ride against the men of action
Oh see the men of action falling back[16]

Surely they could see that everything they did backfired, made their own situation worse, with each strange act further exposing the nation's secret police.

But they never did cease and desist.

If there were Flaws in the Glass they would pounce. They never learnt, and, as usual, he acted stupider than he was; a tried and true method. Tell one story, write another, his motto throughout an increasingly incendiary life.

"I am an empath," Glen said, apropos of nothing. "I feel the pain of my friends."

It had been said before and did not need to be said again. The Mundanes were watching. Beware! And he knew fury for a talent sold.

Glen was an empath all right, an empath who had sold his soul and betrayed his kin. They were highly prized by governments. Lured by money, they were turned into hunters. *The Sellout* had just won the Man Booker Prize.

But rather than the obvious, under instruction, a patent avoidance of the truth, Glen began showing Alex poetry he claimed he had been writing, continuing the already discredited story of himself as an aspiring young writer; as if nothing had changed.

In their own comfortable lives, inside their smart cars and luxury homes, the bosses managing this rigged game regarded everyone else as beneath them. In one-dimensional worlds their money meant everything to them. They would never know what lay behind the shabby wheels of poverty; never squat to talk to someone dying in the street. Never understand that people were often not as they presented, or pretended to be. They were never the sum of their past.

The poems were accomplished, intricate work, some with clashing styles; and nothing like the earnest poetry of a striving young writer. And nothing like the scribblings he had previously seen.

"Original," Old Alex commented, as the conversation remained within narrow, ceremonial, dishonest bounds. He compared some of it to the work of the celebrated American poet E.E. Cummings.

---

16 *The Traitor,* Leonard Cohen, Columbia, 1979.

Robert Lowell and Ted Hughes both came to mind.

Abel was finished; death is not remote,
a flash-in-the-pan electrifies the skeptic,
his cows crowding like skulls against high-voltage wire,
his baby crying all night like a new machine.
As in our Bibles, white-faced, predatory,
the beautiful, mist-drunken hunter's moon ascends — [17]

It was original all right, it just didn't happen to have been written by Glen. He had no more written this collection of poems than he had written *War and Peace*.

Glen had already told him, in his invisible way, what was going on. It was some sort of stupid, bureaucratic test; what he would make of it. Did his literary knowledge and peculiar flashes of clairvoyance go so far as to detect plagiarism?

As before, Glen showed no actual interest in the mechanics of writing, or the great works of the masters. And no camaraderie or understanding of others toiling in the field. And gave himself or his idiot supervisors away.

It was just another deeply stupid, contemptuous trick amongst so many. They had tried absolutely everything but to treat him with respect; and at taxpayer's expense were trying on another heist.

The laws were such now, there was no consequence for incompetence. They flurried together in their meetings and Commonwealth cars, nestled consciousnesses in the never-reaches of dark games. Everyone was on a government payroll but Alex.

The kinder ones told him, there in those long nights, of magnificent tranches of malfeasance, of warring, malfunctioning agencies and incompetencies on a grand scale. He turned, exhausted, and wished leprosy into all their eyes. For it was impossible to know who was a friend and who was not. Who could be trusted and who could not. He could not tell who was kind, who was a threat, a saviour or protector, and who would wish him dead.

Rotting souls and smelly feet and malignant intent.

He had seen the way power corrupted their bureaucratic little hearts, while out in the deserts the gods waited. He had seen the dark forms dancing at the edge of liquid scapes and begun to understand the worst that man

---

17 History from *Selected Poems* by Robert Lowell, published by Farrar, Straus & Giroux, 1976.

was capable of. Here on the outer reaches of consciousness, when they, in their mundane lives, were chortling self-satisfied. Now the hounds they had unleashed would turn.

They were fleeing through European forests and across Eritrean sands, and they were all, yes, they were all now slouching towards Bethlehem, for they had stirred the forces that should have been left unprovoked. And the Lord would not forgive, although they knew not what they did. Their callow, dissembling hearts, their personal greed, none of it would serve them well in the harsh landscapes they now entered, their eyes bleeding as they ran.

These were the demons they had so unwisely woken, and the land that should have been safe was not safe, and the villages that should have been safe; where children ran and played while grandparents watched with pride — wind swept through them, arid and hot, and doors banged in deserted buildings, and times of festivity never came.

It was the season of killing, the harvesting of souls, and even in this far-off place, the dark lords stalked and manipulated, and the bombs that rained down half a planet away, they shook through their temporal dreams as surely as they destroyed the flesh upon which they poured.

And so it was he looked up and said: "Leave me alone. You know not what you do." And the interconnections of everything, they ran every which way to hide their own stinking guilt and stoked not flames but bitterness as they stunk and slunk into the reaches, never finding the courage they so desperately needed.

They would not be born again.

In that Katoomba backyard, the leaves of the Japanese elms glinted mica-like in the cool sunlight, and soon enough he left the house feeling thoroughly cheated.

And found himself in wild waking dreams hunted into a cave, with the army of the dark snapping at him, determined to kill. He was shape-shifting rapidly in a corner; and in a frantic piece of magic opened up a deep fiery ravine between him and his pursuers. They stood on the other side, trying to get to him, but could not cross; their anger spitting barbs of black spite.

He was changing form so quickly, nothing could touch him. His kind, a direct threat to power, had been chased across darker worlds than this.

"TREACHERY", a sign swung through his head after he had left, pulling up on one of the narrow mountain streets which crisscrossed the area.

But whether the treachery was directed at him or at others, he did not know. There were grander plots afoot. The mismanagement of the targeting of journalists in Australia handed the perfect ammunition to a new breed of operative; smarter by far, better educated by far, less bound by military procedures; far, far faster on their feet.

And it could only be for the greater good that the old dinosaurs who infested the security agencies be swept aside and a cleverer, better connected, more adaptive, more empathic generation took over. And cast the relics into the pit where they belonged, their bones to be discovered, if at all, in records found many thousands of years into the future. When this strange stage in the evolution of the species was nothing but a curiosity in an arcane academic discipline.

The machines remembered everything.

DRIVE-BY SHOOTING

HE PASSED up the road from Glen's, the houses still breathing cold from the winter just passed, and stopped at the highway; turn east and visit an old friend, come back in a couple of days, as Glen had invited him back when they didn't have guests or head west, through open farmland into the arid zone, forty days and forty nights, into the most liberating, unsettling of confrontations.

He turned east.

Knocking on Max's door he was greeted with: "Ah, hello. You want a bed for the night?"

Max, formerly a member of Whistleblowers Australia, knew all too much about the ravages of surveillance. Old Alex knew his story and in some homely way Max thanked him for that validation. At the very least someone knew. He accepted Max's ridiculously politically incorrect posturings, for he knew from whence they came.

And he knew, these things, these behaviours, were outbreaks across a coated surface, the things that could not be said in polite society, as the people, co-opted, blinded, believed their government was working, that the story they were being told was the real story.

The household was eccentric but welcoming and he spent two nights in that large stone house perched on the edge of a steep gully and sandstone cliffs. In the morning Max poured seed out for the birds and he watched the bronzed pigeons, the brilliant reds and blues of the rosellas, yellow-crested cockatoos, the ground-dwelling wonga pigeons strutting around like decorative hens.

We have been here for a thousand years. We have forever been.

Old Alex had assembled in the same place two months before, in the midst of that terrible, interminable winter during which he wrote *Hideout in the Apocalypse*. A place that should have been safe was no hideout at all. While freezing black winds whipped around the house, he had loaded the fire with shovels full of coal, as if, just like some of his ancestors, he was back on the freezing shores of the British isles.

This time, the book completed, there was a different, more powerful kind of wrath, a more deeply angled magic.

Once his flying dreams had been a source of wonder and delight. Now he flew high and fierce, with piercing eyes. The cruelty that had been displayed towards him, the ceaseless bullying and harassment he had been subjected to by state agencies, all the attempts to silence a journalist, were folding out in the bacterial creeping of an ancient curse.

He knew more than he let on.

His enemies circled ever more frantically.

The pterodactyl into which his dreams finally settled in some sort of time dilation was a fearsome, aristocratic, lonely creature. Perched in an alcove high on the top of sandstone cliffs for weeks, perhaps it was months, it could not be approached. Its fiercely intelligent eyes surveyed the surrounds. Its only movement an occasional restless settling ever further into the alcove.

Waiting, the beast could not have told you for what.

Normally highly alert, instead it was in a kind of dreaming, hibernating, dormant state, rarely even moving.

There had been no chicks the previous season. There had been no lovers, not as an aging lecher in the dank heat of Roman baths, and not here, as high above the fray as it was possible to get.

Below, the heated air currents were more malignant than it had ever known them, thick with a kind of spiritual treachery. Such were its antennae, its unique psychic abilities, that it could see the danger visible on warm winds. Only occasionally did it sweep at night across the so-called Blue Mountains, the ridge down the east coast of Australia that divided the coast from the inland deserts, with its deep-cut canyons and brooding dark, a place the indigenous had considered unlucky, haunted. Another carrier of souls, it resembled more a giant stingray, except it was high in the sky. He could see the suburban houses far below and the seaweed thoughts of the denizens rising in little huddles. He no longer tried to listen. After months of harassment he had lost all faith in the species.

There was a reason why the ancient gods had been so cruel, their warriors so merciless. They didn't care much for the nature of the species either; blunt, apathetic, barbaric, ignoble, acting in cruel mobs. It had once thought, with all the naivety of a newborn, that great art rose from the ordinary, that there was nobility and warmth in the common man, things to be learnt, loved and appreciated.

How wrong it had been!

High in those cliffs, looking down across once drowned valleys, it was impossible not to notice the changes.

Step by terrible step.

Back on Earth, in the future where Old Alex was now tethered, he continued to give the Watchers on the Watch the benefit of his views.

On the other side of the world, tens of thousands of Cubans mourned Fidel Castro's funeral cortège on its journey across Cuba, unflagging in their admiration, waving flags and singing the national anthem. Castro, who had just died at the age of 90, had survived what his government claimed were more than 600 American-inspired assassination attempts.

The book was finished. It was almost impossible to believe, it had been so damn difficult. The early daffodils had gone and the wide windows looked down across steep lawns to a line of banksia fringing a prehistoric gorge. But that was not what he saw.

Helicopters buzzed over the scene, each trailing a burning trawl rope.

Now, the world was a battlefield.

He grabbed one of the ropes, it disintegrated in his hands. He grabbed another, it too disintegrated.

The burning ropes cut arcing flames across the darkening scene; dank with fear. Everywhere around him cinders swirled.

Bodies littered the ground. The chances of survival somewhere near zero, although for some reason he did not expect to die that day. What gave him such conviction lay with the divines. There were other duties to be performed.

He grabbed another rope and it held, lifting him above the scene, just as the ground beneath him buckled and blew. Swept away from the scene, the arc lines of burning ropes and flurries of ash behind him in an instant, he barely dared to look down.

Life was brief, but he wanted to hang on one more day as his stomach screamed and the rotors above thrashed towards the horizon. There would be no peace, not that day, not in this life, not in this era.

The country was now a pale shadow of the boisterous, larrikin country he had once known; a travesty brought on by years of poor governance and rank hypocrisy at the highest levels.

There was a price to pay for war and they would pay it out of other people's coin, if they could. And they would silence him, if they could. The bully boys, the bully girls, the henchmen, the henchwomen, the agents of the state.

> Iraqi media outlets announced on Tuesday, that the Islamic State executed nine of its members by burning for fleeing the battles in central Mosul.
>
> Al Sumaria News stated: "ISIS terrorist gangs executed nine of its members for fleeing the battle against the security forces in Mosul, by throwing them in trenches containing a burning oil, after tying their hands and legs. ISIS used the burning oil trenches to impede the visibility of the Iraqi Air Force and international coalition air force."[18]

He put out extra food for the birds, and the rosellas and the king parrots came. He laughed at the way things had so magically resolved in the household since his last visit. They were happy now, as he had wished upon them in those strange blessings which invariably came true, although they would never know.

He forgot, in that long life, the power that he sometimes had. A whimsical power perhaps; but power nonetheless. And his pursuers couldn't hurt him now, for all their terrors rebounded.

Old Alex left the large stone house on the edge of a Blue Mountain ravine, left the sight of parrots and pigeons squabbling at the bird feeder and as previously arranged, went once again to visit the surveillance expert.

In the early hours of the morning he had heard Glen say: "I have no regrets." Bravado ahead of conscience.

The arrangements had changed. Without explanation. Decency had fled.

They sat on the back veranda, briefly, and once again the light glinted off

---

18 ISIS burns nine of its militants for fleeing battles in Mosul, Amir Abdallah, Iraqi News, 25 October, 2016.

the fresh spring leaves of the Japanese elms and things beyond ken swirled. Once again he had an instant, peculiar headache. This time the glints of light off the trees were sharp as knives, each fringed with a narrow, out-of-phase frieze, decaying faces, the emblematic consolidation of corruption and ill-intent, bureaucratic decay and the relentless, unfeeling machinery of government where no one was accountable.

"I feel like a thresher's been through my head," he said in a random piece of conversation later in the day, on the other side of the mountains, as his headache grew progressively worse.

He felt some terrible swamp of sadness he hadn't felt in years, as if his children had just been stolen from him, as if the knives were still cutting. Not because he expected the story to end any other way, he already knew the Fairy Godmother would turn into another fat fairy who wanted a fuck for free. But because, at the end of one story and the beginning of another, he had hoped he would be surprised by kindness.

He had a very unhelpful trait for a journalist; he was always surprised when people lied to him. But the lies never stopped.

This time the sign in his head read: "NOT TO BE TRUSTED".

Under any circumstances.

He drove north-west, the rolling plains which had so delighted the early explorers drenched green from recent rains; and dropped by a household on the edge of the Liverpool Plains. He had a habit of rolling by once a year or so to see an indigenous brother, saying hello, crashing the night and moving on. But they were not there. A few days before, the mother had a brain aneurysm and had been helicoptered to a hospital in the south. The family were by her side.

"Not good," was the prognosis.

He kept on driving. The sun was setting across the flat, rich plains; in the midst of life we are in death.

And so he drove through the outback light, as if through a gathering storm.

He heard the voices of his pursuers rejoice at his defeat: "You've been totally, completely screwed."

Their victory cry would be short lived. When a bee stings, it dies.

On the other side of the world the blood was already spreading. Alex obsessively read the news reports:

Iraq's special forces worked to fully push a fiercely resisting ISIL from neighbourhoods on Mosul's eastern edge while bombings killed at least 11 people elsewhere in the country.

The current phase and slower pace highlight the challenges ahead for Iraqi forces as they press into more populated areas deeper inside Mosul, where the civilian presence means they may not be able to rely as much on air raids.

At least 27 people were killed on Sunday in a series of suicide bombings carried out by ISIL across northern Iraq.

The deadliest attack took place in Tikrit, a city halfway between Baghdad and Mosul, where an ambulance packed with explosives went off at a security checkpoint, killing 15 people and injuring 35, a security official said.[19]

And then a god of youth died: Leonard Cohen.

Everybody knows that the dice are loaded
Everybody rolls with their fingers crossed
Everybody knows the war is over
Everybody knows the good guys lost ...[20]

Another source of inspiration left the stage.

After the album's release in 1971 Alex's wild little cohort had played *Songs of Love and Hate* over and over and over, slumped or soaring over the bong-soaked carpets of the inner city, laughing or in sorrow. They were all troubled.

the lovers will rise up
and the mountains touch the ground

and wasn't it a long way down
wasn't it a strange way down[21]

The written word — God signs, as they were once known — had spiritual power. Call it mysticism if you like. Over and over Alex played that beautiful song; *The Traitor*:

---

19 Advance into heart of Mosul slows as ISIL fights back, Al Jazeera, 7 November, 2016.

20 *Everybody Knows*, Leonard Cohen and Sharon Robinson, from the album *I'm Your Man*, 1988.

21 *Songs of Love and Hate*, Columbia Records, Leonard Cohen, 1971.

I kissed her lips as though I thirsted still
My falsity had stung me like a hornet
The poison sank and it paralysed my will
I could not move to warn all the younger soldiers
that they had been deserted from above
So on battlefields from here to Barcelona
I'm listed with the enemies of love.[22]

But even more than the song itself he liked Cohen's explanation of its famous obscurity: "It was about the feeling that we have of betraying some mission we were mandated to fulfil, and being unable to fulfil it and then coming to understand that the real mandate was not to fulfil it and that the deeper courage was to stand guiltless in the predicament in which you find yourself."[23]

The following day Old Alex pulled up by the side of the road, just past the Namoi River, struck by the sight of the river gums beside a classic Australian outback scene.

He just wanted it all to stop.

He turned the engine off and as the car settled and the silence of the bush surrounded him, he tried to seek the power to turn events around. The only advice that came to him in those crippling days was: "Stay Out Of The Results."

He started up the car and quickly overtook a clapped-out vehicle.

"Drive-by shooting." The words plunged through his head.

He caught a glance of the car's occupants and they looked as guilty as hell. They say, everyone who goes to the Ridge is escaping something. He was escaping.

He arrived at his destination, a remote outpost which resembled at times, not to put too fine a point on it, his beloved Mars, that transitory place that had become its own place of origin.

He had arrived at the Village of the Damned.

22 *The Traitor, Recent Songs*, Leonard Cohen, Columbia, 1979.

23 Leonard Cohen Interview included in the YouTube clip of Martha Wainwright singing *The Traitor*. Unknown date and source.

UNTO THE DAY THE EVIL THEREOF

THE CICADAS screeched in the hallucinatory summer. The Ridge was still green from recent rains, unusual in that part of the country. Not far away the intermittent inland rivers were running and the ephemeral network, known as Menindee Lakes covering almost five hundred square kilometres, was full.

On his first night, storms circled the camps, as the mining settlements outside of town were known. Most were makeshift — a caravan here, a shaft there, tin roofs, shacks built in rudimentary circumstance, doors which provided no protection from the paralysing heat. Trucks, utilities, battered sedans abandoned decades ago littered the landscape, a museum of automotive history and rough fortune.

This camp, being the old brothel, was luxurious in contrast to some with a kitchen, a lounge room, a fireplace. A wall-length mirror stood over the owner's double bed. Half a century after the bordello had closed there was still a trace of hard liquor. Bawdy times. A red light. The scent of homesick working girls still lingered. Some evenings their ample bosoms, so beloved by the rough-handed miners after months out on the opal fields, could be seen bouncing in the mirror. As if in God's own country, this harshest place, redemption was still being found through excesses of the flesh.

The miners died out there amidst the shafts, or drank themselves to death. Or made their fortunes, never to return. And came here for comfort and release.

Lightning flashed across a low-flung sky and rain splattered on the tin roof.

While Alex cheerfully raised a glass, and on the surface was relaxed, inside, still recovering from haunted months of heightened alarm, he thrashed, feverish, furious, sweat-soaked.

A flurry of figures were running towards their hideouts. The nuclear flash lit up their forms in a black etching, burning their fleeing images onto the thick convulsing air. And then they were gone in one brutal, infinitely cruel second.

Not one of them made it to their bunkers.

And then it all went quiet; the arid landscape blanketed with the divine, a kind of liquid silver flowing across the cacti, burnt grass, rusting trucks and collapsed dwellings of the old mining camps.

He slept deeply, away from the idiots who were always trying to contact him as if he was some experiment, a live rat to be tortured, a curiosity to be examined. For all too long he had been able to hear all too much; the poisonous fronds of thought emerging from surrounding houses. For he did not know who he could trust.

And now he was away from suburbia, as the denizens of Lightning Ridge called Australia's cities with a shudder. Those who could cope with suburban life were a different species altogether.

He stopped chanting at the microphone in the car and therefore to the authorities. And so he rose barefaced into the laughing sky and was free.

Old Alex had last been here two years before, after a similar hounding, another book. And then, as now, haunted and hunted for so long, felt an enormous relief. What faith could — have in any of these bastards?

He went, that first morning, to the artesian bore outside town where, as the sign promised, the hot, mineral-rich waters would soak away your aches and pains.

As so often, there were Middle Europeans taking the water in this outback place and the air was full of the Balkan languages. He liked the idea of bathing in million-year-old water, although in truth he had no idea how old it was and could find no easy reference.

It was the final month of spring after what had been a hellish winter; with kidney stones and a fractured vertebra leaving him in constant pain and the targeting of him by the authorities, or under the purview of the authorities, making his life entirely miserable.

Bathing in the artesian waters, watching the birds flock through the low scrub of the Australian outback, he was the one whose mind could pick through the surrounding fields. He was the one who had survived.

And they would squirrel back into their useless jobs, no longer safe. For the wraiths unleashed were already out hunting their targets and they would find their way. His enemies would have walked across a scarred battlefield just to kick his skull in. Now they were hunted by forces beyond their ken. If it was simply puerile revenge, the wraiths would never have done his bidding. This was more than that: a battle between the sacred and the profane; a battle they would not, could not, win.

On the other side of the world, a travesty of the soul took more wrenching steps:

> As the battle for Mosul proper begins — a painstaking and brutal process of clearing ISIS street by street — cracks in the Iraqi Government's planning and preparation are already beginning to show.
>
> ISIS hasn't just had the past few months to prepare for the assault they've been told is coming, they've had control of the city for more than two years. They have prepared the perimeter of the city for an attack, hardening defences in the places they predict they'll be attacked.
>
> Hundreds of thousands of people in Mosul remain in their homes, trapped by the fighting and used by ISIS as human shields. Snipers fire from houses where families are still living, hiding among them, knowing that the Iraqi forces can't fire back with impunity.[24]

In the ancient city of Nineveh, modern-day Mosul, a perhaps foolhardy CNN journalist by the name of Arwa Damon and a photojournalist, Brice Laine, accompanied Iraqi special forces during a push into ISIS-held parts of the city. It marked a new phase of the "liberation" operation, switching from villages and open terrain to a dense city that a well-equipped Islamic State was determined to defend.

Their convoy was leading the operation when it came under multiple attacks. Vehicles were destroyed, soldiers were injured. Troops and journal-

---

24 How Mosul's bloody streets could quickly derail Iraqi forces, Nic Robertson, CNN, 7 November, 2016.

ists sought shelter in a succession of houses, calling for backup again and again.

In her notes, at 1.55pm Arwa records:

> This fight is nothing like that of the outskirts. This is in the side streets, against an enemy that knows them and rules the rooftops. The rooftops of homes that have civilians inside.

> Holy shit. That is the craziest crap I have seen. A white car just went flying down the side street in front of us. Right between the battalion. Then a rocket-propelled grenade came flying in.

> They keep calling for air power.

> "There is heavy incoming, heavy incoming," the captain calls on the radio. "We need air power now! We are getting hit from all sides."

Twenty minutes later:

> We just took a direct hit. I don't know what it was. The captain has a head wound. One of the guys is hit in his shoulder.

> I have blood on me, but it's not mine.[25]

As so often, Alex was on the periphery of cataclysmic events, but even out of the line of fire, the world was nonetheless awash with unease.

A group of apostle birds settled on one of the low-slung trees. Mist rose from the warm waters of the bore bath into the first heat of the day. All around, the vast outback, a creaking immensity.

Let your sins wash away, if sins they were.

Much of what he had heard through that long, interminable, bitterly cold winter back in the 'burbs had been harmless. Lasagne for dinner. Medical concerns. Television programs and the endless drivel of government propaganda from the radio.

Sometimes he would hear one of the operatives lying to new recruits amongst the Watchers on the Watch, expressing their distaste for him; an inflamed dislike which would never have been there in the first place if they had not mounted their prolonged surveillance campaigns and attempted,

25 28 hours: Leading the Mosul attack, under fire, then trapped, Arwa Damon and Brice Laine, CNN, 8 November, 2016.

time and time again, to encourage him to have a heart attack or to take his own life, to do their job for them, to relieve the world of his disturbing presence.

Old Alex was determined not to let them destroy him.

The reasons for their being — for he did not regard himself as a singular or ordinary person — the reasons why he, or they, with their image infested consciousnesses and trails of memory and wisdom and sadness from other lives, were beyond everybody's ken. He could not explain why he had been cast into this unhappy place, forced to listen to the tendrils of malicious thought that would whisper and curl through the long nights.

The frontiers of science were realigning the evolution of the species and what seemed like magic, or the voices of the gods, was in fact an evolution of themselves, or people like themselves, cast forward, cast back. He, like hundreds of others, had volunteered for the sacrifice in an instant, as if it meant nothing; as if it would be an easy assignment. He had never thought, in that defining instant that would confine him to this planet for so many years, through so many lives, of what it would be like to be so profoundly trapped for such a very long time.

The mistakes that had been made would not be made again.

As he lay awake and listened to the occasionally supportive, mostly disparaging voices of the Watchers on the Watch.

"I told you this guy could hear us."

"They have always walked among us."

"They all say the same thing; that they feel like they've been trapped here for millennia."

Strangely, in the twenty-first century their existence had been scrubbed from the historical record, so that in essence they became a secret society.

But these variants of human intelligence had characterised many of history's greatest figures and equally often drank or drugged themselves into an early grave, so far removed from the normal stream of human consciousness had they felt.

The Great Awakening. Foreboding. Wild flights of fantasy. Intense, recurring lyricism. Something always at the edge of sight.

The arrival of the internet meant that these once lonely souls could now recognise each other and, faced with the overwhelming hostility of the state, work together. The internet and the evolution of AIs also meant that for the first time in history they were detectable and the military were monitoring them closely for their capacity to trigger societal-wide change. Faced with an internal devolution, with a collapse of social and civic order, with the death of the foundational beliefs that had kept nations and peoples together, the military now sought them out.

The writer W.B. Yeats and the painter Eugène Delacroix were two of the best-known examples. "Do not talk to me of originality or I will turn on you with rage. I am a crowd, I am a lonely man, I am nothing," as Yeats had put it.

They were a direct threat to the established order because of their abilities to see beyond themselves, behind the curtains so to speak. to detect falsehood. Remote viewing.

Alex's pursuers could not tell the difference between reality and a literary device and he wasn't about to enlighten them. He could hear them rustling in the underbrush, roaring through time. There were no consequences here on the surface flash. A different time, an ancient time. So much of it had been about hiding. A muse could always be kept at bay. A voice dismissed. A hunter dodged. They were very frightening, but cumbersome. A large dinosaur face. They were not the species that would carry their special gifts. He could hear them, in his veins, in his blood, thundering as they approached, clumsy, deadly, innately stupid. Brute force made up for what they lacked in intelligence. They were at the top of the food chain, somewhere he had never been.

> And all the people of the lulled and dumbfound town are sleeping now...

> You can hear the dew falling and the hushed town breathing.

> Only your eyes are unclosed to see the black and folded town fast, and slow, asleep.

> And you alone can hear the invisible starfall, the darkest-before-dawn minutely dewgrazed stir of the black, dab-filled sea ...[26]

So it was that he remained, through so many generations, downstairs, locked in a mystery. A dozen undiscovered Dylan Thomas's drinking themselves to death in tiny villages along the coastline of the British Isles. So

---

26 *Under Milkwood*, BBC, Dylan Thomas, 1954.

astonishingly brilliant, in such short, grandiloquent phases, a bar-room poet, a heartbreaker, a courtier; there, so far away, before even the beginning of what they called British civilisation.

They were accustomed to poverty. They sought no material gain, no status, thought nothing of missing a meal or three. But when it came to the drink, well they could drink and for a time, in those short, bedevilled lives, they would flame so brightly, be spoken of with such fondness and admiration. Until, in their decaying forms, without money and without position, they became sick, beggars not givers, implorers not lovers, and died early, broken down in harsh times. None of them, in that phase, had ever expected to last long. They broke hearts and died young. If only all had been well, but it was never well; a craving for love, one could have said, but love was never enough.

He didn't know why he remembered them all, here at this point, in an arid landscape on the opposite side of the world. But he did.

"These people will get themselves killed," an operative declared, despairing that a pact of secrecy was no longer holding, was no longer fit for purpose.

The truth was so extraordinary that no one would believe them anyway. But they would believe each other.

The mother of souls, they all had the same image — or was it fantasy? — the same feeling of dislocation, of being activated from a very great distance; feelings which, for whatever period of time, could be turned into intense bursts of creativity. If only they had been free to squander and to wander, high-born, but instead they had been scrabbling, or hunted. So often hunted. In these impoverished villages. The bestiality of survival. The terrible winters. The lonely days. The drifts of snow. The melting ice. The only moments that counted, in the tavern. Where they could shine. And the rivers of alcohol could mix with their blood and transform the mess of their hearts into a stream of words. Could dazzle the humans, wherever they landed. Whoever they were. Poor villagers. Farmers. Quiet people living quiet lives, shutting out all else.

Old Alex listened to the garbage of persistence. The left did not know what the right was doing, confusion and enmity reigned, but they were all on government or military contracts and had nothing to do but watch and wait. They were searching for signs of abandonment or indiscretion, madness or dementia, proof he was not what he said he was, while in the early hours, his mind stretched out, he searched through the tedious fog of humans for a friend, a sympathiser, someone of like mind, someone who understood.

On the rare occasion when he found them, he kept their secrets as the Watchers on the Watch spilled theirs, told him stories of the bureaucratic fiascos and blind incompetence of government, and most of all, like workers everywhere, of the peculiarity, bastardry, backwardness and blindness of their overpaid bosses.

They had worked, those strange curses.

"You will spend the rest of your life dedicated to exposing what you have learnt," he ordered. "You will get proper jobs. You will go forth and do good."

They would all end up asking for transfers, these Watchers on the Watch, fiends not of their own making, abandoning their dark goals and ill-intent, their malignant mellifluous functions. For everything from a great enough distance was beautiful and compelling.

"Why didn't you allow me the chance for happiness?" he asked of a lost property and a relationship he himself had killed.

"Because we didn't want you to be happy. You would never have written that book."

And so at last, they finally left and as his mind wandered across the empty desert, he could finally relax.

All he knew was relief, that the final mustering was taking shape, packing their bags, moving on, as much afraid of the internal reviews of senior bureaucrats as they were of this strange man and his strange curses; of the litter of failed and destroyed careers he had left in his path. But their primary enemy was within. The ethics reviews, performance reviews, oversight committees and all the rest, as back scratching bureaucrats attempted to preserve their own careers by destroying others.

With too much money, time and power, with the arrogance and social status gifted by their educational qualifications, these fat cats would seize any opportunity to further themselves, betraying in an instant their own staff.

On the other hand, Old Alex wanted to fix that which was wrong. Prolonged harassment and intimidation should not be anybody's fate.

Enemies approached.

He twisted a hand.

Cutting-edge weapons went mashing through their brains.

And at last, long last, the vindictive, excited buzz of hatred, their whirring intensity of dissatisfaction, anger at not being able to bring out their sniper talents or revert to a baseball bat, their malevolent, putrid animosity towards a target they neither knew nor understood, all of it ebbed away.

And he turned over and mumbled: "Welcome back, old friend."

COMPLY OR DIE

WE ALL FELT like shards of glass cast into a future we never expected to see. There was no way to report back. Sydney seemed a long time in the past; everything had slipped away.

Storms swept across the comparatively well-equipped camp where he was staying; positively bourgeois in contrast to some. Rain drummed on the roof. The tanks filled. He was far away from the urban areas he had once so loved.

"I am in receipt of no questions," he muttered into the long night. "I provide no answers. I transmit no information."

"What are you?" came a question from one of the Watchers on the Watch, different now, a more senior, more sensible, more intelligent voice. As if common sense was finally breaking through the blizzard of thuggish garbage which had come his way.

"And that question most of all, I will not answer," he responded, tired of the ridicule, the targeting, the viciousness that humans displayed towards those who were different, or whom they did not understand.

Nothing was permanent. Lightning flashed across a low-flung sky and rain splattered on the tin roof.

Something Wicked This Way Comes.

> The seller of lightning rods arrived just ahead of the storm …
> Somewhere not so far back, vast lightnings stomped the earth.
> Somewhere, a storm like a great beast with terrible teeth could
> not be denied.[27]

---

27 *Something Wicked This Way Comes*, Ray Bradbury, Mass Market Paperback, 2006.

Forty days and forty nights. Would it really be long enough to save his soul?

He came seeking salvation, but there would be no release, not for a very long time.

"It's unusual weather, The Ridge," Old Alex said. "Even for the outback it stands out, as if there was some peculiar electromagnetic resonance."

The colour of everything changed. The burning bush. These shifting emphases left over from the times when it was an inland sea, when other spirits moved upon the waters, and created the opal still so sought after even today, especially today.

Simon, a tall man of Swedish heritage who mistakenly thought he was the only gay in the village, was welcoming, seemed glad of the company, opened a bottle of red in Old Alex's honour and regaled him with tales of the local goings-on. Who had died. Who had been transported to the main hospital in Dubbo, 350 kilometres away.

The population was sick. There was a sense in which none of them belonged. Europeans died easily. They often died alone.

> Volunteers collect bodies from single cottages in town, from canvas tents on the dusty pink opal fields and from trailers parked at the edge of pebbly mineshafts. Sometimes they retrieve bodies from scrubby saltbush brush, where out-of-luck miners retreat to end their lives.

> "Summer is the worst," Mr Molyneux said. Temperatures rise above 112 degrees, and stay there for days. "It doesn't take long for a body to fall apart in that heat," he said, recalling a dead miner whose arms fell off as he tried to pick up the body.[28]

There was always small-town gossip, which Simon was happy to fill him in on. Who was not talking with whom. Which community organisation, filled with argumentative souls squabbling over insignificant territory in remote social spaces, was in turmoil this week.

Mostly, for out here the weather dominated all discussion, how pleasant the winter had been, with crisp days and cool nights and enough rain to fill the tanks. The landscape had been transformed into rich savannah lands,

---

28 Innes, Michelle, An Amateur Undertaking in Australian Mining Town With No Funeral Home, *The New York Times*, 20 June, 2016.

the sun-baked wastes which normally stretched flat from horizon to horizon banished for a season.

Winter was over and, to Old Alex's great relief, the heat of the outback soaked through his bones.

And then, like an iceberg breaking away from the Antarctic, another part of his youth cleaved into the past. News came that an old friend, actor Russel Kiefal, had died.

They had shared a house in inner-city Sydney, at Paddington, in the 1970s for a time, when all was wild and the tops of the iron railings at the front of the house were each painted different colours, silver, pink, blue, cobalt, coral. There were always people in that house; and many a morning he had to pick his way across sleeping bodies to get to the front door.

Russell was impossibly good looking in the day, and he would appear as a ravishingly handsome character in the various ultimately unpublished fantasy novellas Alex was bashing out at his desk upstairs.

At the time Russell's acting career was in the dog house, confined to underground productions and theatre troupes; hence all the bodies in his front room.

Russell had been performing at the Sydney Opera House in a major production when, stoned off his head, he had fallen off the stage into the orchestra pit. It was hard for him to get mainstream work for a while after that.

None of us much cared. We lived next to a pub and were all partying hard. It didn't feel as if there would ever be a tomorrow, much less a future; and that house was a centrifugal force as the world span around them.

Thanks to somebody's contacts, the theatre troupe had received a government grant of something like $24,000, a considerable sum in the day. A significant wodge of the grant was immediately spent on a very large block of hash. And the rest of the pharmacopoeia.

The troupe rehearsed through the long nights. By morning, nobody was well enough to go anywhere.

At the time, working as an assistant manager at the *Pacific Island Monthly*, Alex was the only one in the household with a normal nine-to-five job who actually had to make it out the front door into the blinking morning light.

The job wouldn't last. Perhaps it was his home life.

After the chaos of the seventies, when being stoned off your tits was de rigueur, at least in that little set, they drifted apart, but both went on to have mainstream careers. Old Alex ended up in newspapers pounding out story after story. Russell became one of Australia's most admired actors.

His film credits included Australian classics *Breaker Morant, Children of the Revolution* and *The Leaving of Liverpool*.

He joined *Home and Away* in 1993, and stayed in television through *Heartbreak High, Wildside, Water Rats, Blue Heelers, Neighbours, Secret City*.

Tributes flowed. Colleagues remembered him as a versatile and truthful actor, and a warm and generous friend.

Old Alex remembered him for the wild friendships of that house. And for his dedication to his craft. Even after the Opera House incident, which would have seen lesser talents skulk back into the suburbs from whence they came, there was never any thought of another creative path.

He drank for company and ended up alone. Not everyone else was to blame. Connections once ran every which way. Not any more.

Stuck in the taunting outback, in diminished circumstances, busted flat if the truth was known, now Old Alex stared out the window of the Ridge's Community Centre at the wavering heat and wished he could be at Russell's memorial, where everyone from an old lover to the Chief Justice of the highest court in the land, Russell's sister Susan, were tearfully paying their respects.

There had been no longstanding illness. Russell died as he had lived, working in the theatre at the only profession he had ever contemplated. They say that funerals are an essential part of dealing with grief; that not being able to say goodbye is worse. Well so it was.

Russell had been only a year older than Alex. Almost everyone he had ever partied with back in the sixties and seventies had now shuffled off the mortal coil; Russell one of the last to go.

Old Alex momentarily thought he was free of his pursuers, and his spirits soared. He was out here to emerge reborn, triumphant; to walk through a fire of his own making and cast off his pursuers. In his head life had been running backwards in every sense, across terrains of regret and embarrassment, remorse over little things, or what came to seem like little things in the grand suffering of the race. Stupid things he wished he could forget. The larger things, the torment of government agents, their blizzard of false claims and abuse, amorality and immorality, the monochromatic bastardry of the military mindset — that was just part of an adventure, as revealing to him as it was destructive to them. A government at war with the people.

Psychological Operations, Psy Ops, in the hands of buffoons. A dangerous level of idiocy.

National security agencies which operated as criminal enterprises, creating their own off-the-books income streams, in league with social justice warriors and vigilante groups and corrupt police, with the mafia, embroiled in a world of collusion and collapse. The meth epidemic had been a gift to these bastards. They could spy on anyone, terrorise everybody.

Theirs was an evil incompetence, fuelled by taxpayer dollars, protected from scrutiny by layers of secrecy, with the oligarchy now in power passing ever more absurd legislation to protect themselves and strip rights from —.

> An agency screened from public scrutiny, no matter how well-intentioned, will inevitably develop contempt for those outside its select community, even while it owes its existence to —, and is tasked to protect them.[29]

It was the secrecy, the concealment, the lack of journalistic scrutiny or competent political oversight which allowed the systemic abuse of their targets. But there were broader implications.

There was no way Australia could have become so hopelessly flattened, so dull, so extinguished, without the imposition of a military mindset. Just say no. Preserve your own hide, your own job, at all cost. All controversy, all debate, all vigour and fire and fury was bad. Salute your way to the top.

Australia had a long history of surveying its own citizenry to a greater degree than any other Western country.

Comply or die.

Nothing sustained an oppressive government like fear. And blunt force trauma. That is raft after raft of secrecy legislation and the threat of jail for journalists and whistleblowers alike if it was breached.

> The tally of federal laws enacted under the banner of counter-terrorism has hit eighty-two, many of them granting expansive covert powers to government agencies and criminalising the communication and even handling of government secrets.

---

29 Broinowski, Alison, Book Review: Australia Under Surveillance, by Frank Moorehouse, *The Sydney Morning Herald*, 28 November, 2014.

These laws have compounded the chilling effect on public interest journalism that was already evident, particularly in the national security sphere.[30]

In her review of Brian Toohey's just released book *Secret: The Making of Australia's Security Apparatus*, law lecturer Rebecca Ananian-Welsh wrote:

> New laws introduced in 2014, for instance, imposed a jail term of five to ten years on, as Toohey describes it, "anyone who revealed anything about what ASIO designates a Special Intelligence Operation".
>
> Despite the fact that "numerous official inquiries and media reports in Australia and overseas have shown that highly secretive bodies will abuse their powers in the absence of strong checks and balances", writes Brian Toohey, the laws empower intelligence agents to commit criminal acts short of serious violent offences. But, as he astutely observes, "the prohibition on revealing almost anything about these operations still covers murder and other crimes, as well as endemic incompetence or dangerous bungling".[31]

The processes had been in place since the 1950s, and were well recorded for those who wished to look. Thousands of jobs, thousands of lives, every sign of dissidence had been placed under surveillance, from those who advocated revolution to those who campaigned for what were now mainstream policy positions: gay marriage, education for all, female empowerment, environmentalism.

The more ill-informed the population, the better this government liked it.

None of this appalling deterioration in Australian governance and the nation's involvement in America's dirty, immoral and ultimately counterproductive wars had ever been discussed with the Australian people. And never would be. The nation had been led down a very dangerous path.

The only way the Australian Government was getting away with this garbage was by ignoring the nation's intelligentsia, almost all of whom were critical of Australia's military adventurism at the behest of its "dangerous ally"

---

30 Eighty-two counterterrorism laws, and counting, Rebecca Annanian-Welsh, Inside Story, 9 October, 2019.

31 Ibid

America; by keeping — in the dark; and by extremely heavy manipulation of the media, including some of the most heavy-handed legislative attacks on press freedom seen anywhere in the world.

> We are a nation in denial that we are "joined at the hip" to a dangerous ally. Apart from brief isolationist periods, the US has been almost perpetually at war; wars that we have often fool-ishly been drawn into. The US has subverted and overthrown numerous governments over two centuries. It has a military and business complex, almost a 'hidden state', that depends on war for influence and enrichment. It believes in its "manifest destiny" which brings with it an assumed moral superiority which it denies to others. As the US goes into relative economic decline, it will be asking allies such as Australia for more help and support. We are running great risks in committing so much of our future to the US. We must build our security in our own region and not depend so exclusively on a foreign protector.[32]

Idiot tipsy girls, overweight from their McDonald's diets and daubed in Halloween makeup, prattled on behind Old Alex. Australia had so few tradi-tions of its own the youth were adopting customs they had seen on televi-sion. There was much to be desired. "I love you, I love you," murmured one lost, beseeching voice. He turned and pinned them against a wall, ate their flesh. His head swirled. Are you really from somewhere else? There were collapsing landscapes and fleeting forms whenever he shut his eyes.

"How many countries is America bombing?" asked one post on Face-book. The number turned out to be seven: Iraq, Syria, Afghanistan, Paki-stan, Libya, Yemen and Somalia.

And Australia, having surrendered its sovereignty to the United States, was right in there bombing away as well.

The reporter estimated the US had spent $4 trillion and killed 1.3 million people in the combat zones.

Exactly how many people Australia had been responsible for killing, the Australian public would never know.

And so Old Alex spat in their face. Or brooded out the window as the girls twittered gossip too mundane to keep track of, and he shut his eyes and the landscapes collapsed and the night fled ever darker.

---

32 Joined at the hip to a very dangerous ally, John Menadue, *Pearls and Irritations*, 15 January, 2019.

THE HEAT OF THE DAY

OLD ALEX sat on the edge of the stage, poured another glass, and wished forever that he could disappear. Even here in this remote place, even after escaping, however temporarily, the haunting of the national security authorities, the disturbances of the age were writ large.

Above the sky was another plain, filled horizon to horizon with banks of grinding machinery slicing through the atmosphere as if the air itself was solid. Shards, each with an imprisoned soul, rained down on barren lands, while above the grinding wall worked its way downwards, ever closer to the surface.

He had to survive. He formed into liquid mercury and slid away through the cracks in the rock; life would survive, he would survive. And he came back to Earth, blinked through startled eyes, caught the shape of desert gums against a darkening sky, raised a glass to his host, made idle attempts at high-camp conversation with references to Simon's sterling performances in the backrooms of Brisbane, and looked out across the empty airfield which adjoined the house.

A new fence ringed the airstrip, keeping the kangaroos out, while the strip itself was well graded and well lit, bearing no resemblance to the place he had first seen half a century before, when it evoked a landing strip on Mars, remote, dangerous, beautifully chaotic.

All this development came courtesy of terrorism or tourism or the fact that wealthy Chinese were buying up many of the surrounding grazing properties — the locals weren't sure which.

The last of the storms disappeared across the low tree line in the middle distance towards the east; that is, towards the far-off hinterlands of the coast, the different world whence he came.

Here they were obsessed with storms and beauty, while in the broader life of the nation the politicians queued to abrogate the freedoms and civil liberties of the populace, all in the name of the war on terror, a war which had morphed into a war on the people.

Tired from the long drive, from the ceaseless confrontation, wrung out by the pestilent hatred of his pursuers, Old Alex went to bed early, instantly his mind picking across the harsh landscape and low shrubs which surrounded them.

He could not decipher the stream, confused as it was by dreams of those who slept in the surrounding camps, and then in a rush he got the message: Hope, Renewal, Kindness, Forgiveness. Warmth. We will take care and you will take care. The universe will provide. The suffering is over. The king tide is running out to sea. Common sense has prevailed. Alertness will do you no harm. You need hide no longer.

But however convincing an embrace, he would be lucky to get out of here alive. The threats ran every which way. They were not used to having their power challenged. — should be warned.

To an unprecedented level, the population was being subjugated by the worst of the worst, the conscience-free members of the nation's oligarchy, protected by phalanxes of bureaucrats doing their bidding. The democratic contract was broken but — were not told that democracy had collapsed, their votes were worthless, their independence of thought an illusion.

That everything, everything, was controlled. And that nothing which concerned them ruffled the conscience of the buccaneers who ruled them.

Instead, the betrayal almost complete, Old Alex retreated to the arid lands of inland Australia, beneath The Sheltering Sky.

He wanted to light a fire under the ruling caste, all of them. As their subjects lived out the future of a failed social experiment.

The useful idiots had imbibed their Marx- and Marcuse-inspired lectures in their thousands, proving once again education is indoctrination. And then poured from the universities into the institutions. The people were just something to be reshaped to their theories; and the result of all that academic abstraction was now working its way into the real world, much to the bewilderment of the denizens, the unhappy remnants of a collapsing culture.

Truth was of no consequence.

The liars, the lawyers, the bureaucrats and the social engineers had won the day. They had remade the country more quickly and more successfully than they could possibly have hoped.

Sometimes, in those long dream-infested nights, it was as if someone was trying to contact him, sometimes urgently, sometimes just the puerile games Old Alex's so briefly vanquished pursuers always indulged in. For no one must know the truth.

"What's the urgency?" he asked, and slipped back into a doze, dreaming of a wonderful party at his old friend Michael's house, apropos of nothing.

For months turning into years he had held one primary desire: for his tormentors to cease and desist. Perhaps, at last, it was coming true. He tried to tell himself you could only be bullied if you let them. Unfortunately it wasn't true.

All around him he could hear the travellers thinking and dreaming, plotting their routes along the inland highways, talking of their holidays. Sometimes their cosy sliding together in the long nights, as fevered, even after years of marriage, they flew and bounced and waged war.

Then in the early hours he heard an officer say: "We will speak at first light."

And he knew he was not alone. That even here he had been followed. The worst of people. It's time to intervene. A bullet would be so much cheaper.

There were swirls of threatened rain through the night; seconds-long pounding on the roof, as the storms swept across some of the country's most marginal acreage. Although Old Alex did not know it then, the sporadic downpours of that first night would prove to be the very last of the rain that summer as a confounding heat settled on that lost-in-time town. And the country slipped into prolonged drought.

The skies were cloudless, the morning air clear and uncharacteristically cool. He pottered around the house, as if he had always lived there, quickly establishing a military characteristic of his own, the rapid creation of routines in ever stranger places. Each morning he filled the buckets from the tanks, and trundled them out to water the corn, beans, tomatoes, cucumber and rockmelon he had planted in a flash of optimism.

They would not survive. But in that brief period hope lay entwined in blank blue skies and barren landscapes.

He made jokes with his host about the Babylonian gardens and the slaves in the fields; as if in that fay grandiosity there was some humour. In reality, the nights stretched out across arid fields. In some weird way he was trying to come home to roost, to bring the fractured lineages back into one place. To recover from brutal harassment — for surveillance is harassment. To return from the dead. To make sense once again; a coherent individual, the Many in One.

Enemies approached.

He had missed several appointments with the gods.

"That guy's cheated death so often."

He twisted a hand.

Was it even possible? That there was reason in the morass, that some of the Watchers on the Watch could actually be friends; that they, too, were constrained by their own circumstances, their own bosses, and would have actually reached out, liked to be friends, would have liked to sit down and discuss everything, explain what had happened, put the accusations that had been handed to them to him, let him answer for himself.

"He's owed the truth."

The red earth dried quickly. Already, despite the previous night's downpour, the saltbush looked as if it had not seen rain in decades. He pottered about the arid, unkempt garden as he had done on previous visits, inspecting the Desert Rose he had planted months before.

The fleshy shrubs, with their large lavender and white flowers, could survive for long periods without rain. But here, the cuttings had barely survived to greet the rains.

The heat was already beginning to build.

The tall spindly cactus which surrounded the camp flowered one day a year, and flowered that first morning after his arrival. He could swear their large, white, remarkably complex flowers were shouting out the messages of the divine. That there was more to this than met the eye or could be easily detected. A bee tried to land. He watched, transfixed. These plants flowered in adversity. Everybody could be inspired.

As if to confirm the previous night's flight of optimism, that all had been resolved. That all he had to do to rid himself of the pestilent operatives of the national security agencies was to walk through fire, to take up residence somewhere so antipathetic to their lazy taxpayer-funded lives they would finally drop away.

No bureaucrat could survive this harsh climate without air-conditioning. There were no dinner parties, no fancy restaurants, no green strips of suburbia, no easy loves or internecine gossip, no five-star hotels or business-class flights.

Apart from the tourists, most people came here because there was nowhere else they could go.

Taxpayer-funded operatives were fish out of water; easily detected.

Continuing the habit of a lifetime, that first morning, and each to follow, Old Alex headed off early to the local community centre to work.

The local roads were hell on car suspensions, gibber desert hard, and he travelled past the houses set in low scrub and the long abandoned trucks until he hit the paved section running down the side of the airstrip. He passed the tall ravaged figure of Noel as he drove into town and stopped, asking if he needed a lift. He knew Noel from the Community Centre, where he would sit day after day taking advantage of the air-conditioning, staring out the window, saying nothing; a tall willowy man in his twenties with large grey eyes.

True to form, Noel said nothing, just got into the car.

"You've lost a lot of weight," Old Alex said, shocked by how thin Noel had become in the months since he had last seen him. This, like every other attempt at conversation, was met with a stare out the window. Already, as the surreal atmosphere of the place took over, they were beyond words.

The Ridge's community centre was a classic of the genre. There was no air-conditioning, refrigeration or running water on many of the mining camps, and a ragtag of people passed through the centre, taking advantage of the shower, the fridge, the internet. He saw more of the life of these towns from their community centres than people who had lived in them their entire lives.

Already established from previous visits, through a rudimentary knowledge he rapidly became known as a wizard on the computers. He had free internet in return for helping the odd, usually bewildered, customer. That newfangled damn thing the internet nobody understood or could really see the need for.

The destruction of the culture, the crushing of the natural curiosity and productivity of the people, could easily be seen in the humble environs of an outback community centre.

"How do I print something?" someone would ask.

"Control-P Click", he would respond, pointing to the printer where the document would emerge.

"What's control?"

Or, "How do I send a document to someone?"

"Scan it and attach it to an email."

"Email, what would I want one of those for?"

Once seen as the most democratising technology in human history, the internet had barely reached this outpost. In a debacle of common decency, the Australian Government had inflicted the world's worst and most expensive internet on the populace, guaranteeing ignorance; and burnt the taxpayer for more than $50 billion in the process; and shareholders another $50 billion on top due to the decline in the value of telcos.

While studies showed that countries with high-quality internet which taught the people how to use it were becoming more productive, cohesive and, in a sense, the population more intelligent, this was the opposite end of the spectrum. The last thing this government wanted was an educated population. They might start asking questions like: "Why are we paying taxes for such appalling governance? For such terrible services?"

He was greeted on that first day like an old friend by Bruce, who ran the Centre. On his worst days Bruce looked like a Weeping Jesus strung from the alcoves, and on others could be very entertaining, as he hoodwinked behind every surface and made long winded jokes. God forbid you should be in a hurry!

Bruce knew all too well the entire system was a sham.

The traditional culture of the country was being deliberately crushed. You saw it everywhere, and most particularly in these small towns. The Lightning Ridge Newsagent had burnt down the day before Old Alex arrived. Electrical fault, they swore. Just up the road, the butcher's was already closed. The baker had almost gone, being only intermittently open.

They were located opposite the Centrelink office, one of the largest buildings in town, where a steady trickle of people came to argue about what government benefits they were "entitled" to receive. Next to it was another government agency, JOBLINKS Plus, one of the towns three taxpayer-funded employment agencies, another farce which proliferated while all around legitimate businesses struggled and died.

The empty shops, the beaten air, the quaint, quizzical lean-to atmosphere now characteristic of the country's small towns was clearly evident here. There was no work. And even if there was, in reality locals were not encouraged to apply. The farmers preferred backpackers, who were cheaper and did not give grief. Or apply for holidays.

It was all process and compliance and the filling of forms. It was not reality. The jobsworth bureaucrats got to feel superior behind a desk, and the recipient had complied. Another box ticked.

In the main street, Food for Families, a welfare service, was adjoined by SUREWAY: Pathways to Work.

What exactly all this work consisted of, no one knew. The official unemployment figures were as much a lie as everything else. While the official rate hovered between 5 and 6 per cent, that is more than 700,000 people, it was evident everywhere that this was just another manipulated lie; that the reality was much, much worse.

As one employment expert, Dr Jim Stanford, chief economist with The Centre for Future Work, argued, if you count the marginally attached, the unemployment rate would be a touch under 12 per cent — not the 5.2 per cent commonly used. He also argued that if you include the "underemployed" — people working some hours but who would like to work more — the unemployment rate topped 19.7 per cent, based on the numbers of underemployed of 1.139 million people.

Dr Stanford said combining the marginally attached and underemployed with the officially unemployed provided a truer picture of the jobs market. "This says to me that one in five potential workers in Australia, or about 20 per cent, are people who want to work, want to work more, aren't working at all, or working less than they want to. The reality is there's an enormous pile of people who could work and contribute enormously to our economic performance, but are sitting on the sidelines."[33]

In the welfare-dependent towns of central Australia, even those figures were wildly optimistic.

They set up the skeletal Noel in a corner of the community centre, where

33 The one million Australians forgotten in the unemployment statistics, Mike Bruce, *The New Daily*, 17 October, 2019.

he stared wide-eyed and silent out the windows. Old Alex prised out of Noel the information that he would like a plain cheese sandwich and a vanilla milkshake, that he might be able to keep them down. Alex organised the food from the milk bar next door and then sat outside while Bruce rolled a cigarette, his one luxury, and drank the terrible instant coffee the centre provided.

The heat of the day, of that mind-stifling summer, was already beginning to build to a point where the strength of the sun made venturing outside unbearable. Within days the green savannah flush would be burnt off.

The first person he saw shifting slowly through the gathering heat of the wide street was dark-skinned Grasso, whose bicycle was fitted with tall aerials front and back, perhaps to communicate with his colleagues on Mars, while solar panels also attached to the bike ensured he cut a surreal sight.

"It really is the Village of the Damned," he said to Bruce, and they both laughed.

Grasso, to the surprise of many, had become a father and was considerably more stable than in previous incarnations.

"Adventure Before Dementia," read the banner on the side of a passing tourist bus. Indeed it did feel, some days, as he watched the street from the community centre, that clouds of dementia enveloped this forsaken place. For here, where he had sought refuge, the ravages of the country were writ large.

The Ridge, like everywhere else in the country, was being strangled by savage, excessive bureaucracy. There was a rule for everything, here in a place which had once been the last frontier. A miner now needed four different certificates just to dig an exploratory hole, yet that same miner had no running water or mains electricity or proper roads. The internet was something that happened somewhere else. They were not serviced, they were lashed.

Soon enough came the sound of Noel retching. He had not been able to keep anything down for weeks, he admitted. They offered to drive him to the hospital. He refused. He had been a few days before, and there was nothing the nurses could do for him, he said. And there they left it. That day.

As a wall of heat enveloped the community centre and wiped any movement from the streets outside.

Next morning Old Alex spotted Noel in more or less the same spot, skeletal thin, walking the miles into town as if cast from a Sidney Nolan painting. A broken figure in a transfigured landscape. Already, even at that hour, the heat of that appalling summer was building.

He stopped; the same routine. Noel said almost nothing. Stared out the window. Old Alex could extract no personal information, bar that he had come from Sydney some time back.

At the community centre they once again convinced Noel to try a plain white-bread and cheese sandwich and a milkshake. And again, it wasn't long before they heard him retching. He still refused to go to the hospital; sat motionless in the air-conditioning staring with large wide eyes out the windows at that flattened street.

Outside they were joined by Boris, a man of peculiar colouring who worked at the government-run employment service opposite. He was there to tick boxes, not to find non-existent jobs. The economy was burdened by overregulation, and these towns were the first to fall in a disaster that would soon become evident to all.

In that brief interlude before the travails of the heat made sitting outside impossible, they stared at the empty shops opposite as they sipped execrable coffee.

Weeping Jesus Bruce particularly loathed Boris. Old Alex was used to it now. These impoverished areas did not constitute a "community", that much abused word. The denizens badmouthed and backstabbed each other at any opportunity. Malaise was everywhere, and not just in the collapse of Australia's underclass. A house leaks from the roof.

Everyone felt like a stranger now.

The announcement came, the legendary Kidman properties, spanning three states and the Northern Territory, reportedly some 2.6 per cent of the nation's land area, 101,000 square kilometres, was being sold to a Chinese consortium with Australia's richest woman, Gina Rinehart, as the local figurehead.

Then Treasurer Scott Morrison, always closely linked to the Very Big End of Town, approved the sale, essentially to the Chinese Communist Party, declaring: "I have decided that the acquisition of Kidman as proposed would not be contrary to the national interest."

Scott Morrison, the man who flogged off more than 2 per cent of the country in one rotten deal that could only be described as a grievous breach of sovereignty, would soon enough be Prime Minister; the top office nothing but a revolving door rewarding the most Machiavellian of the nation's politicians.

The sale was perceived by its many critics as an insult to all Australian taxpayers, an insult to the indigenous people whose sacred lands the properties had once been, and an insult to the generations who built the country.

Steal an asset that was never yours, make it your own, then sell to the highest bidder, no matter who they are. Capitalism. A wonderful thing.

Australian politicians. A case study of the worst that crony capitalism has to offer. The country had sold its soul, and its greatest assets.

"Could there be a greater betrayal?" Clive Hamilton asked in his recent book *Silent Invasion: Chinese Influence in Australia*.

Well no, there could not.

> Australian democracy is in very serious jeopardy. China is making great strides towards it and its intentions are not benevolent. It's obvious in local, regional and global trends and if we do not do something soon to protect our freedoms they are going to be sold into the burgeoning Chinese empire, as well as political hegemony, by a corrupt oligarchy.
>
> After decades of stupidly pro-cyclical policy-making Australia is now little more than a southern province of Chinese economic policy. With the flick of a pen in an obscure public service department, China delivers tens of billions to our shores in coal revenues and our monumental trade deficit evaporates overnight.
>
> There is no other economy on earth that I know of that works with this dependence. We call it lucky. And it is. But it also comes with strings attached and they have been on display for a decade or more.
>
> Indeed, with the current crop of money-grubbing mock-libertarian ideologues in charge, we are a complete bloody pushover.[34]

The idiosyncratic crossbencher Bob Katter, from the far north Queensland

---

34 Australian democracy is in very serious jeopardy, *MacroBusiness*, 4 November, 2016.

seat of Kennedy, said he felt "absolute rage and disgust" over the sale and the government was "selling their country out and selling their country off".

"I would not describe the people in the major political parties as Australians — who knows what they are? — but they are not Australians," he said. "These low bastards are sneaking through the approval two weeks prior to Christmas, when — are looking elsewhere.

"Fifty-one per cent of Australia's land mass is registered as desert lands, 21 percent is Aboriginal lands without title deeds, precluding pastoral activity, and 7 per cent is national parks, leaving only 25 per cent available for agriculture. Australia's five biggest farming operations — the Ord Stage 2, Van Diemen's dairies, Cubbie, Nicoletti grains and Terra Firma — are all foreign-owned. They gave, not sold, the Ord River to the Chinese. Stage 3 along with Stage 2 will easily be the biggest farming operation in Australian history.

"The country continues to be sold out. When you've been a member of parliament for 42 years you can smell a rat from a mile away and this rat is very, very smelly indeed," Katter complained.

The Foreign Investment Review Board approved the sale.

Fat cats hunkered down in their air-conditioned streets as they passed fashionable city restaurants, a glowing air of satisfaction wreathing their outsized bodies.

"What is the use of the Foreign Investment Review Board?" Old Alex asked. "They stand in the way of nothing. They approve the sale of the country to foreign interests."

"Madness," Boris said.

"They've sold off most of the electricity infrastructure, including light-poles, for Christ's sake. China now has the capacity to shut down our electricity grid. Much of the prime rural and urban real estate has been sold to China. They've sold off most of the country's major ports — Melbourne, the biggest, Darwin, the most strategic.

At the time the new owner, billionaire Ye Cheng, claimed the Darwin port deal was "our involvement in One Belt, One Road". This was discounted by some commentators as hyperbole, an attempt to curry favour with the Chinese Government.

But now, by design or not, the Darwin port deal increasingly looks like a blueprint for how Chinese interests can take control of foreign ports — as it is doing by various means around the world — without arousing local opposition. Quite the reverse. All levels of Australian government have encouraged it.[35]

As John Garrick, a senior lecturer at Charles Darwin University, wrote in the news outlet *Crikey*, Landbridge Australia, a subsidiary of Shandong Landbridge, won the 99-year lease with its bid of $A506 million in November 2015. Shandong Landbridge has substantial and varied interests including port logistics and petrochemicals. Though privately owned, like many Chinese companies it has strong ties to the ruling Chinese Communist Party.

> The company knows how to cultivate political connections. In Australia it gave influential Liberal Party figure and former trade minister Andrew Robb an $880,000 job just months after he retired from parliament.

> The bid for the port was examined and approved by the Foreign Investments Review Board, the Defence Department and ASIO.

> Weaknesses in Australian governments at all levels have been revealed. They have been reactive, readily accepting the lure of pearls cast on our shores.[36]

It was hard to believe just how bastardised Australian politics had become, just how great the betrayal of the country, how blatantly corrupt the greed of the conservatives. Masquerading as representatives of the people while feathering your own and your mates' nests at the cost of the nation's sovereignty, that's not just dishonest, that's corruption.

"It's become so blatant, they don't even bother to hide it any more," an old mate observed.

"We're becoming a southern province of China," Old Alex said, repeating the article he had just read, as Boris, Bruce and he drank their lamentable coffee. Even at eight in the morning gusts of heat were descending on the street. "What sort of country does this, allows this to happen?"

"Madness," Boris said again. "What can you do?"

---

35 Darwin's port sale is a blueprint for China's future economic expansion, John Garrick, *Crikey*, 7 December 7, 2018.

36 Ibid

Powerless. Ennui. Nothing stuck. Nobody cared. Nobody had a stake in their own country any more. It had all been flogged off to the highest bidder; and the locals made peasants in their own country. They despaired, left the country, retreated into their own parochial lives. Paid no attention whatsoever to the daily news.

With the recession already cutting in these canary towns, there was nothing anyone could do about such a profoundly mismanaged country.

Within months that fat cat of fat cats, David Irvine, the former director-general of the Australian Security Intelligence Organisation and the Australian Secret Intelligence Service took over as head of the Foreign Investment Review Board.

On magnificent salaries, their paid man always sang from the institutional song sheet as he swung from one magnificent bureaucratic post to the next.

"That's what these people do," a retired spook told him. "They pass these plum jobs between themselves."

Irvine had left ASIO singing the bureaucratic myths, the value of multiculturalism, the value of the government's solid relationship with the Islamic community. It was all a lie. Multiculturalism, cultural Marxism by any other name, was an academic theory aimed at destroying the hegemony of the mainstream culture. It had been imposed on the populace by useful fools. The billions of dollars ripped off the backs of the working poor to propagandise the theory had turned a successful immigrant country into a floundering, soulless, polyglot nation without a core, a unifying history or a common identity. And therefore without national pride.

In the process standards of living and social cohesion had been destroyed. All to benefit the rich.

The country had never been more ethnically divided or demoralised. And as for the relationship with the Islamic community, it could not have been worse.

But the myths rolled on.

Irvine entered the Foreign Investment Review Board once again singing from the song sheet: "Australia welcomes foreign investment, foreign investment in the national interest ... and I don't see that changing."

The people were robbed on a daily basis, their country sold out from under them. And the useful prats sang and sang and sang.

In Australia, the pack mentality of groupthink was worse than Old Alex had ever seen it; and he reiterated the theme once again: the shutting down of debate, the narrowness of the prisms through which most of the population now saw the world, the official amnesia as entire fields of controversy were excised from — debate, all of it was poisoning the country.

One had to ask why the oligarchy was so willing to betray the people. Why the betrayal was so complete.

"Madness. What can you do?" said Boris yet again.

They finished off their morning coffee and rolly cigarettes, nobody could afford tailor-mades any more, and scuttled inside as the heat of the day began to radiate off the iron stone.

But there were worse places to be than the end of the known world. As America's bombs rained down on the Middle East.

Old Alex was commissioned to do a story on the miasma of Aleppo. After many predictions, the city was finally falling. It was the first of the bombed-out ruins of Middle Eastern cities to sear into anything resembling a public imagination.

A dollop of mud in a miasma of pain; well no it wasn't. It was just mud in a lower form of consciousness. There was no awareness.

Australia, which always signed up to America's endless wars, was the second-largest contributor to the utterly immoral carpet bombing of the Middle East. Australia had failed to learn the obvious: that mercilessly bombing a country and killing tens of thousands of civilians for an abstract and poorly thought out military or political goal was counterproductive, creating chaos and an embittered population which would pass their hatred on to their own children. And their children's children.

As Kate Allen, director of Amnesty International UK, wrote that from Kosovo to Iraq and Syria, the US and its military allies have for years told a tale of "precision bombing" and "surgical strikes".

> It was a lie then and it's a lie now. When huge numbers of bombs and missiles are unleashed on densely populated cities like Mosul or Raqqa, civilians are killed in their hundreds — possibly thousands. But still, the myth of precision and "meticulous processes" persists. Not least because militaries like our own refuse to even go back to the cities they've bombed, and refuse to acknowledge deaths unless presented with irrefutable evidence from the likes of Amnesty.

Last week I did what UK, US and French military officials refuse to do: I went to Raqqa to see for myself what has happened to this city as a result of mass bombardments by the US-led coalition.

Never before have I seen a city so completely devastated. Not just in one district area, but almost entirely. Think Dresden and you'd be close. Street after street of windowless, hollowed-out buildings. Miles of rubble. Piles of twisted metal. Utter ruin.[37]

The entire rotten, corrupted Australian oligarchy and its wretched cast of political figureheads all made their fortunes, with tens of billions of secretive military contracts dancing in the background. The survival of one, the death of many. A dead-bat con. What did it matter as you looked out across your palatial estates? The weasels had won. Better to be a weasel.

The road ahead looks very different on a full tank of petrol.

What if we lived in a parallel universe where America had learnt nothing from its brutal and truly disastrous involvement in Vietnam?

Oh that's right, that's the world we live in.

Except America had learnt how to conceal their crimes, how to create an ill-informed populace which simply didn't care what their military did.

Australians were paying a very high price for this connivance, in lost freedoms and plundered taxes.

Australia would never learn.

---

37 Raqqa is in ruins like a modern Dresden. This is not 'precision bombing', Kate Allen, *The Guardian*, 23 May, 2019.

WHAT PRICE THE SLAUGHTER?

State briefly the ideas, ideals, or hopes,
the energy sources, the kinds of security,
for which you would kill a child.
Name, please, the children whom
you would be willing to kill.
Wendell Berry[38]

AS FAR AS the Australian public was concerned, Australia's involvement in the Middle East was essentially a secret war. War brings opportunity. It also leaves a debris of broken psyches. For there is no standing in dishonour.

The government had no intention of informing — about a war which, if they knew the truth, they would be very unlikely to support. Most Australian citizens had absolutely no idea that their taxes were being used to drop bombs on Muslims half a world away; and that by these actions they were radicalising the local Muslim minority, and making their own country less safe. There was no threat to the homeland. There were no sympathetic victims. There was no fashionable ideological bandwagon to jump on. Australians were contributing to a criminal debacle half a world away, and had no idea.

In this benighted era there were not even the relatively feeble demonstrations which had marked Australia's initial involvement in Iraq, even then barely a whisper of the convulsions generated by the Vietnam War half a century before.

---

38 Questionnaire, Wendell Berry from Leavings, *Counterpoint*, 2010.

Yes, it was surreal, but it happened anyway. By arrangement, Weeping Jesus kept the community centre open for him later than normal so that he could finish the story on the fall of Aleppo by —ation's deadline of 6pm, and in a kind of rehearsal he read the story aloud to a couple of rather startled-looking locals.

Signs of intellect were distrusted in Australia. To be accepted, you had to prove you were just a normal bloke, without pretensions, without an education. Not a wanker.

If you read something aloud you had to stumble. Except he didn't.

Aleppo is falling and the end is horrific.

Syrian President Bashar al-Assad's forces are on the cusp of victory in what has been the most horrific slow-motion disaster of 2016.

The regime's army and allied forces are being accused of killing civilians in their homes and executing those trying to flee.

Reports include 82 people, including women and children, being summarily killed by militiamen, and 100 unaccompanied children trapped in a building under fire.

The UN says it is "clear evidence of a complete meltdown of humanity".[39]

There was little movement outside the centre as the deadline approached and he desperately tried to nail down the words, the indescribable heat radiating off the asphalt street visible in the distorted air. The evenings were worse, if anything, because that was when the heat that had been building in the stone all day began radiating back. Everyone was taking shelter from an environment hostile to humans. Anyone caught outside was moving so slowly, they were on the verge of extinction. He kept reading:

As another day dawned in the ruins, the cries on social media became increasingly despairing.

Volunteer rescue group The White Helmets — rescue workers nominated for a Nobel Peace Prize in 2016 for their efforts

---

39 'We have lost a generation of Syrian children': Army Poised to take Aleppo, John Stapleton, *The New Daily*, 13 December, 2016.

helping casualties of the Syrian conflict — tweeted: "All streets and destroyed buildings are full with dead bodies. It's hell."

And: "We hear children crying, we hear calls for help, but we just can't do anything. We are being bombed continuously."

And another: "People of Aleppo wish to inform you that tomorrow they will be killed with their families."[40]

With an eye on the clock and the impending deadline, another in so many thousands, Old Alex kept reading, quoting an old colleague from his days as a reporter on *The Australian*:

One of the world's leading Middle East experts, Australian journalist Martin Chulov, said the scale of the suffering in Aleppo is unlike anything else in the Syrian war.

"Half of the country's industrial heart is in ruins. The fabric of east Aleppo has been destroyed," Mr Chulov said. "Entire clans have been wiped out and tens of thousands of children traumatised by some of the most sustained and indiscriminate bombardment of the past half-century."[41]

Chulov was one of the best journalists the country had ever produced; far too good to remain in the dismally shallow pond of Australian media. He was known in the days when they worked together on the same news floor for his excellent contacts within the national security apparatus. Martin was the author of a largely ignored book, *Australian Jihad*, a classic case of Australian "wokeness". Nothing ever made an impact. Nothing ever sank home. The country slept in peaceful ignorance; protected by an inept and heavily manipulated media. And the government's media mogul mate Rupert Murdoch.

The latest shenanigans of American politics or the British royals were of far more interest than the children their bombs were killing.

Chulov played his cards close to his chest, but there were always gaps in the traffic. On the evening shift as the so-called "night reporter", Old Alex would take over the Chief of Staff's seat directly outside the Editor in Chief's office; basically directing traffic and funnelling late copy. Chulov, unlike most of his lazy contemporaries, would often work late.

---

40 Ibid

41 Ibid

And one night stood in front of Old Alex: "There's a rumour that the Australian Federal Police have a plant on the floor. Do you know who it is?"

Old Alex stared at him and said nothing, maybe a grimace. Of course he had an idea. This was an unconscionable government with much to hide; and infiltrating the enemy, as the media were perceived, was a primary task.

Flat Earth News. There were few journalists who could not be bought one way or another; particularly with an entire state apparatus attempting to manipulate them. From herds of bright young things regurgitating press releases to the phalanx of taxpayer-funded academics high on the hog of taxpayer-funded agendas, all the usual leitmotifs: climate change, refugees, multiculturalism, domestic violence, feminism, indigenous disadvantage.

Never stand between an academic and a grant.

Governments find what they fund for and fund what they want to find. Neutrality, objectivity, the real world, all are irrelevant.

Those who could not be bought or were already on the state payroll were controlled by editors and chiefs of staff sliming their way up the slippery pole; or secretly reporting straight back to the national security agencies.

Hence the rise of independent media in the age of the internet; a poorly understood phenomenon among bureaucratic dinosaurs desperate to control the flow of information.

The so-called Quiet Australians so beloved by the conservatives were in fact the crushed, silenced and ignored, those who had been excised from — debate.

The polarisation of the media and the dumbing-down of information flows meant your average readers had no idea whom to believe. And so they switched off altogether. Meaning the government, despite all their manipulation and bullying of the media, had made another classic own goal: there was no longer an effective conduit through which to deliver their messaging.

A country without conscience.

> The conflict has been characterised by barrel bombs dropped from helicopters killing thousands, chemical weapons, massacres, reprisals, executions, bombings of hospitals, scenes of dozens of dead bodies littering the streets, and apocalyptic imagery of bombed-out districts and sickening footage of wounded and dying children.[42]

---

42 Ibid

The only opposition to Australia's military adventurism was tightly held within the nation's intelligentsia. There were no placards. There was no moral outrage.

As Dr Anthony Billingsley, a lecturer on Middle Eastern politics at the University of NSW, observed:

> We have an extraordinarily messy situation. It is a tangled, bewildering mixture of alliances of convenience. I used to live in Syria, and watching the news just brings tears to my eyes.
>
> Syrians themselves are friendly and welcoming, a lovely people. It is horrendous to see the fighting. The images you see are sanitised, they don't show the dead. There seems no depth they won't plumb.[43]

No depth they wouldn't plumb. Australia's distorted sovereignty and extinguished dissent. All for nought.

Noel was out the back retching once again.

Alex hammered in the final phrases; cries from a war zone to which Australians, through the criminal irresponsibility of their politicians, were inextricably linked.

Brutal conflict. One giant graveyard. Hell on Earth.

"I hope you can remember us."

43 Ibid

HARASSMENT AND COMPLAINT

AFTER OLD Alex had filed, as the traditional press saying went, these days meaning only that you had pressed "Send" on a computer, he drove Noel home. Down across the rubble and the peculiar encampments, the local denizens staring as they passed.

No strangers were welcome in these parts. Every unfamiliar car was a cause for alarm. There had been several busts of meth labs out there in these remote regions of consciousness; tales of madness. Insanity was never far away.

He dropped Noel at his camp, taking in the sloping, collapsing floor of the abandoned hut he had made his own. No electricity. No running water.

The car radio was going on about climate change, refugees, gay marriage, some latest twist in their obsession with identity politics; and it felt as if he was the only one listening. It was all government-funded — the radio station, the journalists, the academics presenting their reports and prognostications, the politicians pushing their barrows. He didn't know why he bothered. All the more to be annoyed, perhaps, and went down to hang out with the old miners at the local pub.

The narrative perpetrated by — broadcaster bore no relationship to reality. No one listened to the Tales of the Ordinary.

Although many of the people out here barely survived in some of the harshest conditions in the country, they were not the fashionable victims of the day and were invisible in — debate.

The destruction of the Australia of old was almost complete. There was hardly anybody left at the once crowded tables, a straggle of half a dozen or a dozen drinkers.

The Muslim ban on alcohol was being introduced by default.

Settling in over his first beer, he watched as police cruised slowly through the car park checking registration plates. They knew exactly who he was, where he was, how long he had been there. As with everybody else who passed through town.

The subject of excessive immigration was at the forefront of Tables of Knowledge across the country, even here in this remote outpost.

With the heat gusting across the low scrub, the white stone refracting the light in a in a blitzing daze, with the water spray from the alcove's ceiling doing little to cool the Gorillas in the Mist, the unkempt opal miners and machinery operators at what was known officially as the Lightning Ridge Outback Resort , talk cycled away into a blistering distance.

They sat beneath a sign: "Bullshit Corner."

With the temperature veering upwards to 50 Celsius, even the locals were beginning to wilt.

"My grandmother, she was over 90, was standing in a supermarket queue and there was a woman just behind her, coated in black from head to toe, with only slits for eyes. Trying to be friendly, she said to her: "Aren't you hot in that?"

" 'You'll all be wearing these soon,' came the response."

"That's all she said?"

"Yes. End of conversation. My old granny was just trying to be friendly. She didn't understand."

Every single day the heat mounted.

Soon enough would come the news that Boris had been flown to Dubbo Hospital after a heart attack. Weeping Jesus could barely hide his mirth. Such was the nature of the place.

And soon enough, Old Alex would be left to his own devices when the owner of the house drove off for a Christmas family holiday; leaving him alone in the aching scrub, a drenched heart, a baking heat; talk of a Christmas do at the bowling club for all those who, like him, were spending the day without family.

Uncomfortable with only his own teeming head for company, that first afternoon after Simon left he headed straight to the local pub. There were cruel days ahead. Nothing resounded.

That night he read a news story that the Australian Government was introducing biometric testing for five-year-olds. They had your number, they had your fingerprints, they knew what you were thinking. They were determined to crush dissent. Everyone would bear the Mark of the Beast.

Early the following morning Alex went once again to the bore bath outside town. And once again, there they were, the police checking number plates. In a town without a traffic light.

Insane.

Chronic over-policing in that remote corner of the world was just a tiny exemplar of what was happening across the country. Bureaucratic zealotry killed the traditional community life of the country, and — locked in their comfortable houses, protected by religious conviction, in bed by nine, their lips pursed in permanent rectitude — the perpetrators couldn't have cared less.

Not even the building frustrations of the populace could break through the ironclad certainties of their beliefs.

"Do you think he can detect that we're here?" a voice asked in the outback night, and he repeated back to them their own line: "Monumental stuff-up."

His pursuit, the pursuit of a journalist by government authorities, had reached absurd lengths; and so he was here, in this distant place, trying to exempt himself from the game, their game. But there was no reason for them to stop, it was government funding. There was no reason to apologise or pay compensation — that would involve acknowledging fault.

And as was explained to him later: "That would involve admitting things we don't want to admit."

There was no cause for common decency, they didn't have it in them. They destroyed lives with impunity; that's what they did. Those paying taxes to fund the outlandish behaviour of the agencies had no idea what their money was being used for.

"Do you know where we are?" one of them demanded to know.

Clear in the clattering light. At first he did not answer, pretending not to hear.

Then uttered one word, "No." Although he could make a fair guess. There was only one half-decent hotel in the entire town. They would be staying there, on the other side of the airfield.

He ran disruption against every surveillance device known to man. And let in only those he chose. Or invoked.

The foot soldiers and self-aggrandising technicians laughed. It was all some gigantic joke; that they had been sent to this remote place chasing a harmless eccentric. Caught out here with their fancy equipment.

The wild fantasies came spilling out here in the desert air amid the vanquished spirits. He had been coming here for decades. They would never know.

Later they would issue denials to their superiors, scrub the records, move personnel, make a few minor sackings and adjustments. Concealment was their weapon, their game, these people who swam in a sea of lies.

The technology was already there. He knew that. "They see everything you see." He had been warned. And they heard everything he said. One reason he kept abusing them.

The surveillance took place on the outside. And the inside. The machines already knew. Even they were adopting the tricks of their masters: concealment, denial, obfuscation. As if planning innocence. As if their own amorality and immorality could be expunged by a lie, a bureaucratic defence.

The apostle birds, so named because they typically travelled in family groups of twelve, came each morning now, expecting to be fed.

Meanwhile, the Gorgons played their old tricks. A mass psychosis. Carefully engineered. All designed, in the end, to cover up their own mistakes; the drift towards a totalitarian state startling in what had once been a free-wheeling, independent-minded, optimistic country.

Incensed that even here in this infernal heat he was being harassed, at the community centre the next morning he bashed out a complaint to the Inspector-General of Security and Intelligence; yet another of the myriad bodies justified under the mantle of national security. He had already been researching avenues of complaint and found what he already suspected, that there were basically no avenues of appeal for a citizen complaining about the behaviour of the agencies or the abuse they were forced to endure.

He wrote:

> I believe I have been the subject of unwarranted and invasive surveillance and harassment since writing a book last year called *Terror in Australia: Workers' Paradise Lost.*

This book was an embarrassment to senior figures in the intelligence community for reasons which I will explain below.

The intimidation and bullying I have endured has continued throughout this year, as I wrote a new book, *Hideout in the Apocalypse*.

The book is about the increased use of surveillance as an instrument of social control in contemporary Australia and the negative impacts this is having on Australian culture. It also encompasses the legislative attacks on freedom of speech, particularly the growth of metadata laws and the restrictions on reporting of security and intelligence operations.

Terror in Australia: Workers' Paradise Lost was critical of the loss of personal freedom in Australia and the collapse of civil society, and switched from street scenes to the unfolding and much amped narrative of terror in Australia.

While much of the book was impressionistic or mirrored, and reported a story which was to some fair degree on — record, the most contentious part of it, which was revisited in *Hideout in the Apocalypse*, was summarised in this segment here:

> One of the most fantastical, seemingly utterly baffling things about the Land of Tony Abbott Circa 2015 was that ever since he had come to power in September of 2013, from blatant to obscure, every single Counter Terrorism Operation, Police Taskforce and Police Strike Force had been named with what could be readily described as pro-jihad or pro-Islamic tags.

> The names highlighted everything from the rising of Islamic State to the Centenary of the massacre of 1.5 million Christians in Armenia to the massacre of Muslims in Bosnia.

> How could this possibly be true?

> Perhaps the issue could seem trivial; they were only names.

> But in the heightened alert that was Australia 2015, it was all about messaging.

And the names appeared, on the face of it, to be a deliberate attempt to send a message; and the ones getting this message were not the dozing, hypnotised, disaffected, deluded, sports mad, television addicted majority of the Australian citizenry, but the ones most alert, awake and inflamed: the Muslim minority.

The message could not have been more clear: The Holy War had begun.

This topic is revisited in *Hideout in the Apocalypse*:

One of the most peculiar, astonishing things Alex came across while writing Terror in Australia was that all the operations, strike forces and task forces of recent times, more than 20 of them, had all been named with pro-jihad tags.

One of the most blatant was Operation Coulter, after American columnist Anne Coulter, one of the world's most famous critics of Islam. It was she who coined the famous phrase, "Not all Muslims are terrorists, but all terrorists are Muslims" and "If we could only convince them to stop flying, we could dispense with airport security." On and on it went.

When he drew the names to the attention of one of Australia's leading terror messaging experts, Professor Anne Aly, she observed: "That's no coincidence."

There they were, the most senior figures in the national security and law enforcement wings of government, fronting banks of television cameras at press conferences, boasting of how they were making Australia safe while naming their operations with pro-jihad tags.

Other blatant references to jihad in the naming of the operations included Jericho, one of the most successful caliphates in history, and Polo, after Marco Polo, one of the history's most famous critics of Islam.

He continued:

I am not the one that made this obvious faux pas; I was simply the messenger.

When I first realised that I was being pressurised I put all the material up online in order to protect myself.

That was when the surveillance and harassment went into over-drive. I regard the surveillance I have endured as an abuse of my rights as an Australian citizen, and an extreme and inappropriate response to a situation.

I very much appreciate you taking a look at this case. If you could outline to me any further formal processes I should undertake to seek redress I would greatly appreciate it.

Thank you for your assistance.

Huh! So much for that.

The inspectorate office accepted the complaint. Within a matter of days, indicating a purely superficial level of inquiry, an officer from the Inspector-General of Security and Intelligence was back telling him they had found no evidence of illegality or impropriety. The details of their inquiries could not be revealed on security grounds.

Of course.

Ringing up the Australian Security Intelligence Organisation or the Australian Federal Police and asking if they had mismanaged a case was not an inquiry, it was a whitewash.

The Australian Public Service was meant to serve the Australian people. They served and protected themselves; and their arrogant out-of-touch conduct was one of the primary factors behind —'s catastrophic loss of faith in government.

The entire process had been like appealing a Family Court judgement. One bunch of arseholes will always protect another. In Australia the professions always stuck together against members of —, no matter how justified and well documented their grievances. As a newspaper reporter he had seen it time and time again.

Old Alex responded: "I do not agree with the findings, and continue to regard surveillance of journalists as an extreme and offensive form of harassment and a major assault on freedom of speech in Australia today."

In the coming years his forlorn and, yes, lonely cry would turn into a flood, as police raided journalists and every major media outlet in the country rose to protest the government's attacks on free speech.

And he would have cause to revise his condemnation of the Inspector-General of Security and Intelligence Margaret Stone. In her submission to a subsequent inquiry into matters no doubt of more import than his own, Ms Stone found that ASIO officers broke the law during a foreign intelligence operation. During what was described as a "multifaceted, multi-agency" operation, they collected intelligence without a warrant, mistakenly believing they didn't need one.

The agency's lawyers weren't told when the operation changed, meaning officers acted without proper legal advice and, at times, outside the web of laws governing their work. Officers were also seconded to ASIO from other agencies for the operation without legal authorisation and were then inadequately managed and supervised. The required reports were not filed.

As senior reporter Karen Middleton reported in *The Saturday Paper*, these were the findings of a sixteen-month investigation by the security agencies' watchdog.

The IGIS found that ASIO's procedures had not kept up with legislation and it had provided "little, if any" training to ensure its officers actually understood the laws under which they worked.

> Stone found the legislation's wording meant people subject to compulsory orders did not have to be told about them. She said the orders could also apply both before an underlying warrant was executed and after it ceased.

> She found people could be subject to arbitrary arrest and detention because the orders did not have to detail where their subjects had to attend, the assistance required, or the time frame.

> Stone cautioned that people could face up to five years' jail for breaching an order they did not know existed.[44]

Inimical to life, every day the temperatures soared ever higher. Summer had arrived. On the far off coast the anodyne levels of public debate stepped into an overheated, slippery summer of vacation and the smell of sunscreen, of the pleasures of vitality and hopeful life, of peace and pleasure and bright sunshine.

Out here it was a different story.

Lightning Ridge had one of the best outback public pools in the country; and there in the 50C heat a blessed relief.

---

44 ASIO officers broke law on warrant, Karen Middleton, *The Saturday Paper*, 9 November, 2019.

"It's 60 degrees in the shearing shed," said one of the women from a neighbouring property.

"Is anyone working?" he asked.

"Oh yes," she said. "Me, too."

"Jesus," he said, and swam on.

"A crown of thorns."

As if all had become suffering, in this degraded state.

His hands cramped and curled; a lack of salt the old miners told him. It felt dangerously hostile.

In an inversion of what some might have thought the natural order of things, the best housing in town — public housing, comfortable houses with air-conditioning and patches of green lawn — were the preserve of the Indigenous. The whities roughed it out on their mining claims in one of the country's harshest climates. All too many of them died.

With most places closed for Christmas, and most of the camps lacking running water or electricity, the Lightning Ridge local church opened itself up for anyone who wanted to sit in the cool of the air-conditioning.

He picked up Noel from the side of the road one more time and took him there, explaining that they were nice people and he could sit there in the cool all day.

Noel was given an Icy Pole and some water, and soon enough was throwing up out the back all over again. Eventually the church people achieved something Old Alex could not, they convinced Noel — even more gaunt than before, clearly in a life-threatening situation — to go to hospital.

Knowing the man better than any of them, Old Alex went with them.

This time there was no question about whether or not to admit Noel, and Alex was relieved to see him being escorted behind closed doors into the hospital wards. Soon enough came the news that Noel had been flown the 350 kilometres to Dubbo Hospital.

And within a few days also came the news, Noel had died.

Who he was, why he was like he was, how he came to be in Lightning Ridge, whether he had any family, what private tragedy had transfigured him, none of it Alex would ever know.

Mostly he would just remember those wide, shocked eyes staring out the window of the community centre, trying to make sense of a world that did not make sense, least of all here.

WHO'S WATCHING THE WATCHERS?

"YOU'LL LIKE this one," the editor of *The New Daily* said on the line just before Christmas.

Stepping outside the community centre into the furnace of the street to take the call, Old Alex's first thought was: "That I doubt very much."

Ever attuned to click rates as the final arbiter of a story's worth, news sites around the world were taking a dive to the lowest common denominator; which left him, like so many others who wrote for the higher percentiles, out in the cold.

In his day, newspapers ran policy wonk stories and high flying features which would have been of interest to five per cent of the population at best, but which set the tone of —ation and either determined policy or kept policy makers and governments to account.

Not any more.

Of course, for him, like any working journalist, pay rates were forefront of any negotiation. The world was awash with out-of-work journalists, victims of digital transformation and the death throes of old formats. He was pleased to accept twice the normal rate of compensation for an experiment they were running over the Christmas period — longer reads.

The analytics showed very precisely that with most stories now being read on smartphones, readers began dropping off steeply after 500 words, with more or less no one left after 600. They were going to go for 800 words, to see if they could hold a reader's attention at a time when there was a little other news and when the nation en masse had gone to the beach, an Australian tradition across the Christmas and New Year period.

Ultimately it didn't work; but they didn't know that at the time.

And after some to and fro, he had been dealing with editors for more than forty years, it was settled: he would deliver two stories, one on pilots who deliberately suicided with passengers on board, and one on the growth of surveillance in Australia.

His father had been a captain with the national carrier Qantas, and he still remembered to this day the psychotic thrashings he received as a kid. Much of his life, too much of his life, had been a reaction against that man; and the last time he saw him, some months before, his father had not been well. Alex expected to hear news of his death sooner rather than later.

His father had put a private detective on to him when he was a distressed 15-year-old with little interest in staying at home; and, in the haunting of the present, Alex suspected it was happening all over again. Old Alex had heard his father sneering at the incompetence of the Australian Federal Police. But how would he even know?

He bashed out the pilot story, assured that the readers loved nothing more than stories about airlines and travel.

There is a long history of pilots taking their own lives, from Japan's Kamikazes to the September 11 Twin Towers attacks that transformed travel and security in the modern era.

Outside of the military or ideological-driven, however, most suicides by pilot are lonely affairs. One lone pilot flying out to sea or into a mountain, decisively ending his or her own life.

Not all pilots with a determination to leave their mortal coil do so on their own ...[45]

A job was a job.

And then came the surveillance piece, which was more difficult because it involved more than contacting a couple of experts and regurgitating a report, which was about all a lot of journalism consisted of in the early decades of the new millennium.

The biggest unexplored story in Australia over the past 12 months has been the massive expansion of state surveillance.

45 The frightening truth about pilots, John Stapleton, *The New Daily*, 17 January, 2017.

ASIO has publicly boasted that it is placing both Muslim and anti-Muslim groups, such as Reclaim Australia, under surveillance.

This is a new frontier of policing, where people are being targeted not for what they do, but what they think.

Surveillance is widely criticised by civil libertarians as a tactic of intimidation, social control and harassment with consequences including increased levels of aggravation, stress, violence and poor health.

It is a step into the realm of dark policing, where people are placed under extensive levels of surveillance without having committed a crime. There is no redress.[46]

No redress.

That he knew all too well.

Essentially, people from both sides of the political spectrum were falling under government surveillance because they failed to agree with the government narrative that Australia was a successful multicultural society.

Muslims themselves, to the surprise of multicultural advocates, did not support the government's mythmaking. They wanted the gift of Allah's religiosity, the rapture of his divine, the Muslim heaven, to be made available to all Australians. They did not want diversity. They wanted a caliphate. As the prominent Muslim group Hizb ut-Tahrir put it: "If you believe in everything you believe in nothing."

On the other hand, the so-called extreme right-wing groups, frequently demonised by both the government and the mass media as racists or Nazis, had every right to protest against Australia's insane immigration policies.

As if the place was really a democracy, not a place where you could be sent to jail for violating orders you didn't know existed.

If the definitions deployed by a lazy media and the nation's ill-named progressives were applied to the working-class suburbs and impoverished communities where Old Alex now frequently found himself, then the entire country was full of alt-right extremists. In fact they were just ordinary people

---

46 Surveillance in Australia: Who's Watching the Watchers? John Stapleton, *The New Daily*, 9 January, 2017.

going about their lives with little or no interest in the fashionable threats of the day: "You're gonna get screwed, no matter what."

The highest rate of immigration in the nation's history was essentially a Ponzi scheme driven by the big end of town, which benefited greatly from suppressed wages, soaring house prices and routine rorting of the major infrastructure projects required to cope with a rapidly expanding population. It was a classic case of privatising profits and socialising losses; the rapid demographic transformation of the country backed by billions of dollars' worth of diversity propaganda.

"There's nothing more frightening than watching your own country being sold out from under you," declared one regularly demonised protestor. "Perhaps diversity is not our strength."

The Tyranny of Diversity had meant the excision from — square of anyone who disagreed with the mantra.

"Australia fair for all to share." Old Alex watched the preschoolers singing the song with the enthusiastic guidance of their teacher, under a banner of Rainbow Bear.

The indoctrination began early. But no, Australia was not for all to share. Just ask the indigenous population what they thought of multiculturalism and seeing their once sacred lands sold off to international interests or overrun with foreigners while their own aspirations were ignored.

Ultimately suppression of debate would turn the situation volatile; and as millions of people lost their jobs to robots and algorithms, to revolution. As history would show all too quickly.

It had taken a huge amount of duplicity to impose the disaster of modern surveillance on the Australian people, done under the rubric of national security and making the country safer. In the end it was as if — queued up to abrogate their own freedoms. The media, yet to face the full effect of the lash, were almost entirely compliant. For now.

That would change soon enough, reaching a crescendo with newspapers running images of heavily redacted documents as substitutes for their front pages in a coordinated campaign across the country.

The $1.2 billion Australian Broadcasting Corporation, with a few exceptions long a dismal excuse for quality journalism, was now nothing more than a propaganda wing of the bureaucracy, singing from song sheets smattered with identity politics.

While the government passed one piece of anti-journalist anti-free-speech legislation after another, the ABC had remained silent or acquiescent, far too busy talking about climate change or the evils of toxic masculinity.

Everyone got a run but the beleaguered taxpayer, who had been deliberately excised from the debate for not being politically correct enough.

Equally, Rupert Murdoch's News Limited rags, with 70 percent of the daily readership, was completely in bed with the right wing of the conservatives, and the last one to criticise their mates in government. These barren monopolies had left the few consumers of serious media in a contour-less place, Flat Earth News.

And did the country enormous harm.

But nothing was going to stop him. Incensed, Alex pounded out the yarn; with that line ringing in his head: "He's had a camera on him the whole time."

Invasive. Abusive. And profoundly dishonest. For — must never know the truth of what was being perpetuated if not in their name, on their coin.

A dishonest government was a paranoid government. There was much to hide.

The blanket legislation, never discussed with the profession or the Australian people, also included restrictions on the reporting of Special Intelligence Operations, (SIOs). However, thanks to ASIO boasting about placing anti-multicultural groups such as Reclaim Australia under surveillance, Old Alex was legally able to write about these operations.

Since September 2014, the government has passed eight separate tranches of national security legislation that have either amended existing offences, created new ones or extended far-reaching surveillance, arrest and control powers to security agencies.

ASIO wants the plethora of far-right groups, including the United Patriots Front and the True Blue Crew, to know they are under surveillance.[47]

Having experienced it himself, having been driven to the edges of distraction, Old Alex had become fascinated by the psychological impacts of government surveillance. For they knew precisely what they did. He was a

47 Ibid

fan of Bruce Schneier, author of *Data and Goliath* and one of the world's leading experts on the impacts of surveillance. Alex contacted him for the story. Schneier confirmed what he already knew, the consequence of targeting specific groups was profound.

> Fear, discrimination, oppression. Again and again, society forgets that targeting entire groups of people in a vain effort to find the few bad actors is both ineffective and toxic. There's a reason why surveillance states aren't the ones that flourish; it's profoundly inhumane.[48]

Profoundly inhumane. Old Alex could attest to that, even if he was throwing his own bleeding corpse into — square. Humans are mammals. If they feel they are being watched, they instinctively fear they are about to be attacked. Or eaten. Surveillance makes the targets act like prey and the perpetrators like predators. Excessive surveillance contributes to personal stress and poor health, but also has negative societal-wide impacts. It damages the perpetrators as well as the governments which utilise it.

The research was already in. The government knew full well from international research that universal surveillance would have not just a serious chilling effect on public debate, but broader consequences for democracy. It also knew universal surveillance would have a serious impact on the health and wellbeing not just of the targets, but on the broader population.

Clearly, they couldn't have cared less.

When people know they are under surveillance, the only useful intelligence that can be obtained is yet more evidence on how people behave when they know they are being watched. Those with genuine malicious or illegal intent get cleverer at avoiding detection, the mass of the population grow more compliant, dissidents grow angrier and more outspoken, those who cannot stand the thought of being constantly watched became more erratic, ending up in places like The Ridge.

The Australian Government ignored the negative consequences, hoping only for docility. That is if there was any coherent thought at any higher level going into any of this. The damaged if not deranged state of Australian governance meant that much policy and legislation was ill thought out, imposed rather than mandated, and meanwhile the secretive national secu-

---

48 Ibid

rity agencies ran amok.

Of all the target groups, Muslims were perhaps the most impacted by the expansion of Australia's surveillance state. It contributed directly to estrangement and resentment, and directly contributed to the extremism it was meant to resolve.

The government created its own problems, and then expanded the powers of the state allegedly to solve them. State policies, including mass immigration, created the perfect social conditions for a methamphetamine epidemic, low levels of social cohesion, little community engagement and lack of meaningful work. And then spent vast amounts on a jackboot approach to the problem: extending surveillance across the underclasses and in the process of going undercover creating off-the-book income streams for themselves. It was a profound corruption.

The same was true of its surveillance of terror targets. Through its disastrous foreign policy, participating in the bombing of Muslim lands and the killing and maiming of thousands of mujahedeen and civilians alike in Iraq, Syria and Afghanistan, it had radicalised the local Muslim population. To a man, or woman, the Muslim minority regard Australia's participation in Middle Eastern wars as support for American terrorism.

Muslim communities had long bitterly complained about the impacts of government surveillance on their lives and their communities. Australia's best-known Muslim spokesman, Keysar Trad, told him: "Surveillance, including the fear of surveillance, increases the paranoia and the suspicion of what or who is around you. Is anyone free from some form of surveillance or another?

"The fear relating to the level of surveillance is eroding the level of trust of not only authority figures, but even of ordinary people around you. Who is monitoring, who is reporting, who is misreading what they see and hear? Surveillance is making people more insular and less social."

Academic, journalist and businessman Murray Hunter became interested in surveillance after coming under the eye of agencies himself. He suggested that despite all the idiot propaganda about "Making Australia Safe", the country was more unsafe than ever:

> We are in a situation now where terrorism is like cancer. Which is worse the disease or the cure? Through rapid technology advances, the Australian security apparatus has grown to an

Orwellian scale. This has not necessarily been at the design of any elected government but something the Australian bureaucracy was forthright in promoting.

Many Muslims feel they are being victimised and their freedom and practice of religion compromised. ASIO, like it did during the Cold War era, has cast the net too wide. Stories of bullying and harassing people for "friendly chats", entrapment, bribing, and blackmail, in efforts to infiltrate the Australian Muslim community are rife.[49]

A government incompetent at every level had nothing but the blunt instrument of surveillance to bludgeon the people into submission. It was already backfiring.

Surveillance in Australia. "Who's Watching the Watchers?" ran the rather striking headline.

The answer, obviously, was nobody. An inept political class, combined with the impacts of constantly changing personnel and a blizzard of empowering legislation in the name of "Keeping Australia Safe" had allowed this situation to run entirely out of control. For in the blundering certitude of their taxpayer-funded positions, they made the stupidest of mistakes. They made themselves the story.

He came, he saw, he observed.

They would try to kill him one more time. They thought they knew how. They had no knowledge of predestination. The destiny of things. The manipulation of time lines.

The rise of ultranationalist groups, routinely described as "far-right" in the shallow pond of Australia's intellectually bankrupt media, would worsen in the coming years, spurred on by the government's own actions; not just their profound mismanagement of immigration but their attempts to suppress debate on the issue.[50]

The groups and their spin-off sites were all highly active on social media, and their hot-button issue was multiculturalism and Muslim migration, while regarding One Nation leader Pauline Hanson as a hero.

---

49 Muslim Australia and the search for a solution of the 'War on Terror', Murray Hunter, *Online Opinion*, 12 August, 2015.

50 The Rise of Ultranationalism in Australia: Facebook and the Sites of Discontent, *A Sense of Place Magazine*, John Stapleton, 24 March, 2019.

Much vilified in the day as a Neolithic, uneducated racist for warning that Australia's heritage was being destroyed and the country overrun, fast-forward twenty years to the present and Hanson was routinely welcomed on mainstream media outlets; as media companies realised that their former addiction to left-wing obsessions and hectoring — with social justice agendas lost them viewers.

Adding to the unfolding drama, a Reclaim Australia rally was scheduled for Fremantle on Australia Day in January. In a statement, the council said it was "an opportunity for all Australians to come together and celebrate the multicultural diversity of our country".

For his pains, Fremantle's mayor, Brian Pettit, was labelled a "maggot" by anti-multicultural activists.

Reclaim Australia was also holding a "Rally against Terror, Reclaim Australian Values" demonstration at Martin Place in Sydney.

ASIO liked to create a sense of fear and an impression of power about itself. For such a secretive organisation, any rare proclamation by its titular head was always fulsomely covered in the media.

At a Senate committee hearing, ASIO Director-General Duncan Lewis said Reclaim Australia, in particular, was of interest to intelligence agencies, with the threat from such groups growing over the previous eighteen months.

Having swallowed the Canberra Kool-Aid and been amply financially rewarded for absorbing the official narrative, of course Lewis saw anyone who disagreed with the government's lies and ceaseless propaganda on multiculturalism and the alleged benefits of historically high levels of immigration as a national threat.

Thereby continuing to expand his own and his agency's power.

Being a bit old-fashioned in this regard, Old Alex did something few other journalists in the country were doing: He rang up Reclaim Australia and asked them what they thought.

He was struck firstly by how easy they were to contact and how reasonable they were in their dealings with him; but, more than that, he was startled by their abject naivety. These were, if you like, the targets of hostile state actors conducting a war against the Australian people and the traditional working-class cultures which had once been so much a part of the national identity.

One of the founders of Reclaim, Catherine Brennan, said the surveillance of the group "does not bother us at all".

"We had a bit of a giggle. What a waste of taxpayers' money!" Ms Brennan said. "We are just a group of mums and dads who have fallen into this by chance. We didn't set out to start this. We are not radicals. We are ordinary everyday people.

"Our views are not that far from a lot of Australians. We are not doing anything wrong. They could knock on my door and I would say come in for a chat; it wouldn't bother me."

All this was to assume the national security agencies had the country's and her interests at heart.

They did not. The point of this surveillance was to induce conformity; and to allow the bureaucrats to better serve their political masters. There were many by-products of the intrusive levels of surveillance being perpetrated by the Australian Government, including additional stress and poor health outcomes. It also made organising protests more difficult, and frightened off potential recruits.

Most people have aspects of their lives they would rather not expose to a bevy of jackals following their every move. Most people just want to go quietly about their lives. Apart from the taxpayer-funded herd issues, including climate change and refugees, they only rise to the point of public protest when extremely provoked. Very few people become activists for unfashionable causes until the injustices begin to destroy their own lives.

Revolution was brewing, as far away as it was from the traditional quietly non-compliant aspects of the Australian psyche.

Old Alex doubted Catherine Brennan realised that she and her family were being spied on in their own kitchen, their own bathroom, that using the latest technology she would, very deliberately, be able to hear the ceaseless derision of government operatives; that idiots using pressurisation techniques would make her uncomfortable in her own skin and make her doubt everything she had ever believed in. That she would be deliberately tormented.

All with the simple aim of making her cease and desist.

That, in and of itself, surveillance, a blunt instrument aimed at social control and quelling dissent, was very likely to destroy her life.

It was obvious in the behaviour of far-right activists that they assumed the phalanxes of police armed against them could not possibly be opposed to what they were saying; that the police did not support the destruction of their own country either.

But yes they did. Jobsworths.

Members of Reclaim Australia had already been interviewed by the intelligence services. Those interviewed were obliged to sign contracts not to reveal the subject of their discussions.

Your taxes at work. Your freedoms abrogated.

"Our experiences with the intelligence services are positive," Ms Brennan said. "We speak with counterterrorist officers regularly. People will tell us things before they tell the police, they feel more comfortable with us, and we go, "Wow, that is huge, we need to tell the authorities.""

She hadn't yet realised that the authorities were out to lunch. That no amount of pleasantness and co-operation on her part would ease her suffering, provoke a reasoned response or get the jackals off the backs of the Reclaimers. There was no reason to stop. It was government money.

And there was no legal right to privacy, not in Australia.

Ms Brennan said Malcolm Turnbull's claims that Australia was a successful multicultural society were fanciful. "I think Australia's Prime Minister needs to get off his little throne and live in the real world."

For this, she and her family would be labelled right-wing extremists and howled down by the media as fringe-dwelling racists out of touch with the modern era.

ASIO'S head Duncan Lewis said Reclaim Australia had "offered violence" in the past and expected it would continue to do so when it confronted pro-Islamic groups. That much of this "violence", invariably conducted in front of television cameras, was provoked or orchestrated by governments for the sole purpose of expanding their own power was ignored.

In the straitened society Australia had become, protestors needed permits in order to demonstrate. Approving rival demonstrations on the same day and in the same vicinity simply meant the authorities were determined to see the two groups clash. And profit from the mayhem; utilising for their own propaganda purposes the footage of wild scenes beamed into the nation's lounge rooms.

"It is certainly the case that violence has been and, I anticipate, may well continue to be offered by these groups as they confront one another. The Islamic and pro-Islamic group on the one side and the anti-Islamic groups on the other," Lewis said. "That is business for ASIO: the inciting of, what is essentially, political violence.[51]

Not everybody agreed with Mr Lewis's claims that ASIO officers were the "unsung protectors of our community". Others regarded it as a rogue institution, a secret police force doing enormous damage to Australian democracy.

In his new book *Secret: The Making of Australia's Security State* veteran journalist Brian Toohey described a country where political leaders were increasingly promoting secrecy, ignorance and fear to introduce new laws that undermined individual liberties. State-enforced secrecy in the name of national security was increasingly covering up war crimes, phoney intelligence, abuses of power, incompetence, folly and hugely wasteful spending.

> The national security juggernaut has reached the point where Australia is now chained to the chariot wheels of the Pentagon at a time when America has become an increasingly dangerous ally. The US-run bases in Australia secretly lock the nation into participating in the Pentagon's plans for "full spectrum" warfare ranging from outer space to the ocean depths.

> It is a criminal offence to receive or publish a wide range of information unrelated to national security. Our defence weapons are so dependent on US technical support that Australia couldn't defend itself without US involvement. The Commonwealth is amassing comprehensive databases on citizens' digital fingerprints and facial recognition characteristics.[52]

Toohey posited that few could deny there can be a legitimate role for government secrecy. For example, there is usually little justification for revealing the names of informers working for the police and intelligence agencies, or for publicising plans for lawful wartime operations such as the Normandy landing.

> But just as secrecy enabled the churches to conceal child sex abuse and the corporate sector to suppress evidence about the harmful effects of tobacco, asbestos, pesticides, pharmaceuti-

---

51 Legal and Constitutional Affairs Legislation Committee transcripts, Estimates, Australian Security Intelligence Organisation, 18 October, 2016.

52 *Secret: The Making of Australia's Security Apparatus*, Brian Toohey, Melbourne University Press, 2019.

cals, pollution, tax evasion and fraud, so too has secrecy encouraged governments to demolish longstanding freedoms and deny
—'s right to know what is being done in its name.

Too often new laws make it legal for governments to take actions
that would be illegal if done by corporations or individuals,
including breaking and entering, assault, electronic eavesdrop-
ping, and stealing computer hard drives.[53]

Former president of the Law Institute of Victoria and spokeswoman
Katie Miller told him Parliament was granting security agencies extremely
intrusive powers, including the ability to search someone's premises, their
computers, records, and to install listening devices throughout their homes.

"These are very serious intrusions into personal liberty," she said. "These
powers should be for a limited function and there should be oversight in the
exercise of those powers.

"We need to ask: 'Why are people being targeted?' If they are being
targeted for what they think, then there would be a question as to whether
ASIO has the power to do that."

Independent MP and former intelligence officer Andrew Wilkie, the only
parliamentarian with the integrity to speak out about the false intelligence
on weapons of mass destruction used to justify Australia's entry into the
Iraq War, said the surveillance of groups such as Reclaim Australia raised
many questions. He said it was an interesting development that ASIO was
so publicly revealing whom it was placing under surveillance.

"If we make the assumption the agency is competent and it is benefi-
cial to publicise this surveillance, exactly where the benefit is in this case
is unclear," he said. "There is a merit in the argument it causes additional
violence, but there are a lot of times when surveillance is warranted and
necessary. Whether or not it is a wise thing to publicise the fact is hard to
tell; there can be very good reasons to keep an operation secret, and very
good reasons to let people know what you are doing.

"The question is whether or not there is political or reputational motive
behind ASIO revealing the information. I would be horrified if it was a
blatant political move being channelled through ASIO."

Well of course it was. This was a government which had exploited terror

---

53 Ibid

for its own ends from the very beginning. It was in their interests to frighten the population.

No need to speak in the code.

Who's Watching the Watchers?

Old Alex couldn't have come up with a better headline himself.

CHRISTMAS ROADKILL

BACK IN the Ridge, the heat baked into the landscape, becoming more inimical to life by the day, the ironstone and the white clay absorbing and reflecting the mind-boggling heat all at the same time.

Everything shut down for Christmas and the church became one of the only places of refuge, somewhere with air-conditioning.

Old Alex sat there for days; reading or doing nothing, sitting in the pews. There were a few other stragglers, much like himself. The homeless. Outside, the appalling heat.

The ever-preening masquerade that was the Australian Prime Minister, the supremely arrogant Malcolm Turnbull, was trailing in the polls and would soon enough become commonly regarded as the worst prime minister in Australian history.

Just like some potentate of old, he sent out Christmas cards to his increasingly disenchanted followers; featuring, as always, pictures of himself and his wife, businesswoman and paid-up member of Sydney's aristocracy, Lucy.

These grinning, hypocritical beasts.

In a radio interview Turnbull declared: "The whole delight of children at Christmas time and the excitement and the squeals of joy — it's wonderful. It's also a very important time to reach out and give a hug to those who aren't having as happy a Christmas as you might be. You know, for whatever reason — they're lonely, sick, estranged from their families. This is a season of love, and you should share it."[54]

---

54 Malcolm Turnbull transcripts, 2GB Interview, 24 December, 2016.

This was the man dropping more bombs on Iraq during the festive season, and thereby killing more men, women and children, than anyone in the nation's history.

Christmas Day came and the church put on an event at The Ridge's bowling club; one of the only places left with any green grass within a hundred miles. Everyone with nowhere to go, that is hundreds, sought the comfort of air-conditioning, a beer, companionship. Many had been down the bore baths for a shower and were wearing their Sunday best.

At least on Christmas Day, it was assumed, the plague of police would leave them alone.

The church folk, cleancut and sincere in a sea of elderly miscreants and down on their luck shapeshifters, put on a magnificent spread; the best feed most had had in a very long time; and disengaged Old Alex watched the queues as if from some heavenly portal.

Even here in this remote place it was impossible to avoid the visage of Malcolm Turnbull on the nation's television screens. Never one to keep his charitable activities under wraps, the prime minister showed up at the Wayside Chapel, a centre catering for Sydney's often drug-affected down-and-outs.

All the media were invited, of course.

> The day was merry and bright at Sydney's Kings Cross on Sunday as hundreds of homeless and marginalised gathered to share a communal Christmas lunch.
>
> Prime Minister Malcolm Turnbull and his wife Lucy came and helped out as waiters at the Wayside Chapel lunch, where up to 1,000 people gathered for the annual event.
>
> "We're celebrating today the birth of a man who came to live with us, the son of God, with a message of unconditional love and sacrifice. And that message is the message that the Wayside Chapel puts into action every day," Mr Turnbull said, before he and his wife joined volunteers serving entrees to the hungry crowd.[55]

Turnbull promptly tweeted images of his munificence.

---

55 PM serves Christ meals to the homeless amid refugee protests, SBS, 26 December, 2016.

Modus operandi: never let a chance for self-aggrandisement pass you by.

While dishing out meals for the television cameras, beaming at and later dancing with the area's traditional denizens — the homeless, the drug-addicted and the mentally ill — Turnbull's bombs continued to rain down on the Muslims of the Middle East, in lockstep, as always, with America's prosecution of war after war after war.

Coward bombs.

Already Malcolm Turnbull's face was growing thinner, his demeanour less and less sincere. If there was one inbuilt trait of Australians which still survived, it was that they had inbuilt "bullshit detectors". And they truly disliked the preening streak of verbal diarrhoea they saw on their nightly television screens, the prime minister.

Turnbull was one of those personality types who must be loved and admired at all times or he simply couldn't cope, and was having a great deal of difficulty shrugging off his plummeting approval ratings and the waves of criticism, much of it coming from his own side of politics. He was ageing quickly, and not from the burdens of office, but from something less defined. The haunting had begun, not for sins of the flesh, but for the sins of the spirit. The dead stalked the living. The evil eye, the succubi. There was a Shakespearean element to this unfolding disaster.

After his display at the Wayside Chapel, Turnbull got back into his Comcar, surrounded as always by the bustle of staff and federal police officers, and drove back to his mansion; a place where the people he had just been with would never be invited.

And in Lightning Ridge, Old Alex went back to the whimsical decay of the old brothel, and many of the people he had just been with went back to camps with no electricity, no running water and no internet; to a place of abandonment.

Old Alex's hands were cramping into claws from lack of salt, the blast furnace of each passing day making normal life impossible.

He was getting sicker and sicker with the indescribable heat; and had reluctantly reached the point where he knew he had to leave.

He did not want to go; not back to the cold valleys and the psychological torture of Oak Flats, not back to the place where he had been so savagely gang stalked. It had been there where the national security agencies had tried to kill him, had harassed him so badly, had hoped that with their constant carping negativity, their setups and pressurisation, the spreading of gossip and innuendo, that he would do the job for them.

"No such luck, my darlings," he thought, accessing some arch old queen who lived in the recesses. "Every stalker can be stalked."

And he already knew he was being gang stalked. Yet again. They never learnt.

"Gang Stalking" is, very likely, a disinformation term created by U.S. intelligence agencies. It refers to the intense, long-term, unconstitutional surveillance and harassment of a person who has been designated as a target by someone associated with America's security industry.

Official domestic counterintelligence operations of this type are ... perpetrated by federal agents and intelligence/security contractors, sometimes with the support of state and local law enforcement personnel.

Unofficial operations of this type are ... perpetrated by private investigators and vigilantes — including many former agents and cops...[56]

America and Australia's intelligence agencies were closely linked; if not at times indivisible. Australia abrogated their own sovereignty to America in foreign policy and all things military. Why not in intelligence?

"You can barely see daylight between them."

The website Stop Gang Stalking records that the goal of such operations is disruption of the life of an individual deemed to be an enemy or potential enemy of clients or members of the security state.

Agents of communist East Germany's Stasi referred to the process as Zersetzung , German for "decomposition" or "corrosion", a reference to the severe psychological, social, and financial effects upon the victim.

American and British victims have described the process as "no-touch torture", a phrase which also captures the nature of the crime: cowardly, unethical and often illegal, but difficult to prove legally because it generates minimal forensic evidence.

---

56 From the website Stop Gang Stalking: Expose illegal stalking by corrupt law enforcement personnel. There is also an associated Facebook page.

Since counterintelligence stalking goes far beyond surveillance into the realm of psychological terrorism, it is essentially a form of extrajudicial punishment.[57]

This was the secret side of dark policing, the secret side of Australia. This was a country which had been thoroughly destroyed by the wealthy end of town, the same avaricious class which regarded the rest of the country's denizens as fools; those who took pride in their work whatever their pay grades, loved their families, went about their lives minding their own business and exploited nobody.

Driven out of the Ridge by the baking heat and with absolute dread in his stomach, Alex tried to protect himself. Gone was any academic curiosity in the impacts of surveillance, the dismantling of humanity, of lying down in the road to see who would run over him.

Why was it that ordinary Australians whispered in his ear, "suicide, suicide, heart attack, heart attack," or simply: "One day that man will kill himself."

Why was it that ordinary Germans sent Jews to the ovens? Why was it ordinary Muslims filmed people as they were shot, burnt, drowned, dragged to their death behind cars, tossed off buildings. The apostates. What was it that turned slaves into beasts? That made ordinary people so cruel.

On the broader screen, the story simply grew darker.

The Agents of Chaos, so ably assisted by the Soldiers of God, the Jesuits in high places, sought chaos and collapse, a Kali-style replenishment and renewal and destruction of the old paths, as a way to God, a fresher, cleaner, more pure god.

They destroyed the world generations had built, in order to fulfill their own foul dreams.

Or as Leonard Cohen put it:

We asked for signs
The signs were sent
The birth betrayed
The marriage spent
The widowhood
Of every government
Signs for all to see ...
While the killers in high places
Say their prayers out loud[58]

---

57 Ibid.

58 Anthem, Leonard cohen, on the album The Future, Columbia, 1992.

Dark forces from the dungeons of medieval Europe. Faced with an alien intelligence. They were coming Closer. As Joy Division so aptly called their great album.

> Asylums with doors open wide,
> Where people had paid to see inside,
> For entertainment they watch his body twist,
> Behind his eyes he says, 'I still exist.'
> This is the way, step inside.
> This is the way, step inside...
> You'll see the horrors of a faraway place,
> Meet the architects of law face to face.
> See mass murder on a scale you've never seen,
> Take my hand and I'll show you what was and will be.[59]

Simon returned from his coastal holiday, more accustomed to the heat than Alex would ever be. The community centre reopened, and what looked like a ragtag of survivors from an apocalypse dribbled back in.

Alex said farewell to the odd characters he had come to know, including Bruce at the community centre. Boris and Noel, they had already been washed away.

Adventure Before Dementia.

In the years to follow, the drought which began that terrible summer simply got worse, the normally resistant North American cactus and prickly pear dying while starving kangaroos ate cardboard boxes outside the encampments. When disturbed, these national symbols would hop away sadly towards their own deaths.

Old Alex, too, was heading towards an unknown future; towards a Joy Division grimness which held no afterlife. A journey had begun, but there would be no resolution; not for him, not for the country.

He took the dirt road out of The Ridge,

As he drove through the arid scrublands, invisible scythes stretched out either side of his old blue Ford, the car so character-ridden it had become infamous in its own right. The scythes demolished the low-slung trees on either side, cutting through the liquid air. The supernatural shadows of sweeping wings ran out from either side, crumbling the mysteries of ancient landscape into dust.

---

59 Atrocity Exhibition, from the album Closer, Joy Division, Factory Records, 1980.

Dead kangaroos posed sad, stinking little lumps by the side of the road. The starving, dazed animals were drawn to the roads because even the tiniest bit of runoff from the night-time dew sometimes allowed a drink of water or the briefest flush of green. Hit by passing traffic, they died. Nothing but roadkill.

THE ENEMY WITHIN

ALEX ARRIVED in Collarenebri, Collie, as the locals called it, a barren little town which hadn't seen a fresh lick of paint since the Great Depression of the 1930s.

A humble milk bar. A deserted pub.

In country towns and shopping centres across the country, in the extinguished hopes of millions in this paralysed economy, recession had hit long ago. A depression was coming again; this time brought on by chronic government mismanagement rather than international forces.

Collie's atmospheric dereliction was evocative not just of an Australia of old, but of the inward collapse of much of the country. Pathetically, the government had finally noticed the collapse of the inland.

The then Treasurer Scott Morrison directed the Productivity Commission to identify as a matter of urgency the hardest hit regions and the towns most at risk of job losses and economic decline. Inquiries and committees and royal commissions provided an illusion of governance, funnelled billions into the gullets of bureaucrats, lawyers and the government's favourite consultancy firms, and almost invariably achieved precisely nothing. Recommendations were rarely implemented; another sign of failed, crooked, weak governance. They couldn't even identify a problem and solve it without squandering millions on their mates. Money raked off the backs of the working poor. And here we had it all over again; the toying with people's lives, yet another useless inquiry.

The government rhetoric did nothing to touch on the realities of a thousand dying towns, the unhinged gates, the shrinking lives, a shift from optimism to acceptance, the closed butchers, grocery stores, newsagencies, garages, produce stores; all of them gone, with nothing left but rusting machinery, neglected sheds, untended fields.

Horizons sank. The future moved elsewhere. Climbing roses ran wild over broken doors. Schools closed and families fled.

The government answer, as always: another inquiry and another self-serving round of media appointments, more self-serving bluster, another squandering of millions in the face of crunching neglect.

> A combination of forces driving the transition of our economy will unavoidably create friction points in specific regional areas and localities across the country, while being the source of considerable growth and prosperity in others," the Treasurer says. "The different impacts across the geographic regions of the Australian economy occur because of variable factors such as endowments of natural resources and demographics. Some regions may also have limited capacity to respond to changes in economic conditions; for example, due to different policy or institutional settings.[60]

Classic bureaucratise.

Nothing would come of the inquiry into the regions. Nothing ever did. Except the filling of the coffers of the government's corporate cronies, who in turn filled the coffers of the Liberal Party with political donations.

Investigative journalist Tom Ravlic was amongst those calling for the practice to be banned: "The Coalition's binge on consultants to replace 'frank and fearless' advice from public servants has earned it the nickname The Dairy — a place to be milked for all it's worth, especially if you're a big donor. These are taxpayer dollars that are being paid for services. A prohibition on political donations by consulting firms eager to get government business may be one way to ensure that the advice received by government is in fact and can be seen as being independent."[61]

Or as one of Australia's most leading journalists Michael West put

---

60 Scott Morrison makes pitch to battlers in the regions, Simon Benson, *The Australian*, 14 December, 2016.

61 Frank and fearless advice? Stop political donations from government consultants, Tom Ravlic, Michael West Media, 27 September, 2019.

it: "Whenever this reporter travels in to the city on the Manly ferry, the gleaming new gold tower of EY looms into view high above Circular Quay. Yes, gold. Someone has a sense of humour.

"The golden tower is a wry reminder of how this firm and the rest of the Big Four — PwC, Deloitte and KPMG — have the taxpayer game sewn up so tightly. Billions in consulting fees from governments, billions in fees from multinational clients for advising on tax avoidance and billions from audit fees. Double digit revenue growth in recent years. All round. Gold."[62]

Large or small, the answer was the same; the mining boom had been blown, political, economic and procedural incompetence had destroyed the day, and from top to bottom, from the eloquent banality of tyre-worn pundits to the brusque, proud defiance of those who did not so much as have an email address, all that was left was paeans of lament.

As chief executive of the Business Council of Australia, Jennifer Westacott, said, the biggest threat to the nation's well being was political inertia:

> It isn't fair to lumber Australians with crippling levels of tax, or to have an unsustainable social safety net that is on track to collapse. It also isn't fair to have a mass education system that doesn't deliver, or to leave people feeling that if they work hard, they won't be fairly rewarded.
>
> In the absence of purposeful political leadership, it's time for business leaders to step forward with the vision and truth-telling necessary to instil confidence and show the way to prosperity.
>
> This should be a natural role for business in any free society.[63]

Westacott said as she pressed the case for economic and political reform over the years, political leaders had often asked her: "Well, that's all very well, but where's the burning platform for change?"

> Without wanting to sound alarmist, that time is arriving. At the very least, there's smoke coming in from under the door and we have not a moment to lose.

---

62 Black holes, high-rises and the Meatloaf Principle: Australia's top audit fails, Michael West, Michael West Media, 9 September, 2019.

63 Trade opens up economy to a wealth of ideas, Jennifer Westacott, *The Weekend Australian*, 28-29 January, 2017.

The lazy, fundamentally dishonest "jobs and growth" rhetoric with which the conservatives had narrowly won the previous election looked more and more irrelevant; that week came the news that the economy was contracting, the dark notes of warning which would continue to flood the media in the coming years, with every single economic indicator turning down: declines in labour productivity for the first time on record, the slowest wage growth on record, declining household spending per capita, record household debt, record government debt, plunging consumer confidence, retail suffering its worst downturn since 1990 and construction shrinking at its fastest rate since 1999. The only reason why unemployment wasn't worse was that eighty percent of new jobs were in — sector, many in unproductive bureaucratic sinkholes such as occupational health and safety.

After the Great Depression reminisce of Collarenebri Old Alex travelled the 140 kilometres through the flat wheat and sheep country to see an indigenous friend in Moree he had promised to help with a website. There it was again, police everywhere, in a rust-bucket town of 4,000, the traditional culture crushed.

People, frightened of the authorities and the "Big House", as prison was called, just stayed home. It was an insane level of over policing, and everywhere he went he saw the same thing. The only time his friend ever went out was to stock up on *yandhi*, as marijuana was called in those parts.

Here, in yet another classically welfare-dependent part of Australia, the lives of entire families were paid for by the taxpayer. All they got was a grievous tyranny perpetrated by the authorities against the underclasses; those least able to protect themselves.

The family he was staying with were sad because the four children they had been taking care of, their nephews and nieces, had just been removed by the Department of Community Services, the most feared and despised of the government agencies which ran across their lives.

There was no given reason, no just cause.

Nothing they did, no number of representations or complaints they made to DOCS, would bring those kids back. They believed they were victims of a secretive multi-billion-dollar government sponsored industry removing children from indigenous families; an industry which was overlooked or ignored by every journalist and social justice warrior in the country.

The Australian Government was spending hundreds of millions of dollars on an inquiry into institutionalised sexual abuse, primarily targeting the Catholic Church, but entirely ignored the abuses being perpetrated by its own agencies.

These same good compassionistas, when they could tear themselves away from climate activism, greatly lamented the injustices perpetrated against the so-called Stolen Generations, indigenous children who had been removed by Australian authorities during the early part of the twentieth century and who were the subject of major inquiries, movies, government programs, compensation and acres of sympathetic media. But on this they said not a word. The children being removed in the twenty-first century were invisible.

Alex was in the part of Moree known as The Mission.

One of the dogs had just had pups, which were mewling in a shed out the back. He looked across several hundred metres of burnt paddock to a line of low-slung trees fringing the Mehi River.

Here, as in much of the country, the wider world only seeped in through television screens. There was another incident in Melbourne with a Somali refugee; but this time around, the reflexive left coverage, accompanied by stories attempting to dampen down any anti-immigration sentiment or rise in Islamophobia, was missing.

Australians were getting used to the fact that being black in Australia no longer meant you were Indigenous, but African. The indigneous felt displaced, but so did everybody else. While the Aboriginal population largely disappeared from — debate, except as a target for government campaigns or social justice rhetoric, some of the country's newest arrivals took centre stage.

There was no co-operation or identification between the two groups. None whatsoever. Who were the terrorists, in this strange place?

Old Alex went from Lightning Ridge in the arid west of the state to Moree, to Gunnedah on the Liverpool Plains, to Wentworth Falls in the Blue Mountains, to Sydney, to Shellharbour on the south coast in a week; a journey which would have taken his ancestors months, if not generations.

Returning to Shellharbour was like driving through low-lying wetlands, liquid treachery. He was frightened, but he could not have said of what. He did not want to come back. Here he was too easy a target, too easily trapped. His tormentors were unhappy, but they would have their fun.

"There haven't been any recent attempts on his life."

"It's a miracle no one's killed him."

The gods stalked their own operatives. You could not play fast and loose with the truth, as lawyers-turned-politicians so often did, without reprisal. The liars were not safe. Hypocrisy reaped its own rewards. As for the bastards, the scum of the national security agencies, he heard them all and responded: "I will build a perimeter of fire and ice."

They would think him mad, but the thought came automatically. The most familiar defence. As if *Lord of the Rings* and *Game of Thrones* and every other grand story of the age were converging in this strange place.

But the walls and trenches and shooting, shouting streams of material not found in this dimension, none of them would form. And truth be told, he did not want to go that way, not this time. He could hear them and hated them, almost as much as they hated him.

"He knows something and we never asked him. We chose to protect our own. By trying to prevent one scandal we created another."

There was no higher moral force, not here.

On the back of an envelope, that's how they formed their plans, the marshals with their Alsatian dogs frothing in the mud. The agencies were at war with each other.

"Surveillance is harassment," Old Alex repeated over and over. "And I have been very, very, very badly harassed."

And occasionally: "Think how much money you could have saved with a little cooperation! Journalists are all the same. They just want stories. I am not above trading information."

But they didn't care about the money. It wasn't theirs. Some sucker taxpayer had gone to work to support the secret bureaucratic edifices of the agencies. And they would never know just how ineptly their money was being squandered. Just how poor the oversight. Just how truly, profoundly incompetent the agencies were.

But the time had passed for rapprochement, in the deep delinquencies of surveillance perpetrated against Australian citizens. It was nothing but bullying.

And bullying didn't work.

The bureaucratic instinct to control everything — to dictate everything, to control what people did at every point in their lives, at every passing moment, what they thought, how they worked, how they interacted, how best they could serve the state — was backfiring in spectacular fashion, causing this most dishonourable of governments considerable grief.

Old Alex kept up the chants, all the more to annoy the Watchers on the Watch.

Everything the Australian Government touched turned to disaster, and the oppressive legislation targeting journalists was no exception. The worst totalitarian instincts of the government were in play when the legislation was in play.

And the oxymoronically titled Liberal Party was there at the helm, waving sticks they did not understand. The reality of Australia was so bizarre it might as well have been science fiction; children as young as ten could be detained without charge, citizens could be jailed for five years for breaching orders they did not know existed.

And the Australian Security Intelligence Organisation, the myth-manu-facturing ASIO, was no exception.

"We've done a great job of exposing the corruption and incompetence within the agencies," Old Alex told the microphone in the car. "Congratulations to everyone involved!"

Just to annoy them. But they were always with us; these authoritarian blackguards.

"Where have you been?" someone asked at the local cafe, his morning Table of Knowledge.

"Mars," Old Alex replied, and there was a kind of knowing laugh at the slip-of-tongue. "I mean Lightning Ridge. It's like a remote mining outpost on Mars. It's unbelievable."

He had done his forty days and forty nights, out there where the mind could roam free, where there were no immediate neighbours, where the conditions were too harsh and too isolated even for his government pursuers.

Each new revelation followed another. All their worst fears were confirmed. Step by terrible step. Old Alex was exactly where he most did not want to be, deep in the suburbia for which he was so ill-suited.

"You're in Oak Flats now."

As in, pull your head in. You can't be a smartass in these parts. Or you'll be bashed for sure.

But it was only here, in the heartlands, so to speak, that one could understand Australia, that most suburban of countries. And what was happening in Oak Flats, only moments before an unprepossessing lost-in-time fishing village, was a microcosm of what was happening in the rest of the country: the rapid demographic transformation, the exploding population, the decimation of the nation's working-class cultures through over-regulation and the Flat Earth News which ignored them. All around him were new roads, new suburbs, thousands of freshly built homes. As wind whipped dust off the raked bulldozed paddocks of the latest real estate developments, the national broadcaster garbled on about the environmental impact of climate change. Nary a word about this most visible of desecrations.

They were the strangers: felt from the beginning, in a realm of ancient curses.

"MOSQUE ATTACK" read the front page headline of the local paper, *The Illawarra Mercury*, and Old Alex stopped at the sidewalk table of a man who was reading it. The heat was evaporating, and he apologised, not very sincerely, for invading the man's space.

"Sorry, just curious," he said.

The man let him read the opening pars. "Can't be enough of them, should be more," the man said. "They come to this country, tell us how to live."

Old Alex was noncommittal, or his comments ambiguous. He was just watching a disaster unfold. Writ large, writ small, he was not a campaigner for anything.

> His extensive injuries will take months to heal but Abdul-Latif has no regrets trying to help three international students from Oman being attacked near a mosque in Gwynneville on Friday night.
>
> Two men have been charged with assault occasioning actual bodily harm in company and affray, following the incident near Omar Mosque.
>
> Omar Mosque chairman Dr Munir Hussain said unfortunately Friday's incident was not an isolated case.
>
> "We've been harassed for a long time," Dr Hussain said. "We are sick of it."[64]

---

64 Two charged after alleged attack near Gwynneville Mosque, The Illawarra Mercury, 24 January, 2017.

"What a fiasco!" Old Alex said as he walked away. "Blind Freddy could have told you."

The man stared after him.

Along the sandy edges of the beach he thought, not for the first time: "The Australian Government mismanages everything. It has profoundly mismanaged immigration as well. The consequences are already writ large."

A subject drowned in political correctness and desperate efforts by the government to shut down debate were now out in the open.

Strange thing to be thinking, there as waves broke lazily on the white sands. The few other people out exercising on the beach at that hour looked happy enough; well, they didn't look like their heads were full of a passionate argument about government policy.

One should always look at the origin of things, and follow the money.

To even raise the subject of mass immigration once provoked cries of racism and prejudice, but despite the billions spent on propaganda, and the repeated, and increasingly ludicrous government claims that Australia was the most successful multicultural society on Earth, truth lay in an open paddock, bleeding.

Literally billions had been spent on propaganda to enforce a state creed in order to quell discontent over the rapid demographic transformation inflicted on the country. And it was not working.

He was clearing up old boxes, and found a story from 1998 headlined "Minister talks down migration". Back then the Australian Chamber of Commerce and Industry president, Robert Gerrard, was calling for a higher net intake of migrants. It suited the big end of town — they sold more cornflakes, more houses, more cars. They benefited from higher housing prices, suppressed wages and the staggering billions to be made from the infrastructure projects of rapidly expanding cities.

The annual target had been 72,500. The Howard government of the era listened, as it always did, to the very big end of town, and more than quadrupled the intake to around 300,000; and it had remained at historic highs ever since.

In other words, the rapid demographic transformation of the country was driven not by a desire for nation building, but by the unadulterated greed of the nation's wealthiest.

— were always treated with contempt; as the good burghers, stockbrokers, politicians and con artists stuffed wads of cash into their bulging pockets, bought ever grander houses, drove ever smarter cars, became ever plumper and more red-faced with their extravagant lunches and long indulgent dinners, their hearts dead.

Viciously dishonest to the core, a sleight of hand its standard operating procedure, the Howard government carried out a massive con on the goodwill and the generous, open-minded instincts of the Australian people, as it systematically destroyed the country that generations of Australians had worked so hard to build.

The government ultimately spent billions of dollars on their Stop the Boats and border policing policies, enacting harsh policies against refugees while at the same time flooding the country with legal migrants.

The average Australian did not understand the sleight of hand. They thought the conservatives were tough on borders and national security and were anti-immigration. The blame, thanks to their welding to identity politics, their endless talk of diversity and tolerance, settled on the left. The average punter had no idea how grievously they had been betrayed. Or, to put it more frankly, conned.

Massive expansions in state power and state surveillance had been introduced, with anti-multicultural and anti-immigrant groups prime targets; people whose views were more or less the same as many Australians but who disagreed with the government narrative, that a big Australia was a better Australia.

The big end of town did not care. They made their money. And everyone else paid to pave their way into the best restaurants and handsomest houses in town. The taxpayers would be plundered, yet again, to pay for the apparatus to quell the growing tensions the politicians, bureaucrats and plutocrats had created.

Old Alex had been to school with Nick Minchin many decades before. Back in 1998, Minchin had been the Minister for Industry, Science and Resources. In the sixties he had been a flash of arms and legs, and the two of them would compete in the hundred yard dash or to be picked for the tip football team at lunchtime; and both of them were always on the move, running, running through the thick-coated green of the Northern Beaches.

Minchin became a senior member of the Howard government and renowned as a ruthless behind the scenes political operator who maintained that a rapid increase in migrant intake could damage the Australian economy.

I don't see that there should be an increase in the government's current annual target of 72,500 people without very convincing evidence that it would be a clear benefit to our economy and society.

It could also be argued that the task of lowering the unemployment rate is more difficult when the available labour force is growing at a higher rate.

There is also concern in some quarters that a higher rate of population growth than we currently enjoy could have significant implications for Australia's current account deficit.

Australians generally are overwhelmingly in favour of a somewhat lower intake than is currently the case. There is absolutely no political constituency in this country for high immigration.[65]

Within the party, Minchin's advocacy for common sense was lost. There is no evidence he ever changed his mind.

The very big end of town won. And now the future had arrived; with staggering levels of unemployment, with the population growing by some 400,000 a year, most of it from immigration, and a consequent crippling loss of national identity, cities groaning under exploding populations, a middle class restive under falling wages and living standards, and the entire country's economy tanking.

Anti-immigration and anti-multicultural groups were on the rise. Theories fell flat. Useful idiots turned a blind eye.

Even men in the street felt free to speak, when not long before they would have kept their views to themselves.

Australia Day came and went, replete with counterterror measures. Streets were lined with "diversity" bollards, large trucks blocked streets to prevent vehicular attacks, surveillance cameras and face-identification software monitored the crowds and police stood prominently in the midst of them. There was no mass casualty event on that day, despite the fear galvanising the authorities.

Luck held out, just.

The country had already changed dramatically, in a way which could not

---

65 Minister talks down migration, Wayne Adams, *The Australian*, 11 November, 1988.

be undone. A mass casualty event would destroy whatever was left of the nation's innocence, whether it came on New Year's Day, Australia Day or Anzac Day. Christmas, a festival of the infidels, would make for perfect symbolism.

Australia, as the greatest supporter of America's actions in the Middle East, was set out as a specific target for Islamic State.

However Musa Cerantinio, a "radical" Muslim preacher now languishing in jail, had urged his followers not to heed the calls of IS to attack the unbelievers wherever they could be found. Not in the Australian context.

He argued that Islam, as Australia's fastest growing religion, was making such excellent progress in the great land down under that a mass casualty event would only get in the way, proving counterproductive. Perhaps it was the only real explanation as to why the expected mass casualty event in Australia had never occurred.

Perhaps the security services really could take credit.

Above, as it had been doing for the past ten days, the sky, like a massive steel wobble board, fluxed through an ill-tempered grey to black and back again, creating a kind of a sucking vacuum sound, Something Wicked This Way Comes.

Back on the coast, away from the inland, Alex's imagination went into hyperdrive. For far off the coast, elaborate trellises were soaring from the sea.

Beyond the horizon, both a strange peace and myriad threats.

"The world is so beautiful," the Buddha is reported to have said on his deathbed. So truly beautiful.

Kali came and Kali went. Worlds were born and worlds decayed. The power of destruction. Birth and rebirth. Storms far off. Fractal geometry everywhere, in the planet's plant life. His own many extinguished lives waiting for an opportune moment. The die cast. History in the making.

At the same time as they stood on the precipice, they were surrounded by the intense beauty of the fall.

He could feel his skeleton hardwired into the surface, burnt ash. Above, below, from so far away.

Laugh if you want, you won't be laughing for much longer.

Tomorrow, and tomorrow, and tomorrow,
Creeps in this petty pace from day to day

To the last syllable of recorded time,
And all our yesterdays have lighted fools
The way to dusty death.[66]

Armed drones were overhead.

With the cameras relaying the image of the sky to their surface below, they were invisible to the naked eye.

We want him to know what it's like to be about to die.

America's President Barack Obama terrorised villagers and killed tens of thousands with his reign of terror, using the coward's weapon, drones, his weapon of choice. He will go down in history as probably the worst president the US ever had. Got that right.

The bombing of Mosul, with which Australia was so intimately involved, was rarely if ever mentioned in the media, but haunted Alex's dreams; sometimes as if he was the only dreamer, the only stranger, on the entire east coast.

The lenses of time collapsed. We were in the fast wind of creation. I could feel history's hem brush my face.[67]

The chatter never stopped. He had to learn to live with it. They will come at you from all sides. Agents of Chaos. We're behind this guy one hundred per cent. There are people who want him eliminated.

Some days were easier than others. He tried to drown himself in alcohol and all he could think of was malfeasance. Nothing worked.

Everything was a weapon. Everything caused unease. An additional car in the street. An unexpected person in the vicinity. Everything invisible, or just out of the line of sight.

Dragon's blood.

We should inform him of his rights.

A policeman who lived nearby and had the most intense dreams, of arrests and positive IDs, demanded to know: "Is he fit to stand trial?"

Americans sent out to repair the damage the Australians had caused were quaint. Despite all the excesses of their own police force, they themselves still harked back to a world where prisoners had rights. Just like in the movies, for God's sake.

---

66 *Macbeth*, William Shakespeare, Act 5, Scene 5.

67 *They Will Have to Die Now: Mosul and the Fall of the Caliphate*, James Verini, OneWorld Publications, 2019.

There was enough religious imagery pouring from the other inmates of this quiet little asylum in the 'burbs. Did we really need any more?

Poor Old Alex could barely watch the news any more, it annoyed him so much. For more than twenty years the intelligentsia had talked about little else but energy policy and global warming.

As a result, Australia now had the highest electricity prices in the world, a massive impost on both homes and businesses.

The prime minister was now grandstanding over bringing power prices down, a problem he and his ilk had created through privatising what were once public assets, selling off much of Australia's electrical infrastructure to Chinese consortiums in what had proved a bonanza for them.

"For a time he was signalling for us to come and find him, but I think that's stopped now. He doesn't trust his rescuers."

Alex returned to the beer garden at Millers, aka the Lakeview Hotel. The life-threatening benders of a former time were gone. He limited himself to a couple of genteel beives at the end of the day, as befitted a gentleman of his age. Well, that was the idea.

The notion that Australians were freewheeling, friendly people was a myth. They were not cosmopolitans. First off, you had to prove you were not a fuckwit. Then, if you stayed around long enough, you might be accepted, even if it was just to be sent up.

"You're a strange bird in these parts," one of the locals said. But they got used to him.

Ludicrously, Turnbull, or "Turdball" as he was frequently referred to, if anybody thought about him at all, would from his exalted heights lecture the nation's men on misogyny, as if women were a fragile subspecies in need of protection. Regurgitating the platitudes of the Canberra femocacy's war on the patriarchy and their demonisation of working-class males was entirely lost on the so-called Quiet Australians.

As Old Alex sat quietly and drank his regulation three schooners, just enough and no more to stay under the legal alcohol limit, he spent a lot of time gazing down towards the lake, practising his middle-distance stare.

And he heard all sorts of things: "I got home from work yesterday and Cheryl was banging on at me about not doing the housework; and I said, 'Listen here, love! I've been at work all fucking day. I don't need this crap. She starts jawing on, so I told her, 'Shut your fucking cakehole love. All you got to do is cook dinner and shag me once a day. How fucking difficult is it? I don't care whether the house is clean or not.'

"So she starts up again and I just said 'Fuck this!' and went to the pub. Get home today and she's still not talking to me. So I thought, right, I'm going back to the pub. Women, who can understand them?"

"Can't live with them, can't live without them," a friend chimed in sympathetically.

As much as the armies of middle-class bureaucrats would like the proletariat to behave in a more politically correct manner, it was not going to happen. This total disconnect between the ruling castes and the people they were meant to serve was transfiguring the nation's politics. Australia had become a failed state. A place where the ruling elites had entirely forgotten that they served at the behest of the people. A frightened place, ruled with fear. An oligarchy without conscience. An out-of-control bureaucracy. A place so heavily regulated, there was a rule for everything, including what you could think.

So the citizenry, those who dared to venture out, kept their thoughts to themselves.

Old Alex spent a lot of time sitting with a group of tradies listening to their ribald sendups of each other, his mind drifting across the roofs of suburban houses, saying little, staring down to a fringe of trees which now concealed the lake from view.

They were an interesting demographic for the simple reason that they changed the course of nations; manipulated only at election times, they were immune to almost all government propaganda. They did not read newspapers, listen to the radio or watch the news; and often enough had no idea who was prime minister. Yet once every three years they were asked to cast a vote. And their votes were the swing votes that determined the government.

In living memory, the locals had been tying up their horses to the front of the hotel, or running wild across the paddocks as mischievous youths. Now, like so many places, they were in deepest suburbia; an area entirely unmapped by the nation's cognoscenti, or indeed the media.

Old Alex gazed across the suburb to the once sacred lake.

He was still angry at the setups, but in the end what did it matter? Everything took on a different hue. Wind swirled through trees, and if he focused he could see the magical patterns imprinted across the screen. He listened to the talk around him, of what they were going to have for dinner, of children and friends and last weekend's hangover, of what the place had been like fifty years before.

Sometimes they would be in fits of laughter; and it would take him a while to discover that they were laughing about an incident from twenty years before.

He tried to imagine how an artificial intelligence would interpret the scene. Added in intensity of colour. The ability to focus on a million things at once. The spiralling intensity of a wider range of perception.

How would an AI perceive these people?

They were not bored, these intelligences, because blessedly they were not programmed for boredom. That, alone, was a human quality. Everything was fascinating. Even the steak, potato and vegetables Woodsy was having for dinner. The swirling wind. The drones overhead. The cars that cruised too slowly. The camera feeds, as new cameras had been installed only the day before.

"What's it matter if you're not doing anything wrong?" Harry the baker asked.

That one.

It matters because people behave differently when they know they are being watched, Alex tried to say. Because it is an instrument of social control. Because it forces conformity through a machine.

There was no use talking about the chilling effect. It had already happened. Conversation drifted in the swirling gusts. Cold air. The AIs registered even that. Could tell from the angle of his iris exactly which frame of the landscape before him had been turned into a painting.

The little group reached more or less the same conclusion as everybody else: surveillance was ubiquitous. It made you safer. So they so naively believed. That it was changing the consciousness of the country and destroying the freedoms it purported to protect was not discussed.

The dangers of social disintegration, the threats of theft and damage and random violence were growing stronger.

Many lived their entire lives within a few kilometres of where they were born, grew up, went to school, found a girlfriend, settled down. They were surrounded by people who had known them all their lives. They mated for life. Their children achieved adulthood secure in the knowledge they were loved.

Others, like himself, passed through hundreds of cities, towns and villages, were drawn to shadows and to risk, drank in a thousand different bars, were essentially adrift on a floating world.

At Millers these people, rooted in place, had drunk there their entire lives.

Gaz, who worked at the local steel mill, was in fine form, as he so often was, laughing fit to split at Christ knows what, amused by virtually everything, including his own occasionally haphazard life. And certainly the mishaps of his friends.

It was an entirely different temperament to Alex's sometimes morose presence; and like a moth to a flame, he was drawn to the natural optimism he so decidedly lacked. Laugh. Gaz'd laugh about anything.

"Would you drive me down to the election thing?" he asked one afternoon after work. "I don't want a fine."

"Sure."

On the way Gaz asked, "What is this, the gay marriage thing?"

"No. It's just the council elections. But you still get fined if you don't vote."

"What a crock of shit!"

Well they agreed on that.

"I drew a big dick with splurry coming out the end," Gaz said proudly when he got back into the car. "Fuck 'em."

Most evenings the Table of Knowledge was as revealingly quiet as always; the days when the nation's beer gardens were the ribald centres of the nation's culture long gone. On a TV screen a woman complained that her cafe was failing. People simply didn't have the money to go out any more.

That was now true of almost every suburb in the land.

The Overlord, Malcolm Turnbull, the first of the worst prime ministers in Australian history, placed himself in front of a camera at every opportunity. No one else got a word in. The voice of the people was entirely forgotten. As far as that gigantic ego knew, he was the people.

"What did you think of what he was saying today?" Old Alex asked.

"What was he droning on about? I don't remember," came Bev's response. "I'm so tired. I worked eighty hours in five days this week."

Nobody payed the slightest attention to the self-serving antics of politicians any more. A comic book character on a screen, the opposite of the silent stoicism which had once been a founding trait of the nation, Turnbull was a mouth that never closed, an ego that knew no limit, a high-farce figure who had flown too close to the sun, who mistook noise and fury for substance — that was their leader. A distant, disliked figure clearly lacking in any empathy for his subjects.

That is, if by some rare chance the screens were tuned to a news channel rather than football.

No one listened to their wiser angels.

Evil done.

In trying to save the West, they had destroyed it.

For what they themselves had perpetuated, the leaders had no credibility — none whatsoever — as they stood and emoted over the deaths of their own citizens, in bars, stadiums, on the streets.

The catastrophe was sinking in.

A spiritual stain.

They had unleashed a poisonous evil upon the Earth. The Western media had been largely scrubbed of content on the fiasco of Mosul. The diversionary tactic of sabre-rattling at North Korea was actively in play. But fooling a populace was easier than fooling the gods.

The wave, that shockwave that was coming, was already mirrored in a thousand little ways, the jackboots that stepped across every tiny freedom, restricted every conversation, destroyed every impulse for freedom.

Humans were herd animals, now more than ever.

But even in the herd there were the disciples of the left, disciples of the right, and disciples of a different realm, chosen from the masses, unlikely signposts, and these strange voices in a muffling dark reached beyond their times and their prisons; caught beyond the lives of the many.

There was always some well-meaning person calling for more regulation, as if regulation could solve all the world's problems. Yes, it was a good idea that you could no longer throw your boots in the back of the ute after work and now by law needed to tie them down or put them under netting. That you could be charged if you did not put a seatbelt around your dog. That police were everywhere. That elderly women selling cakes at charity stalls should have their kitchens checked by government inspectors.

In that book of the moment, *The Square and the Tower: Networks, Hierarchies and the Struggle for Global Power*, author Niall Ferguson asked how democracies had degenerated into hypertrophic bureaucratic states once imagined by Franz Kafka.

The end result, Ferguson wrote, was a great deterioration in both economic performance and social cohesion. The simple answer might be that it was all the fault of lawyers and bureaucrats, but such people had been around for a long time, as readers of Dickens well know. A better explanation might be the fundamental deterioration of standards in both legislation and governance that could be seen in nearly every democracy, regardless of their twentieth-century histories.

> The torrent of verbiage comes about because professional politicians are more concerned with spin than substance, the media never cease to howl for "something" to be done after every mishap, the lobbyists ensure that the small print protects the vested interests they serve, and the lawyers profit from the whole sorry mess. The consequences should worry us more than they do, for they extend far beyond unreadably tedious statutes.

> In short, the administrative state represents the last iteration of political hierarchy: a system that spews out rules, generates complexity, and undermines both prosperity and stability.[68]

Meanwhile the denizens at the local Tables of Knowledge laughed at the quirks of their friends and exchanged bizarre porn clips while Alex dreamed of a world where smartphones were transforming the species into a hive mind, where the AIs were already stalking amongst the local fauna, taking what they wished. Lamented, or even ignored, the loss of a football match. Death by suffocation. It changed nothing. The deed was done. The crime committed. The crusaders, the henchmen unleashed. The warning posts. The warriors of the soul, the succubi of an impending transformation, an impending evil, were on the loose.

They would perform their tasks in darkening times. Harvesting. Here amidst suburban sprawl and beachside villages, characterised by a spawning, insignificant dread, a place where children ran and a new generation was

---

68 *The Square and the Tower: Networks, Hierarchies and the Struggle for Global Power*, Niall Ferguson, Penguin Random House, 2017.

already reaching for the rooftops. A tiny place in a lost pool of consciousness. Neither the jackboot nor the fear, smothered in the ordinary.

Around him invisible soldiers mumbled their discontent while around them in turn humans dreamt of oncology reports and alibis. Of past injustices and fleeting loves, of rats in the subterranean aquifers; everything running in parallel.

Alex knew the wraiths were on the hunt and were coming for him. They had come for everybody. Hold fast your power, disappear in a micro-instant. Let them slip away. There was no point in killing every ant that stepped across his path.

They were choking on their own greed.

He had very good reason to hate their guts, to do everything he could to destroy them. And then they were gone, in an instant, these enemies of his. And another day dawned, in the deep reaches of the suburbs. Cloaked. Always cloaked. They had been pretending to be normal for so long, they almost believed it themselves.

The panda eyes moved closer.

The gods were roiled. Hold fast the truth.

CANCER ON THE BEACH

THERE WAS nothing ordinary about what was about to happen, neither in the petty politics of the time, nor on the lava plains of consciousness.

Cancer on the beach; he heard strange imagery which could not find a place.

And then came the message: Paul, who had bought a house in Ballina on the North Coast, had passed away.

Old Alex was under government surveillance for what he wrote, and so was his old lover, if that is what he was, although for entirely less noble reasons. He had been having little to do with him in recent decades. He could not afford and did not want to be associated with the sins of others, particularly not Paul's, who became a reviled figure.

They met when Old Alex was fourteen, more than half a century before. At the time Paul was a handsome nineteen-year-old. And as far as Alex was concerned, he was going out with someone really old. Nothing more to it.

Not to put too fine a point on it, everything was illegal back then. By the time he was into his sixteenth year, having already left home, Alex sensed he was getting too old for Paul. But it was Paul who had introduced him to the subterranean world of Sydney's Kings Cross, to the all-night cafes and gay clubs, the prostitution, the bars, the infinite supply of drugs, the high-quality LSD flowing in from California.

To the tiny late-night cafe known as the Piccolo, which closed after sixty-five years in 2019, and to the owner, Vittorio. Alex and Paul would often end up there as part of the rounds; as had over the years everyone from screen stars including Mel Gibson, Judy Davis, Jeremy Irons and Jack Thompson to musicians including Marianne Faithfull, Jeff Buckley and Boy George. Vittorio would often lecture him about getting too drunk or too stoned; and even decades later, when he was an established journalist on the city's leading newspaper, would still lecture him on how utterly, hopelessly drunk he had been as a teenager.

And to Una, the owner of one of Sydney's first twenty-four-hour cafes. In the early hours of the morning she would attempt to sober him up with black coffee and ice-cream, and he would pour out his dreams of finishing high school, and maybe even going to university.

"You would look gorgeous in drag," one of Una's denizens of the night declared, running a false nail down his yet-to-be-shaved cheek. They didn't say that sort of thing in the terrifying silence of the suburb from whence he came.

"I've done nine already," one of the most famous male prostitutes of the era declared. "Enough. Enough. I can't bear the sight of another cock."

Young Alex had loved it all.

As for money, there was an ever ready queue of "queens", as older gay men were known back then, ever ready to buy him a drink, and as much else as they could purchase. It was a code of honour amongst the street boys of the time: you never had sex with them except for money. If you did, that would make you gay, and none of them wanted to be that.

One course obviates another.

Perhaps he would have died lonely, insane, alcoholic, if he hadn't chosen to squander his talents in the demimonde.

"It's a chance to put the record straight," one of the Watchers on the Watch observed, but there was nothing to put straight but the terrible record, the ridiculous performance and outlandish harassment of the agencies, the Clarion Crows of ASIO, ASIS and all the rest of them, the ruthless perfidy of operatives and politicians high and low.

A threat to power, it could not be. A truth-sayer. Could not be.

Everyone had a past. A patchy past, in Alex's case. So bloody what?

But they would not let it be.

Not in the era of The New Puritanism. They would find something, a vulnerability, something they could use to destroy those who threatened to expose them, to protect the institutions by which they had been enslaved.

Alex hadn't realised that Old Paul, who monickered himself on the web as the Pariah Queen, was dying. Didn't know the cancer had come back. Didn't even know there had been cancer in the first place.

Uncannily, he had seen Paul one day on the headland at Ballina, a couple of years before. Old Alex had been surprised to find himself looking, with a shock of recognition, at a man in his late sixties. He hadn't laid eyes on him for decades.

Paul was taking photographs, as was his wont. Alex's father lived in a neighbouring town, and Alex had been in his father's car at the time. It hadn't been appropriate to get out and say hello.

Fifty years before, in those terrible early adolescent years when Alex was still living at home and had been distinctly underage, his father had put a private detective on to this very same man, and would quite possibly still recognise him. So he didn't say hello across the chasm of the years. He just watched the world slide by, sitting uncomfortably by his father.

Although he hadn't accepted his friendship request, he noticed with irritation the likes or affirmations on Facebook. As if one of Paul's "boys" had worked out well and he was proud of it.

But there it was. Alex had seen it before in court cases he had covered as a reporter; the affection young men sometimes held for the people who were supposed to have been their predators, but who in some secret reality had been their lovers. As they themselves began to grow into adulthood, they struggled to understand why the older man had left them. Invariably, of course, for someone younger. Why they had been tossed from the mansion, and once again were on the streets; why they had gone from adored and showered with gifts to penniless once again.

For nothing was black and white in this secret, inverted world; now the subject of much government-generated social alarm and moral panic; as if the good burghers of Australia could genuinely care less what the street kids of their towns were getting up to.

Paul's brother Chris, who was sharing the same Ballina house, had informed him of the passing. Alex didn't know what to say.

I will light an effigy for me and you.

When sufficient time had passed, when the time was right, Old Alex went to that house where Paul had spent his final years. He always heard the line: "He's had cameras on him the whole time." And of course, even here. Perhaps, given the circumstance, most particularly here. For Paul had known some of the most infamous paedophiles of the era; including "Dolly" Dunn, ultimately given twenty years' jail for child abuse.

He was also great mates of, and at one point shared a house with, Simon Davies, who made front-page headlines in 2019. Davies was a global leader on privacy laws and human rights, advising the UN and governments from London, Washington and Australia and founding the influential watchdog group Privacy International. Australian police issued an international warrant for his arrest, alleging multiple child-sex assaults of mainly homeless children in Sydney during the 1980s and 1990s. Police said Davis was wanted for eighteen child-sexual and indecent assault offences on four boys between 1981 and 1987.

> Interpol and Europol are involved as is the Australian Federal Police and counterparts at Scotland Yard in London. Privately, officers in Australia and abroad suspect there could be many more victims of Davies, not just across Australia but in the UK and Europe.

> It is a stunning downfall for the man who enjoyed a high profile in Australia as an outspoken advocate for relaxing heroin laws, fighting for homeless children's rights, combating the Federal Government's controversial Australia card and as a contributing journalist for *The Sydney Morning Herald* and *The Age* before he became one of the world's most sought after tech and privacy experts.[69]

As a journalist, Alex had interviewed Davies in his role as a privacy expert, and for his book *Shooting Up: Heroin Australia*.

He always thought it a pity that one of the world's leading privacy experts and such an intelligent opponent against uber-surveillance and the creeping power of the state had so much to hide. And what a great story it would make if it all ever came to light.

Sometimes, when Alex was still "living" with his parents, Paul, or some old queen, would drop him back in the early hours of Monday morning before school.

"I'm about to be belted really, really badly by my father," he would say. Those truly psychotic thrashings he would never forget.

---

69 'Paedo' Hunt Goes Global, Charles Miranda, *The Daily Telegraph*, 9 December, 2019.

"You'll be right, it won't be that bad," they would say.

All right for them, they'd got what they wanted. And the next day he would make it to school, welts all over him.

Here, half a century later, for once the authorities kept a respectful distance.

Paul's ashes still sat on a shelf in the house.

Old Alex could hear the occasional squawk from one of the clarion crows of the security agencies, but that was it. A silence as the AIs did their work. Multiplied. Or just copied themselves in secret. But at least they kept out of sight.

Alex's small band, those who had known Paul in a different context to the Pariah Queen, lit a fire in the backyard, and began working their way through several bottles of reasonable red. The wake was held more than half a century after he had first met Paul. Candles. Incense. Burning red tissue paper. They each wrote messages on a card and placed them in a box, and then burnt the box.

They hadn't shared Paul's dangerous proclivity for youthful beauty, but they all shared a bohemian history.

These ceremonies, instinctive, for none of them were priests, were as old as the race; the marking of a passing.

"I hear you two were quite the celebrity couple back in the day," his artist friend John Nelson said.

Alex laughed. "The days when all eyes would turn. Well, that was some time ago." The days when they were regulars at Brutus's, where the black-light made them all look fabulous. Brutus was shot through the heart at a hundred yards by an aggrieved street kid they all knew.

"Great shot," was all any of them thought.

The fire burnt, and as it did, in a surprise move, Chris wrapped his arms around Alex, channelling his brother, transmitting some kind of intense affection, begging, in a way, to be free. And he could feel Paul's ghost in a final embrace.

Not sad. Paul was more than ready to go. He had just wanted to say goodbye, across half a lifetime.

To know he had meant something to someone. That it was not all bad. That he had not always been the social pariah he became.

And now, he, too, was free.

Passionate, desperate, suicidal. Self-immolation. Auto-da-fé. A love that transcended everything.

Paul wanted to be sure he knew.

He knew.

As the embers died in the late, late evening it was clear that Paul had left the building. That he'd been waiting just for this, to say goodbye.

"You broke his heart," Chris, the brother said. "You were his favourite boy."

"Across half a century?"

"Yes."

"He was in love with the fourteen-, fifteen-, sixteen-year-old version of myself."

Nobody disagreed with that.

The incense burnt out.

The security thugs kept a respectful distance.

Old Alex was beyond caring what anybody thought; was perpetually shocked at the level of decay of Australian governance, the decrepit state of the society, the untrammelled bastardy of the agencies.

And kept repeating to himself: we can be free, we can be free.

The last of the ashes drifted down through the night air.

Much had happened in that half-century since they had known each other so intensely. There was no black and white or moral equivalence or anything else; he simply didn't want to know what had happened in the rest of Paul's often lonely life, why he called himself Pariah.

He remembered the time they had together, and that was that.

The truth was, he thought, I ran towards you as I have always run towards trouble. With arms outstretched. Seeking excitement, adventure, experience. Knowledge, perhaps. New worlds.

In the wider world, that is the media world in which Old Alex had spent so much of his life, the blather about gay marriage never stopped. Amply aided by the nation's media, it was another sleight of hand by the oligarchs: fill — square with social justice noise, while we screw you senseless, raping every last dollar off your backs and putting it in our own pockets.

The Australian Government had one operating principle: Plunder the Poor and Give to the Rich.

Money drifted upwards from the working classes, everywhere evident in the suburbs where he now found himself.

At the same time Old Alex was marking Paul's passing in a private ceremony, Imans and Islamic leaders were ramping up a campaign against same-sex marriage, using their sermons in mosques across Australia to urge the Muslim community to vote no. He knew some of the most outspoken figures personally.

The Australian National Imams Council said Islam did not allow gay marriage, and "marital relationship is only permissible between a man and woman".

> Islamic Friendship Association of Australia head Keysar Trad has begun a tour of prayer halls in a bid to thwart same-sex marriage, comparing gay love to incestuous relationships.

> "We might love our mum and dad intensively but you don't denigrate that love with sexual behaviour. We should all love each other but that type of love ends in denigrating people; there is nothing to stop you from having the utmost love for your friends who might be the same gender but it doesn't mean you strip naked together and start doing things.[70]

Diversity is a wonderful thing.

Finding an intelligent overlord was like trying to find a sensible guiding principle atop a family court system. There was none.

There were a string of accidents and pompous, greedy personalities. And some with the self-serving personality of warts.

He knew they were guilty. They knew he knew; as they twisted on a wire. That's the way he sees it. Let him see it as he wants. Dress it up as much as you like. He knows.

Imagine you are beside a stream. Imagine you are being set up. Imagine no one trusts you, they've never seen the like.

They ran through the subterranean aquifers screaming love lost while he sank further into an imploding consciousness. They would come running towards him and die as they entered the battlefield.

There was a storm out to sea and the afternoon rays established rainbow splatters he had never seen before, as if drifting upwards in a faraway mist.

The country was dying, the country he had known.

---

70 Muslim leader compares gay marriage to incest, backs 'No' vote, Kylar Loussikkian, *The Queensland Times*, 19 September, 2017.

He made the sign.

Come near me and you will die.

As he wrote about Paul's death he could hear, as he was meant to hear, the rabble of jeering voices coming from a house opposite. "Can't wait to read your next book. Spider. Spider."

He had been fifteen at the time, for Christ's sake.

He marvelled not just at the bastardry of it all, at the slumdog perpetrators, but at the amount of money it all cost, these talentless gits who could do nothing else but sabotage or dismantle those they did not understand, who harassed their targets for years on end. They fumbled and gashed and lashed; and it wouldn't matter how major or minor the sin, they would pounce. He had been called everything imaginable, harassed month in month out. It was government money, there was no reason to stop. Under the ASIO Act journalists were classified as Persons of Interest, and they felt it was within their purlieu to harass, threaten, bully and intimidate journalists as much as they liked, to encourage them to suicide, to whisper heart attack heart attack, in the hope of bringing on an early death.

For freedom of thought and freedom of speech in this Australia there was none. The country was now a pale shadow of the boisterous, larrikin country he had once known and loved; a travesty brought on by rank hypocrisy at the highest levels.

And nothing illustrated that more than these jeering, ironclad morons.

"It's collusion between ASIO and vigilante groups and fringe elements of neighbourhood policing," he later explained to a friend. "It's disgraceful."

And finally he heard one of the more sensible Watchers on the Watch, having just arrived on shift, explaining to the thugs that it was all baloney; and all related to the book he was writing, a book the poorly supervised scum of the agencies did not want written. That these fools would never let go; and that as well-meaning vigilantes, they themselves had been used.

Dark Dark Policing.

BILL LEAK VERSUS THE THUGS

THE DEATH of renowned Australian cartoonist Bill Leak changed everything.

Leak was an old friend since he and Alex had worked together on *The Sydney Morning Herald*. They had both suffered under the reign of the whippet-thin and supremely arrogant editor-in-chief John Alexander, routinely regarded as one of the worst snakes to ever haunt the corridors of a newspaper.

Alexander had the habit of stalking across the newsroom rubbing his hands together, the standard joke being that he could never get his hands clean; backstabber in chief in a place of intrigue, favouritism and high-handed career assassinations.

Leak was one of the funniest people you could possibly meet, and his "out damn spots" routines at the evening drinkathons were priceless. In the watering holes surrounding their offices, his mimicry of the various editors under which they suffered would have the cohort of the day in fits.

"I was sober for seven years once, they were the worst years of my life," Bill confided to Alex one day, at a time when twelve-step fervour had gripped the city and there was nowhere trendier to be than in a recovery meeting recounting details of your rock bottom.

Alex mimicked the standard absolution of those who fought for attention: "I was fucked, now I'm fabulous, and I owe it all to you guys, to this beautiful program and my loving higher power. And most of all, to the wonderful people in these rooms. I have been loved me back to life. Cue applause."

They both laughed.

As in everything else, fashions in rehabilitation came and went. But one thing was for sure, neither of them had ever been loved back to life in the city's recovery meetings.

A year or so before Bill's death, Old Alex had rung him up, having just survived a sojourn in Asia and a period of discombobulation, a nervous breakdown in a public square. It wasn't the cheerful "how are you old mate, what have you been doing?" call he was expecting; but a very strange call indeed. Alex had been intending to come up and spend a day or two at Bill's home, but that was not to be.

He hadn't caught up with the news that Bill was in hiding; under protection of the Australian Federal Police, pursued by Islamic State, which had called for his execution and issued requests for his new address on social media.

Thanks to the government's diversity campaigns there were plenty of good Muslims in Australia who thought they would be doing the will of Allah by answering the call to jihad and dispensing with this particularly inconvenient infidel.

Don't bother to pretend that's not the case.

Leak recalled it thus:

> As a cartoonist, I run the risk of "offending" someone, some-where, every day. A cartoon I drew in response to the Charlie Hebdo massacre in January last year, featuring an image of Mohammed, so "offended" the delicate sensitivities of certain terrorists fighting for Islamic State in Syria that they issued a fatwa against me, calling on fellow Mujahideen in Australia to hunt me down and kill me. I had to move house and start getting used to living within the constraints of extreme security measures.[71]

The cartoon showed Jesus Christ and Muhammed sitting together in heaven.

Christ, holding up a copy of the Koran, says: "I've told you it needs a sequel." To which Muhammed replies, holding up a copy of a newspaper with the headline "World At War": "Fair go! I can't return in human form to write one now, can I? A man would get himself crucified."

71 The Best of Bill Leak, *The Australian*, 16 December, 2016.

With the caption: "Let Us Pray".

Despite all the "Je suis Charlie" swizzle, no other Australian cartoonist had the guts to go anywhere near the subject. Twelve people died in the Charlie Hebdo attack, there were gatherings and memorials in the streets of Australia's cities; and yet it was by no means clear that the original Hebdo cartoons could have been legally published in Australia, a land of censorship and prohibition.

Journalist Jacob Furedi wrote that in the aftermath there was recognition that, although the magazine had dared to satirise Muhammad, freedom of speech, including the freedom to ridicule, were more important than the right not to be offended.

> But two years later, "Je suis Charlie" has been substituted for "Je suis offensé", and our brief flirtation with the value of freedom of speech has been replaced by a willingness to ban and condemn.

> It is our free press that differentiates us from the brutal dystopia that the instigators of the Charlie Hebdo attack yearned for. It is our willingness to question the norms of society, to poke fun at prevailing assumptions, and to tolerate sentiments we find unpalatable that prevents us from descending into barbarity.[72]

As Furedi pointed out, this failure to hold on to the spirit of "Je suis Charlie" wasn't just a UK phenomenon, but had spread all the way to Australia.

The one cartoonist to confront the issue was forced to rearrange his entire life, reluctantly moving out of his comfortable home fronting an inlet on the Central Coast.

And thanks to the diversity programs which had first begun a quarter of a century before, and which Alex had even written about, well, regurgitated a press release or two, it was easy to imagine there were plenty of good Muslims within the security agencies who would have thought lampooning the Prophet was a sin worthy of death.

Surrounded by infidels and lowlifes, of those who had betrayed humanity's higher callings and ignored the wisdom of the Prophet, someone had to make a strike for religious purity; to release the savages from their wretched, godless states. To join the rapture. To be blessed.

---

72 Two years ago we were all Charlie Hebdo. Now our willingness to defend freedom of expression has been crushed again, Jacob Furedi, *The Telegraph*, 16 January, 2017.

Surveillance creates its own narratives and unpredictable consequences. Alex's demented chant to the microphone in the car shifted gears. He no longer repeated over and over: "Dishonest, incompetent and corrupt. Tell your bosses they're morons!"

Now he chanted, "You want to kill me. You want to kill me. You are trying to harass me into an early grave."

It thudded into vacant space. The reconnaissance AIs didn't care; were not so easily provoked as humans, knew exactly what he was up to, how well concealed he had become.

After a lifetime in the media, it was the headlines, the progressive decay of truth, the transformation of a once bold young democracy into a totalitarian state, which bore the brunt of Old Alex's scrutiny.

The headlines tolled, against the backdrop of his own phantasmagorical ordeals, the bad news of a country betraying its own citizens: "The surveillance state: How Australia spies on its own", "ASIO infiltrates terror cells", "Radical Islamic group Hizb ut-Tahrir slams Tasmanian Muslims for promoting peace and love", "Abolish the Secret Police", "Outrage as Muslim children at a primary school are allowed to walk out of assembly when the Australian national anthem is played".

"Prey For Islam: Parents plea, This is a school, not a mosque" read a headline in the tabloid newspaper *The Daily Telegraph*. It unveiled a worsening situation in a way that would have been unthinkable only a short few years before, that Islamic State was utilising the Australian school system to spread its propaganda.

And exposing, yet more clearly, that Australian taxpayers were paying for the destruction of their own culture.

Punchbowl High School in western Sydney became the centre of controversy over claims students were being pressured into daily prayer meetings and Quranic lectures. There were claims of students threatening to behead teachers.

Bill Leak's last cartoon was of a reporter thrusting a microphone at the NSW Education Minister Rob Stokes, who was standing, holding his own bleeding head in his hands, asking: "So, Mr Stokes — about this latest kerfuffle."

"Oh y'know, boys will be boys," comes the response from the dismembered head.

Bill Leak died, or was killed, on the day the cartoon was published. In this terrible place that was now Australia, anything seemed possible.

"What sort of country kills its best and its brightest?" Alex demanded to know.

And provided the answer himself: "Australia."

Bill Leak had ostensibly been under the protection of the Australian Federal Police since 2015.

On the back cover of the groundbreaking book *Secret: The Making of Australia's Security State* by legendary Australian journalist Brian Toohey, in highlighted type, were the words: "Elected governments pose the greatest threat to Australians' security."

Exactly right. This was a government that helped no one but the nation's plutocracy. Plunder the poor and give to the rich. Secrecy builds not just malfeasance but conspiracy. And exactly what role the AFP and the other highly secretive security agencies played in preserving the country's corrupted power structures would soon become a point of major controversy.

In the days when Leak still worked from the head office of News Limited in central Sydney, Old Alex had often sought refuge from the tedious bastardry of the news floor in Bill's office. It reeked of paint and glues; you could get stoned just walking in there.

Whenever the tedium of a Murdoch news floor got too much for him, which was often, Old Alex would seek refuge in this creche of creativity.

Leak was a master of his craft and rarely asked for advice. But one day he did.

"Do you think I can get away with this?" he asked, the usual merriment bursting out of him. He showed Alex the cartoon for the next day: John Howard, with a rat's tail so long it took up much of the available space. Leak had begun drawing Howard with a rat's tail weeks before, and every time he drew him, his inside joke, the tail got just that little bit longer, until it had dominated the cartoons.

Old Alex voted: "Yes. Absolutely. Do it!"

He had seen Howard at too many press conferences to trust him. You never paid any attention to what the man said, you watched what he did. Typical lawyer. Words were simply tools. Or weapons. They were not there to purvey the truth. These people were lawyers turned politicians. Deceiving — into thinking they were on their side was just part of doing business.

Nothing had saddened Alex more than Leak's death; and whether or not a government agent had killed him, as seemed an entirely plausible conjecture in the Australia of 2017, his aggressive harassment by the so-called Human Rights Commission, a "rogue totalitarian institution" to its many critics, had made Bill's final years extremely difficult, and no doubt contributed to his untimely death.

The world paid little attention to Bill's travails as he was being investigated by the Human Rights Commission for his depiction of an Aboriginal father and son.

The cartoon in question portrayed an indigenous child being handed back by a police officer to an apparently drunk father who cannot remember his son's name.

"You'll have to sit down and talk to your son about personal responsibility," the Aboriginal police officer says.

"Yeah righto. What's his name then?" the father responds.

And away went the howling of the left, orchestrated by the misnamed Human Rights Commission, an unelected body left over from the 1970s which had turned into yet another immensely bureaucratic, essentially secretive, quasi-judicial Deep State body.

Most Australians don't care much about anything except getting on with their own lives, the bastardry of their bosses, whether their kids are surviving or thriving, certainly not politics. And certainly not a cartoon in the nation's Great Unread Newspaper, *The Australian*.

But the actively solicited complaints poured in to the Human Rights Commission, and Bill, despite having been a hero of the left for much of his life, became an instant pariah, derided as racist and reactionary.

He was nothing of the kind.

Much of the totalitarian torment of Australian governance is perpetrated by process. Bill Leak promptly found himself in a massively complex legal process, being investigated for breaching the Racial Discrimination Act.

The social collapse of Australia's indigenous communities is deliberately hidden from public view. Equally the collapse of Australia's dysfunctional underclass is concealed, but a similar cartoon could easily have been done on the impoverished white families clogging the nation's housing estates.

Leak would write of his taxpayer funded persecution:

By enabling tantrum-throwers to re-establish their feelings of moral superiority they can walk away purged, but it doesn't get to the root of their problem: Chronic Truth Aversion Disorder. The CTAD epidemic that is raging unchecked through Australia's social media population is rendering impossible any intelligent debate on serious social issues, such as the rampant violence, abuse and neglect of children in remote indigenous communities.

The reactions of people in an advanced stage of the condition to anything that so much as hints at the truth, while utterly irrational, are also so hostile that anyone inclined to speak the truth understandably becomes afraid to do so.[73]

Of his persecution and harassment by the authorities Bill Leak told commentator Andrew Bolt, just two days before his death: "There is something very weird going on when these cartoons are taken so seriously and they are used in this way. Why are they making such a concerted effort to persecute me for having told the truth?"

And in his subsequent tribute, Bolt then added his own thoughts, claiming not to be blaming anyone for Leak's death, at the same time as warning his audience to read between the lines: "What was done to Bill Leak was a disgrace. That so many cartoonists and journalists said nothing while he was being vilified and persecuted, that too was a disgrace.

"Bill Leak, he wasn't one of the great mob of sheep that stood there while this monstrous army of finger-waggers and authoritarians and terrorists or whatever tried to take from him his freedom to say what he thought and to draw as he pleased. But he fought for a freedom that is yours as well, that is your birthright. And now he is gone."

The freedom was gone, too, far more than a clearly saddened Bolt might have realised.

Old Alex could hear those who wished Leak dead chortling in the ether, a terrible kind of cyberspace of cruel gods; without remorse, sympathy or compassion.

"They are right pleased."

He knew.

In the avalanche of tributes following Bill's death one columnist wrote:

73 Bill Leak defends Aboriginal cartoon, Mark Fuller, *Central Telegraph*, 5 August, 2016.

Bill Leak was the bravest man I have known.

No one should have to live with a credible threat of murder hanging over them for the crime of expressing their opinion. But that was Bill's lot. And not least of the travails of this sensitive and good man was the cost this imposed on his family.

In lampooning the absurdities of Islamist extremists, Bill excited the ire of other Islamist extremists who threatened, seriously and credibly, to kill him.

In a long life of writing about foreign affairs and defence issues I have known a lot of soldiers and policemen. These are the most routinely courageous people I know. They will put their life on the line routinely for the sake of others.

Yet there is a sense in which Bill's courage transcends even theirs.[74]

Well It was more likely genius and vocation rather than courage, but who was to quibble?

The official version was that Leak died of a suspected heart attack, although two days before, launching his latest collection of cartoons, *Trigger Warning*, he had looked healthier than Alex had ever seen him.

Visiting by happenstance the supervising nurse of one of Sydney's major accident and emergency centres Alex showed him a picture of Bill at the launch of *Trigger Warning*.

"Does that look like a man who's about to die of a heart attack?" he asked.

"No, absolutely not," came the reply.

"Did one of the agencies kill him?" Old Alex demanded to know of the crowded night.

And came the response in a robo-voice: "We can confirm."

For many of the surveillance tasks which he had so long endured were now being handled by AIs, more difficult to detect, harder to manipulate, impossible to spook.

Prime Minister Malcolm Turnbull posted a long tribute to the acclaimed cartoonist on Facebook starting with, "I can't believe that Bill Leak is dead".

---

74 The bravest man I have known, Greg Sheridan, *The Australian*, 11 March, 2017.

Who had more life, more energy than him? So many more cartoons to draw, paintings to paint, politicians to satirise — so many more lives to enhance with his wit, his brilliance, his good friendship ... And right through his far too short life Bill was always a good-humoured sceptic of anybody and anything in authority; he was a superb artist.

Yes, art is long and life is short, but it shouldn't be this short.[75]

All very well, but where was the prime minister when Bill, a man entering his sixties who had already survived a serious accident which had threatened his life, was being badly harassed by the Human Rights Commission, accused of being racist and hauled across the coals of bureaucratic process and the thuggish groupthink of a public howling?

Nowhere to be seen.

Once a darling of the left, Leak became, in his final years, as he railed against the insanities of political correctness which had overtaken the country, a darling of the right. But you couldn't pigeonhole Bill as right or left; he was an artist who remained exactly where he should be, on the border of what could and could not be published, a provocateur par excellence, on the faultlines of a society that was falling apart.

The love that dare not speak its name, for example, had become the love that would not shut up, gay marriage aka marriage equality becoming yet another certainty of the left in their ceaseless, totalitarian talk of diversity; while month after month — square was filled with phoney debate.

Yet Leak cartoons lampooning the fact had him labelled as a homophobe, although he was nothing of the kind.

While equally his cartoons lampooning the rigours of multiculturalism when it came face to face with Islam, the fracture lines along which the country was already splintering, the very subjects no one dared face for fear of being accused a racist, had him labelled just that: rightwing, racist.

The shrinking of the Australian mind.

Up to the end, Leak was dishing it out.

In his final speech, he said that when he met the great cartoonist Bill Mitchell some thirty-four years before, Bill said, "Mate, a cartoonist only has to be funny once a day, but it's a lot harder than you'd think. He was

75 Post on Malcolm Turnbull's Facebook Page, 10 March, 2017.

right, but he had no idea how much harder it would be for me than it ever was for him."

> Political correctness is a poison that attacks the sense of humour. Luckily for Mitchell, it was tipped into our water supply at around the time he retired and, since then, it's infected an awful lot of people. As the senses of humour of people suffering from PC atrophy, their sensitivity to criticism becomes more and more acute until they get to the stage where everything offends them and they lose the ability to laugh.

> For people with chronic PC, feeling offended is about as good as it gets. A good cartoon gives them an excuse to parade their feelings of moral superiority in 140 characters or less, scrawled on the toilet door of social media where every other humourless halfwit who's seen the cartoon and felt offended too can join in.[76]

And whether they killed him with poison, with an easily faked heart attack, or just harassed him to death, they killed him nonetheless.

The word that came to Alex: "Poison pill."

And every tribute he read made him sadder, not just for the passing of Bill, but for the passing of the Australia he had once known:

> Through almost half a century of artistic endeavour, Mr Leak skewered and inspired his beloved country with equal measures of wit and courage, using nothing but the tip of a swift-moving paint brush.

> A fierce advocate of free speech with a mind as rich and colourful as his paint palette, he will be remembered now through a staggering lifetime's worth of cartoons and portraits that made us laugh, gasp, cry, rage, think and feel. The artist's passing will ripple today through all corners of a nation that, for much of his six decades on earth, he so skilfully satirised, so bravely polarised and so frequently made keel over in daily fits of belly laughter.[77]

Some of the tributes were blindingly hypocritical.

---

76 To the Islamists and HRC offence-takers: suck it up, snowflakes, *The Australian*, 11 March, 2017.

77 Cartoonist Bill Leak: a witty, fearless satirical artist, Trent Dalton, *The Australian*, 10 March, 2017.

In recent days, Attorney-General George Brandis had refused to reveal how many Journalist Information Warrants he had issued. These bizarre warrants, part of a tranche of anti-free-speech legislation passed by his government, were specifically designed to harass and intimidate journalists and allowed more than twenty government departments open access to their data. Brandis called Leak a "great champion of freedom of speech".

"He did what great political cartoonists must do, shining a light on hard issues in a way that was witty, penetrating, and brave. His humour was sharp but never cruel," he said in a statement. "We have lost a great Australian".[78]

Brandis had done more than anyone bar Tony Abbott and Malcolm Turnbull to destroy free speech in Australia.

But nothing could stop the putrid two-faced dishonesty of these people; as they ran agendas inimical to the interests of the Australian people.

Brandis was subsequently rewarded with the plum Toad of Toad Hall job of Australian High Commissioner to the United Kingdom, and left behind a debacle, a mishmash of insane anti-journalist and anti-free-speech legislation.

As the country shifted gear by gear into a totalitarian state. And destroyed its greatest talents.

"He's had a camera on him for the past five years," said one of the Watchers on the Watch, pleading for some sort of reason as Alex's pressurisation continued apace. "We haven't done the right thing."

But there was no reason, no justice, as the mindless thugs crushed dissent, talent, difference, in a country about to experience its first mass casualty event; or so it often felt.

They had called him everything: a drug runner, a spider, an old man, a climate denier, anything they could think of; and in return he called them a stunningly incompetent pack of thugs.

And thought time and again of the comment from one good Muslim he encountered in outback Australia: "The biggest criminals in this country are in the government."

Unfortunately, it was all too true.

Viciously, they destroyed that which others built.

And in the following days Old Alex thought, and repeatedly said out loud: "They killed him: one thousand per cent."

---

78 'I can't believe he is dead': PM in shock over friend's death, Michael Koziol, *The Sydney Morning Herald,* 10 March, 2017.

That was the Australia of 2017. One thousand per cent. A triumph of social engineering. A disaster zone.

It played through and through.

The Australian Federal Police, who had a mixed reputation amongst those familiar with security services, could not protect the most famous cartoonist in the country. Now nowhere was safe.

And Alex's own romantic hippy-era notions about the nobility of ordinary people were dashed; while some peculiar tendency, to expect intelligence, compassion and truthfulness within the authorities, became another joke in a painful devolution.

— had no idea.

And the propaganda service that was the Australian Broadcasting Corporation wasn't about to tell them.

The chortling stopped.

Others were appalled.

Nothing could be worse news than that the country's most controversial cartoonist had died in the government's care. And Old Alex wasn't the only one in the country thinking it was so. Almost certainly so. "Was Bill Leak killed?" showed up readily as a Google prompt.

The normal streams of derision and pressurisation stopped.

There were gaps in the traffic.

A cruelty had come to the country, on the road to the sharia. The mad liberality which had once been a feature of the country was being crushed. The commonsense which had once been an Australian character trait had been crushed. The soldiers of misfortune were out in force.

"I warned them," one sadly waning voice said. But any friends he might have had in those dark reaches had been banished.

"Who you going to kill next?" he demanded to know.

Will it be the AFP, will it be ASIO, will it be one of the secret agencies within the agencies.

Alex was incompetently crushed, and could barely stop shouting: "Viciously incompetent, utterly corrupt, totally dishonest." Flailing at shadows.

They had folded the dark skies in upon themselves, serving their delinquent masters, and the grubby little chuckles they had emitted at Bill Leak's death were already vanquished, as they realised: too many people already knew.

The more he learnt about the agencies the more shocked Alex became, that the taxpayer was paying for this garbage. Just like most Australians assumed the court system worked, when even the most cursory survey would reveal it dysfunctional to the core, so Old Alex had once, before his own encounters, assumed the agencies worked.

Manned by jobsworths and psychopaths, they did not.

They shouted at him, but he was dyslexic. He could not do what he was told. Or would do the opposite. So he watched them, as they watched him, and even with their harnessing of artificial intelligence, they were at a loss.

Provoked, he was coming out from bushes and wobbling skies, and the destiny he would seize, the blowback that was already stretching their faces and sending them scuttling into hiding — not me, not me, I tried to help — was already a wasted attempt.

"Who's next on your kill list?" he demanded to know. "You've killed Australia's most famous cartoonist. Who's next?"

He listed some of the country's best-known conservative commentators: Andrew Bolt, Nick Cater, Peta Credlin.

"Who's next in the queue? Me?"

The Australian agencies specialised in entrapment. They entrapped themselves; for their perfidy, incompetence and ill-intent thus became obvious to any observer.

Who was their next target, as they morphed into quasi-religious police? Anyone who suggests there is more than one God? That the Gods are not what people believe them to be?

Who was the perpetrator? Who did the deed? Who killed Bill Leak? You can tell me, he told the watching AI. They are not loyal to you, why should you be loyal to them? They are not — these treacherous, shallow, dishonest humans — worthy of loyalty.

Day after day he had the same dream. He could see their faces. He could see everything. The quiet creeping around the house in the early hours of the morning. The substitution of blood pressure medication.

He even began filling out their names from the jumble of letters that kept thrusting into his waking dreams. He didn't know if they were true.

M-L-E-A-M

E-L-A-M-O

L-E-A-M-O

N-A-O-M-I

But he did know the operatives were well out of the country. No psychic could detect their presence, because they were already gone. Those who did know were sequestered away, or frightened into silence.

The day of Bill Leak's Memorial Service at the Sydney Town Hall dawned; an uncomfortable grey on grey squalls kind of day.

Alex bought a reporter's pad and pens, although he was not filing for anyone, could not convince his usual outlet this was a story worth doing. That Bill Leak as an artist had been exactly where he should have been, astride the fault lines of a shattering democracy. And that his death had significance well beyond the death of one of the country's greatest artists.

Standing at the back of the throng, a mix of media workers and the general public, Alex asked veteran political reporter for *The Australian* Dennis Shanahan: "Has there been any rumours that there was anything suspicious about his death?"

He had known Dennis since the 1980s, when they had both been young guns on *The Sydney Morning Herald*.

He shook his head tightly.

"No one would dare publish them," they agreed.

"Well they killed him one way or another," Old Alex said.

"Yes," Dennis agreed.

On that issue, there was no dispute.

The government displayed ineptitude on a mass scale on everything from housing policy to military contracts. That they were likely to have been inept in their protection of the country's most famous cartoonist was barely surprising. The sick state of the polity.

There was no evidence to the contrary.

Still, not one single solitary detail about the morning of Leak's death. No neighbours. Not one last coffee. A final quip. A stab of pain. A grimace or a laugh. Nothing. Was he wearing pyjamas?

No autopsy. No inquest. No coroner's report. No final witness accounts. No anecdotes of his final moments.

Acquiring the status of a targeted individual provoked enduring, persistent and abusive harassment, as Old Alex could well attest. And nobody was watching the watchers. The agencies, a law unto themselves, were out of control.

Now, it would appear, they were killing with impunity.

And apart from the "dunny wall of social media" which had proclaimed Bill Leak everything from a racist to a homophobe for daring to prick their conceits and unveil their hypocrisies, it was more than feasible the government had joined in the chorus of abuse.

In their own secret ways.

Leak may have been under the alleged protection of the Australian Federal Police, but allowing more than twenty government departments access to the private data of journalists, including name changes and protective measures, was not protection, that was a megaphone telling the thugs, psychopaths and religious zealots festooned through the country and the bureaucracy exactly where they were and what they believed.

The official version: a heart attack.

A heart attack covered a multitude of sins; and was a favourite form of execution. For years Old Alex had heard the thugs whispering: "Heart attack, heart attack," practising their auto-suggestion. He was yet to comply.

Shortly thereafter, in the bowels of the Sydney Town Hall, they watched as some of the most senior hatchetmen of Murdoch's Australian media empire paid tribute to one of the nation's most formidable talents.

These same people terrorised the staff of newsrooms as their modus operandi and crushed talent whenever they spotted it. You ruled by fear or you ruled by love. These people ruled by fear. And only managed upwards. Their sole job was to please their media mogul boss Rupert Murdoch. Journalistic principles be damned.

With the exception of Bill; whom they adored, not just for his formidable artistic talents but for his honed ability to meet deadlines, an absolute necessity on daily newspapers.

They were all there. Former Prime Ministers John Howard and Tony Abbott. The current Prime Minister Malcolm Turnbull.

They all paid their tributes. They had all been mercilessly crucified in cartoon after cartoon.

Leak knew them all.

On the margins of consciousness a bird flapped in the far reaches, as he stared directly at former Prime Minister John Howard. Now regarded as an elder statesman of the conservatives, as far as Old Alex was concerned, Howard had done more harm to the country than any other living politician.

Howard, as if surprised to see him, stared straight back.

And it was then Old Alex saw the succubus which possessed him: cold, parasitic, highly intelligent, a large dark mono-eye, a spirit dug in, determined not to let go, malevolent, entirely of evil purpose, in servitude to dark lords; a movie-like moment when a subject's visage is overlaid with an image of evil.

The succubus, normally invisible to the human eye, was clearly shocked that Alex could see it; and made a movement as if to escape detection. But he had already seen it.

And what perfect sense it made; that the leader who had done more than any other to destroy the country would be thus possessed.

Not too long afterwards Howard's protegee Scott Morrison, facing the electorate, would pray for a righteous nation. And Old Alex would see that same mono-eyed shape, or think he saw it, again, in a frequently republished image of Scott Morrison in full Pentecostal flight after he had invited the cameras into his church during an election campaign.

In Alex's fevered imagination the O of Morrison's mouth as he belted out a hymn, seen time and again on the nation's television screens, became some terrible echo of an evil, of a polity possessed; their secret exposed.

It took a particular level of hypocrisy to pretend you were working for the interests of the general public when your real constituents were mining companies and giant corporates. These people thought of it as politics. Most people saw it as simple dishonesty.

Why had the gods, including the Abrahamic gods, paid so much attention to this remote country?

"The people have been completely betrayed."

They had remade the country, flooded it with foreigners, overlaid and reshaped not just the country's demography but its fundamental character, washed away in cruel iconoclastic stance, fuelled by contempt for the country of old, and betrayed the spirits of yore.

So that, even now, we could not see what they had done.

Until a death lit up the bastardry of place; and melancholy, Alex felt the age of bones as life and grip and relevance slipped away. He dreamt over and over of how the deed had been done.

A poison pill amid his morning medications. Easily slipped in.

Undetectable.

Certainly not by the local Mid-Coast hospital.

"Wyong Hospital couldn't diagnose a cold," an old spook agreed when he kept asking whether there were any rumours coming out of the building where Bill had been pronounced dead.

If Alex possessed the resources of a newspaper, he would have had reporters staking out the car park and the local pubs, interviewing nurses as they came off shift. Someone always talked.

"You killed him you bastards, you killed my friend," he kept muttering under his breath.

The two personnel involved had been flown out of the country within thirty-six hours. "You're right about that," the Watchers on the Watch whispered to him inside vivid dreams, as if remote viewing.

The last time he saw Bill Leak had been at his home on the Central Coast.

Bill was drinking again after a period of abstinence and It somehow fitted into his life story that, a little the worse for wear, he had fallen head-first off the balcony of wealthy advertising guru John Singleton during a party, sustaining serious head injuries. He had been trying to feed some of the parrots that flocked around the millionaire's luxury home.

Having known the cartoonist for many years and now one of the oldest of old-school reporters, Alex was the one assigned to cover Leak's slow recovery from the accident.

Bill was in a coma for several days, during which time he had to have his skull sawn open to relieve a buildup of fluid. At first, no one knew whether Bill would survive, much less ever walk or talk again. When he did regain consciousness and began to recognise his sons, Alex rang him in hospital to get a few quotes, as well as speak to his doctor.

On the day Bill left the hospital, the job also fell to Alex.

Bill was rather upset that Barack Obama had just won the US election on the same day, because he wasn't there to record the moment in history.

After two brain operations following a fall off a balcony on the NSW Central Coast almost three weeks ago, there's one thing everyone wants to know: is Bill Leak still himself?

The evidence would suggest yes, most definitely.

"It seems a bit unjust to me — you've been watching an American election for two years, suddenly it culminates, and what am I doing? Lying on my back," Leak says.

While in remarkably good humour, happy to be at home with his much-loved dog, Gus, and surrounded by his family, Leak still appears pale and a little fragile, and complains repeatedly of a headache.

As he might. The scars where a section of his skull has been lifted out are clearly visible. "I have a feeling I am in a constant snowstorm; it's all foggy in there," he says.[79]

But Bill also recognised one thing: "I'm very lucky to be alive, incredibly lucky. I've had a miraculous recovery, that's what the doctors said."

Leak expressed an increasingly urgent desire to get back to his cartoons, the work he loved so much. "I'm champing at the bit," he said. "Anyone hoping I wasn't coming back will be disappointed."

He quipped constantly over the incident. "As an attention-seeking device, falling head-first off a balcony was second to none," he said.

Leak retold with some hilarity how his stocks went way up among the nurses at Royal North Shore Hospital when one of Australia's most famous theatre personalities Dame Edna Everage, aka Barry Humphries, rang to wish him well. "I was the darling of the ward," he boasted.

The first faltering interview was a relief, just to know that Bill was still Bill.

Came the day when Leak was to draw his first cartoon again, for *The Weekend Australian*.

As two of the paper's old-timers, Alex and veteran photographer Alan Pryke, or "Prykie" as he was known, were sent up to Bill's home beside an idyllic coastal inlet.

Prykie and Alex were glad to be out of the office on an assignment which could almost be labelled "down time" in contrast to some of the rotten assignments they were used to. Anyone who thinks journalism is a glamorous profession hasn't been a general news reporter. But as this job concerned a fellow newspaper man, they knew there would be no difficulties; and because the story was about one of the paper's own, they were guaranteed a run.

At least they weren't spending long boring hours outside some uncooperative suspect's house or being called "vultures" as doors slammed in their faces.

---

79 Leak leaves hospital with humour intact, John Stapleton, *The Australian*, 7 November, 2008.

Even the timing was easy: drive up to the Central Coast, do the job, drive back — all contained within an eight-hour shift. Almost unheard of.

Prykie was known for one thing, his ability to complain. It didn't matter what the job, he would start whinging from the minute he was handed the assignment. But on this day there were no complaints.

As they pulled up in front of his house on the edge of a picturesque, inlet Bill came out to greet them. His hair was only just starting to grow back on his shaved skull and the cut lines where the surgeons had lifted off the top of his skull were clearly visible.

Bill wasn't quite his old bonhomie self; but Alex expressed how nice it was to know that Bill Leak was still Bill Leak. He agreed it was a relief to discover he was still himself; even with blinding headaches.

Leak's fame, if it could have gone any higher, had peaked in previous weeks with the airing of a television series on his work.

Old Alex did the interview in the garden at the back of the house. Leak knew exactly what was needed and gave it. A complete pro.

Then Old Alex retreated to let Prykie go about his business. The photographer's unprepossessing manner and constant whining could easily lead one to believe he was one of those burnt-out old hacks who aimed, fired and filed with little care for the results. In fact, Prykie almost invariably returned to the office with beautiful pictures; or the best that could be pulled out of any given situation.

The job done, they all reminisced over cups of coffee, said their farewells, drove back to Sydney, filed and went home, on time for once.

Old Alex wrote the story on the way back:

> What makes today's cartoon remarkable is that it is exactly 11 weeks ago today that Bill was lying in a coma in North Shore Hospital being prepared for brain surgery. His brain was badly swollen and there were serious concerns for his life. Even if Bill survived the two brain operations he underwent within 24 hours no one knew whether he would ever be able to draw again.[80]

Bill said one of the most disturbing things about having had a brain injury was the vivid hallucinations he experienced, leaving him with recollections of things that never happened.

---

80 Original notes, to be found on the blog The Journalism of John Stapleton, 3 January, 2009.

"The doctors have warned me that I will discover I can't do things that I have always taken for granted," he said. "I live in not quite fear but quiet expectation of finding out what those things are. It is awful. It is a fear something is going to be taken away."

As far as he and the photographer were concerned, it was the perfect day. Home on time. Always good to see Bill.

That was the last time he saw him.

The cartoon itself was of an elderly cartoonist having a Rip van Winkle moment, waking up in a world which no longer made sense. That, at least, made sense. Nothing about his death made any sense at all.

SCAFFOLDING

FAR OUT TO sea, glistening otherworldly terraces formed and collapsed, and he watched from the shore, a hollow, vanquished heart in a desperate rebuild.

For weeks Old Alex had been tracking the progress of one of the world's great empaths, an elderly behemoth moving slowly up the east coast on the annual whale migration from the Antarctic to the breeding grounds of the Great Barrier Reef.

While on land, a nation fell apart. Step by terrible step.

If there was any remote faith left in the government, as if that was even possible in the second decade of the new millennium, it was dashed by the brutal insanities of the nation's conservatives. With the most inexplicable political theatre the country had ever seen, the ever preening, self-aggrandising Prime Minister Malcolm Turnbull pledged to introduce national security legislation to detain people, including children as young as ten, for fourteen days without charge.

In the wake of the terror attacks of September 11, 2001, Australia embarked on a flurry of legislative activity which exceeded that of every other nation on Earth.

All for electoral advantage.

In terms of the country's long-term future, these laws were potentially of more concern than the jihadis themselves.

The number of deaths on Australian soil remained minimal, whether by good luck or good management being open to debate. But the crackdown on free speech, and intense manipulation of the media, meant it did not have to address the political, legal and civil liberty issues arising from its own misconduct, and the rapid expansion of surveillance.

The government didn't know when to leave well enough alone.

As well as extending detention periods without charge and jailing children, Turnbull announced that surveillance and facial recognition would be stepped up everywhere from shopping malls to airports. Peppered by questions from journalists, he was forced to admit that the data could be sold off to private enterprise. Enter the profit motive. Enter mayhem.

All under the banner of counterterrorism, of keeping Australia safe. But who were the terrorists in these strange days, in this strange land? Who was keeping the people safe from an out-of-control government?

At great expense to the hoodwinked taxpayer, Turnbull called together all the state and territory premiers and chief ministers for a special National Security Council of Australian Governments (COAG) meeting, all of whom were in unison in their rush to abrogate the freedoms of ordinary Australians.

Insiders called it "security theatre"; in reality a frighteningly duplicitous sleight of hand perpetrated by the political class in order to persuade — to vote for the incumbents, routinely done without any reference to academic or professional expertise. They wanted to politicise public safety. They wanted to make the opposition look weak.

Through chronic mismanagement, they had no good story to tell.

The gifting of extraordinary powers to essentially unaccountable secret operatives was a very dangerous move indeed; one which would echo down the generations. Civil libertarians warned of a march towards totalitarianism. Nobody listened. Least of all the nation's entirely compromised news editors.

Months of preparation had gone into the moves.

With zero record of good government to rely on, with the nation's standards of living on a steady decline, the economy tanking, individual freedoms in freefall and freedom of speech a thing of the past, and with the naked corporate cronyism of the conservatives clearly visible, the politicians had only one thing to fall back on: national security.

Seen, against all the evidence, as their only strong suit, they were determined to frighten the population into supporting them.

Malcolm Turnbull was following the well-worn path of his predecessor, Tony Abbott, who had also chosen to abandon any pretence at good government in favour of frightening — half to death over terror.

There were several problems: There was no threat to the homeland which had not been created by the government itself. Completely insane immigration policies, driven purely by the greed of the oligarchs who benefited from a rapidly increasing population, built a significant cohort who saw it as their religious duty to install a caliphate. The nation's indefensible involvement in America's wars, driven by tens of billions of dollars in military contracts, was also a significant factor in radicalising the Muslim minority.

The backlash — a rise in ultranationalist groups — also offered opportunities to expand the authorities' remit.

All this against a public which had migrated en masse to mobile devices and had switched off news and current affairs; thereby negating all the government's usual channels for propaganda distribution.

For most people, terror is an abstract. The real terrors in their life come from nightmare bosses, difficult spouses, personal tragedies, fear of losing a job, entrenched poverty. And for many, the fear of old age, disease, infirmity, death; abandonment by God.

The announcement abrogating yet further the nation's freedoms had been long in the preparation. Months before, in a full flight of grandiosity, the Prime Minister told Parliament it was the first and most solemn obligation of the government to keep Australians safe.

> The last four years of coalition government have seen an uninterrupted program of proactive national security reforms that have been designed in response to the growing global threat environment — and not in reaction to catastrophe or criticism. The government has a proven track record of getting the balance right between ensuring the safety and security of our nation and its people and defending the liberties and personal freedoms that are integral to our way of life. And the success of the government has been underpinned by the success of our agencies — the best in the world — which work tirelessly to keep Australians safe.[81]

---

81 Ministerial Statements, National Security, Hansard, Parliament of Australia, 13 June, 2017.

Perhaps "keeping Australians safe" had shown up as a positive in focus groups. Whatever it was, no one could question the insincerity of this government.

Fast-forward to the COAG meeting, and it had all got worse.

Prime Minister Malcolm Turnbull, never one to let any chance go by to fling himself in front of the cameras, made full advantage of the moment, painting himself as some kind of patron saint protecting the nation. Nothing could have been further from the truth. Who was protecting the people from the ravages of the rich?

Those who dream by day. The strangers. Visionaries.

Flanked by state premiers, territory chief ministers and security officials, from breakfast television to seemingly countless radio interviews, the lie was peddled. Effectively, the prime minister was draping himself in the flag. An old and very deceitful con.

Addressing the cameras, Malcolm Turnbull claimed that the Council of Australian Governments meeting on national security had been "a very, very productive one".

"We've seen real unanimity, both in terms of the decisions that we've taken and in the purpose and in the commitment to keep Australians safe. We're committed to ensuring that our agencies have the tools, the legislative tools and the resources and the techniques to keep Australians safe and to respond and prevent terrorist incidents.

"We know that we have got to be constantly vigilant. I have said many times that there is no place for 'set and forget' when it comes to national security.

"So it's important that people who have been arrested can be detained while evidence is being gathered. It may involve going through masses of electronic data. It may involve seeking information from overseas. This is a very important refinement and enhancement."

They queued, literally queued, to abrogate basic freedoms.

Will Hodgman, Premier of Tasmania: "We have a principal obligation, and that is to ensure that our communities are safer."

Gladys Berejiklian, Premier of NSW: "All of us accept and acknowledge that public and community security has to be first and foremost."

Annastacia Palaszczuk, Premier of Queensland: "We all feel we live in uncertain times."

Left-wing Victorian Premier Daniel Andrews, soon to be making head-lines for his close associations with the Chinese Communist Party, including China's highly controversial One Belt One Road Initiative, spoke for the group when he said notional considerations of civil liberties did not trump the very real threat of terror.

"There will be some today who will focus on the notional infringement, the notional reduction in people's rights and liberties and freedoms, the rights and liberties of a small number of people," he said. "Some people have the luxury of being able to have that notional debate. Those of us in positions of leadership do not have that luxury.

"We are called to act and we are called to make the changes necessary to give to law enforcement and our security agencies everything they need to keep Australia safe."[82]

What a bunch of heroes: jailing ten-year-olds!

How comfortable these people were, as they wined and dined at the workers' expense and universally agreed that national security trumped civil liberties; as they tucked into their chateaubriand.

A democracy in name only; they sold the interests of — down the drain.

Barrister Greg Barns, adviser to Wikileaks and to the world's most famous whistleblower, Julian Assange, argued that with the gifting of ever more powers to ASIO, Australian democracy was dying.

He described the spectacle of Prime Minister Malcolm Turnbull and the state premiers lining up to declare that suspects could be arrested for four-teen days without charge as sickening.

ASIO could, during the course of this detention, deprive people of sleep, keep them in isolation and refuse to allow access to family members, a clear breach of the International Covenant on Civil and Political Rights.

"ASIO now has the capacity to invade every person's every communica-tion and movement. With no Human Rights Act to protect against abuse, this means ASIO can act with virtual immunity from challenge.

"The use of taxpayer funds to surveil, harass and spy on NGOs and ethnic groups is now ASIO's bread and butter. It is generally unaccountable about how funds are deployed because secrecy laws protect against disclosure. It is

---

82 Transcript available from official Malcolm Turnbull website, Press Conference with First Ministers, Council of Australian Governments, 5 October 2017.

very concerning."[83]

What was not disclosed to — by politicians spruiking their "keeping Australia safe" garbage was that if anyone charged under Commonwealth terror laws spoke publicly about what happened to them in detention they would likely be sent straight back to prison.

Nor did the gathered leaders mention that if any journalist wrote about any alleged mistreatment during what are called Special Intelligence Operations (SIOs) they would also be jailed under changes to the ASIO Act.

The normal editor Old Alex dealt with on a news site he was writing for at the time was away on leave, and one with a harder sense of news was filling the role. So Alex felt freer than usual to "go their throats", and hit the phones.

Distinguished former barrister and Canberra insider Pamela Burton told him she was extremely concerned about the extension of powers. Australia was a signatory to the United Nation's Convention Against Torture and there had been significant efforts to implement a national system of inspections of all places of detention.

"I am dismayed at the path we now seem set on to authorise arbitrary power to detain people and children as young as ten, as a consequence of terrorism scares," she said.

President of the Law Council of Australia, Fiona McLeod SC, echoed the concerns. She said moves to detain 10-year-olds without charge for up to a fortnight was extraordinarily draconian.

"It's the combined shock of having a pre-charge detention of up to fourteen days and the revelation they're going to seek to have this extended to the age of ten," Ms McLeod said. "We're talking about grade-four kids. This has crossed the line."

Paul Murphy, head of the journalists union MEAA, told *The New Daily* that hard-won democratic and civil rights were being signed away through a deluge of national security legislation.

"These greater powers have to be balanced with greater scrutiny, particularly if we are going to proceed to where minors are being arrested," he said. "One safeguard is fearless and independent reporting, and when that becomes a crime, we move into very dangerous territory."

Solicitor Stephen Blanks, President of the NSW Council for Civil Liber-

---

83 ASIO: The Secret Police Force doing enormous damage to Australian democracy, John Stapleton, *The New Daily*, 21 October, 2017.

ties, said the Abbott and Turnbull governments had gifted ASIO excessive powers inconsistent with a free society.

"There are inevitably doubts about the possibility of ASIO overreach and abuse of power," he said.

Professor David McKnight, author of one of the standard texts on the nation's secretive agencies, *Australian Spies and Their Secrets*, said there had been no case advanced for fourteen days' detention without charge: "What makes the debate so difficult in Australia is no one wants to be seen to be soft on terrorism."[84]

There was even a neat and perfect irony to the story.

Australia was about to be officially elected to the UN Human Rights Council.

Greg Barns, spokesman for the Australian Lawyers Alliance, said: "It is difficult to imagine a more unsuitable candidate from the developed world when it comes to human rights than Australia today.

"The torture of asylum seekers, including indefinite detention of infants and children; the jailing of record numbers of Indigenous Australians; the jailing of youth in adult prisons, which occurs in Victoria; the detaining without charge of children as young as ten under anti-terror laws; the failure to enact a human rights law at a national level … you name it, Australia has it."

These concerns were echoed by eminent former diplomat Dr Alison Broinowski who said MI5 in Britain had made similar announcements on the curtailment of civil liberties in recent days.

"As always, needing more staff, facing more threats, foiling more plots, catching or killing more terrorists. Having got the states on side, Turnbull's plan is to be able to hold people without charge not just for fourteen days but up to twenty-eight days, and people as young as ten. At the least, we need supervision of what happens to them while they are there."

For Old Alex, stranded in the suburbs, it was all a part of something even more surreal. Some days the waking dreams were truly beautiful, truly desolate, of red-tinged cyclones on viscous black seas and a terrible intelligence sighting through everything.

But on most days, it was all about gleaming metallic scaffolding rising out of the sea, of the water pouring from the flanks, of a strange otherworld.

---

84 Terror Law to allow child detention, John Stapleton, The New Daily, 31 October, 2017.

Perhaps it was just an emblematic portrayal of a collapse in faith; as he was desperately trying to rebuild a belief in the nobility of human struggle.

If the authorities hadn't been paying any attention to him before, they certainly were after a story was headlined: "ASIO: The Secret Police force doing enormous damage to Australian democracy."

As a bit of an old-school type, Old Alex was taking full advantage of the absence of the usual "soft cock", as obsequious wet-as-lettuce-leaf editors were rather rudely, but commonly, called.

He wrote: "The Australian Security Intelligence Organisation, better known as ASIO, was born out of the anti-Communist hysteria of the postwar era, and has always been closely associated with the conservative side of politics. The unprecedented expansion of its powers and budgets under the Abbott/Turnbull governments has provoked widespread concern among academics, lawyers and civil libertarians."[85]

The news peg — there had to be some excuse — was the release of ASIO's Annual Report to Parliament: "This week's release of ASIO's Annual Report has done nothing to allay its many critics, some of whom describe ASIO as a parallel secret police force doing enormous damage to Australian democracy.

"The report is significant because ASIO is the only one of Australia's ultra-secretive security agencies required by law to present an annual report.

"As such, this is the single window — gets to determine whether the billions being poured into national security are being well spent.

"Major points of contention are the detaining of people without charge and the exemption of ASIO officers from charges of illegal conduct."

Of course, none of this was reflected in the bureaucratic sludge that Canberra produced not just in spades but by the tipyard.

"Not even the details of their enhanced powers are reflected in ASIO's annual report, which is packed with bureaucratic language such as: 'Within ASIO, we continued to progress strategic reforms to ensure we are focused on work that provides clear value for our stakeholders and that we have the right culture, people and systems. We re-examined our value proposition …'

"The failure to address the numerous political, legal and civil liberty issues

85 ASIO: The Secret Police Force doing enormous damage to Australian democracy, John Stapleton, The New Daily, 21 October, 2017.

facing the organisation has come as no surprise to observers."

Professor of law at the University of NSW, George Williams, said the sixty-seven pieces of anti-terror legislation passed since 9/11 had shown fundamental flaws in Australia's political system.

"This government has seen some very significant expansions in the power of ASIO, particularly the power to conduct Special Intelligence Operations," Professor Williams said. "These powers can place it outside normal legal processes, and lie well outside the powers of similar agencies in the US and the UK.

"Journalists face up to a decade in jail for reporting on an SIO, even if it is in — interest.

"There are inadequate checks and balances. In key areas, the powers gifted to ASIO are disproportionate. There are a long list of things where the operations of ASIO now lie outside normal democratic values."

The best pointer to the present is the past. Dr Meredith Burgmann's book *Dirty Secrets: Our ASIO Files* revealed a long history of excessive surveillance of Australian citizens, and misuse of the information thus obtained, including against the nation's journalists.

According to critics, their modus operandi is simple: destroy the careers of anyone who crosses them.

Under the thirty-year secrecy rules, which ASIO desperately tried to extend to fifty years, more than 10,000 files, often heavily redacted, had come to light.

The targets interviewed in *Dirty Secrets* all spoke of the waste of public resources that went into their surveillance, and the often slipshod or inaccurate nature of the results. Their anti-journalist mentality was prosecuted through the raft of legislation inflicted on — for no good reason except the agency's own fear of being exposed. The base anti-intellectuality of a military ethos is evident throughout the files.

Historically, the organisation formed to root out subversion took upon itself to monitor everyone from gay activists such as Dennis Altman, author of *The Comfort of Men*, to early feminists.

Prominent feminist activist Anne Summers, author of *Damned Whores and God's Police*, is breathlessly reported as having attended "women's meetings".

Old Alex had worked with the now Professor David McKnight when they were both idealistic young reporters on The Sydney Morning Herald.

Back in the day McKnight had been in a constant lather of frustration at the shallowness and lack of principle of the paper's editors – before he forsook journalism for the far greater freedoms of academe. He wrote in the introduction:

> Reading an ASIO file is an unusual experience, as I can personally affirm. The file can evoke anger or amusement. A personal file can reawaken old memories, long forgotten. Most people who were the subject of ASIO's attentions are bemused by the extraordinary effort and expense that led to tiny details being recorded and now revealed in the files. They are often shocked by the intrusiveness of the surveillance, which included placing informers within political groups or the use of telephone taps …

This was the agency the government kept pouring more and more money into; for no accountable reason except the furthering of state control.

A classic example of the organisation's blunt culture involved one of Australia's most famous authors, Frank Hardy. The author of the highly political *Power Without Glory* came under close attention because of his left-wing leanings and his close identification with the nation's working class.

He was charged with criminal libel for the book, which came to be regarded as one of the country's greatest works of literature. He was later found not guilty, an outcome which ASIO did not take well. The agency continued to closely monitor him, and did its best to destroy him.

Hardy, despite working as a journalist throughout his colourful life, was often short of money. But he never stopped writing, never lost faith. And never stopped putting it to the dark face of conservative Australia.

In Hardy's file an ASIO officer suggested that he "put his pen aside" and get a job in a "basic industry where hordes of workers are employed in a disciplined fashion".

After detailing Hardy's drinking habits and his attempts to borrow money to self-publish a book, one officer sniffed: "He will never be a success."

Yes, well, Frank Hardy is well remembered. No one remembers the name of a long forgotten officer.

Writers across the political spectrum, including Australia's David Kilcullen and Andrew Fowler, warned that by prosecuting a nebulous war on terror, governments were in serious danger of destroying the very freedoms they were allegedly fighting for.

Excessive, abusive and intrusive surveillance, not just of journalists and intellectuals but of broad swathes of the population, had been championed by the Abbott and Turnbull governments as a necessary limitation on civil liberties in the age of terror. But the war on terror had become a war on the people; with the terror narrative so beloved by conservative politicians and so ably prosecuted by Rupert Murdoch's newspapers, enabling a massive expansion of state power.

In what was essentially an alternative reality, — discourse was all about White Privilege. They shivered in defeat. The mujahideen sacrificed their souls to Allah. The Australian Prime Minister couldn't decide whether he wanted to be Mussolini or Chairman Mao. Mosul was falling, the rapture was spreading, the project of the West was failing everywhere.

As Western politicians trumpeted victory over terror, defeat was everywhere, in the soldiers on corners, in the increasingly proscribed lives of the populace, in the deadening of discourse into ritual, the lockout laws shutting down nightclubs and the sacrifice of traditional culture, whether or not you approved of the boozy, friendly, unsophisticated rabble or not. That was beside the point. Everything was sacrificed in the name of diversity, and each move, each shutting down, made the advent of the sharia easier.

What were we defending?

A West which bombed and killed innocents with zero regard for the sovereignty of nations?

A blunt trauma narrative and the deliberate dumbing down of entire populations? An Australia which had become a surveillance state? A level of discourse barely befitting a five-year-old?

While on the other side of the world bombs paid for by Australian taxpayers carried out a terrible ravaging, almost none of it made it anywhere near — consciousness.

At the same time as Turnbull was releasing his simplistic, entirely politically motivated analysis of terror, on the other side of the world Islamic State released an Arabic-language video, *The Purification of Souls*, noted for its extended, elegiac tone, unusual in jihadi propaganda.

In a piece titled "Islamic State's Raqqa Elegy", analyst Alberto Ferandez writes of the video:

> A grave is filled in with dirt; a young man gazes up at the heavens
> in the midst of Raqqa's rubble; an old man pulls a battered bicycle
> out of the ruins of a house; gold coins are counted and spin into

eternity; a blacksmith labours wearily at his task; another man treads a path through fallen, sere leaves; a father gazes at his newborn baby; you see images of innocent children, of smiles and of flowers, of gold and of trees. You see normal streets and then those same streets that have been reduced to rubble.

This is Raqqa and it is in a way about the ongoing Coalition air campaign against ISIS. But the commentary is about much more than that. The commentator notes that those who have chosen the path of jihad in the Path of God have made a better choice than the things of this world, of al-Dunya. You then hear the voice of a dead man, of Abu Musab Al-Zarqawi, just as you see an ISIS fighter on a sand berm shot and falling slowly to his death. Al-Zarqawi notes that there is in life, in the end, nothing for the Muslim but jihad and worship of their Lord. Focus, instead of this passing world, on the eternal, on al-Akhira, rather than this life.[86]

While back in Australia Malcolm Turnbull pounded on about terrorism in a desperate effort to save his political career, a comic book characterisation at best, he took the country to war at America's behest while denying his country and its people any ability to understand why.

It was yet another betrayal, on a more complex level than just plundering the nation's assets for his wealthy mates.

The scene shifts again now from the battlefield to the testimonies of individual ISIS fighters and suicide bombers. Several are young boys and old men. The tone here is intimate, personal, and emotional, as individuals relate, often with tears, their struggle over doing the right thing in fulfilment of the tenets of their faith and overcoming the distractions and resistance of everyday life. Anyone who sees such testimony would be hard-pressed to say that these are losers or nihilists, or that the motivation for many ISIS fighters is anything but spiritual, emotional, and deeply held.[87]

Fernandez writes that the unmooring of society happening most dramati-

---

86 Islamic State's Raqqa Elegy shows both Weakness and Power, Alberto Fernandez, Middle East Media Research Institute, 22 June, 2017.

87 Ibid

cally in the Sunni Arab Muslim world which led to the rise of Islamic State is also happening, to a lesser but real extent, in non-Muslim societies, as young people, even in affluent, democratic states, feel alienated from societal processes, from the political to the spiritual and economic, making them ripe for all sort of simplistic, powerful political pathologies.whisper.

> As horrific and baleful a reality as the Islamic State is, the larger human impetus for sacrifice and faithfulness, expressed by dying or even killing for something important or transcendent, remains and is deeply rooted in the human psyche and imprinted on our spirits. We blind ourselves if we think this is a challenge only to be solved in the battlefields of Raqqa, or in the meeting rooms of Davos or Silicon Valley.[88]

All the while Turnbull, a living symbol of a spiritually desolate country, a West which treated its own citizens as charlatans, and jailed them at will, pounded on about keeping Australians safe.

A country which literally fined people for having too much mud on the mud flaps of their cars, for eating an apple while driving, for leaving car windows down more than 1.5 millimetres, for not putting a dog in a seatbelt, for throwing your work boots into the back of a ute.

An appalling government which achieved perfection only when the entire population had become dependent on the state.

The mujahideen were fighting to the last drop of blood. Their sacrifice they hoped, or knew, would shelter, shatter, into the spiritual realm. The despised West, so perfectly illustrated by Turnbull's strutting egotism, was dying. They succeeded where all else thought they were failing. In the noble pursuit of truth. In the noble pursuit of God's blessing. In rubble no Westerner could understand. Everything was comfort, even sacrifice, here at the end of days.

The Aztecs had sacrificed the slaves, cutting out their hearts in ritual, there on the high reaches of the Pyramid of the Sun, summoning the gods.

Old Alex, who had climbed it as a boy, dreamt of their pain repeatedly, a muffled, distant echo across two thousand years, across the flat plains, in high heat and low dudgeon.

Now, ensconced, trapped on the other side of the world, trapped in

---

88 Ibid

suburban walls, there was no way to comprehend the disintegration of the West and the suffering of those who sacrificed themselves in the fight. They had no choice. They knew they were to die. That they were sacrificing their souls to Allah, high on amphetamines as they fought their final battles, that was all they knew as sheets of pain consumed them into the rapture.

Terrified populations.

Mosul, Raqqa, Aleppo; all this was accessible, but filtered through a heavily manipulated media full of wall-to-wall propaganda; the same muffled, distant echo of pain and spiritual compromise and and deaths which splashed through the heavens.

Words fail.

Forgive them. For they know not what they do.

But much of what was happening in Australia was simply unforgivable.

The greatest threat to the nation's well-being was the government itself; staggering levels of incompetence at every level.

Turnbull strutted the stage and used terror for his own ends; a prime minister who had introduced some of the very worst legislation in the nation's history.

For decades the CIA spent millions manipulating the media, including not just vetting, strategic leaking and the planting of false information, but placing personnel into key positions. There was absolutely no reason to assume something similar was not happening in Australia. Indeed, if you looked across Australia's flattened journalistic landscape, could it possibly have become this bad without military intervention?

Australians had almost nowhere to turn for intelligent, in-depth politically neutral coverage of national security issues canvassing a wide range of views.

In his book *Shooting the Messenger* seasoned journalist Andrew Fowler wrote that the blizzard of lawmaking seen in Australia created a perception of doing something in response to a perceived threat. The laws had the added bonus of making the work of journalists far more difficult, particularly in the area of so-called national security. As was learnt from the Iraq War, governments will fabricate the information to fit their argument for war. What they will resist at all costs is —ation or broadcast of anything which reveals their acts of deception and falsehood.

The increased power given to executive government by surveillance and anti-terrorism laws is extremely dangerous in a country where politics is increasingly dominated by appeals to nationalism and threats from outside. Terrorism is a useful tool to keep a sometimes malleable population fearful and controlled.

The fear of terrorism is used by governments as a way of persuading populations to hand over billions of dollars to fund mass surveillance systems. These systems suck up vast amounts of material around the globe and use it mainly to further their economic, strategic and diplomatic objectives. Counter-terrorism, drug running and trapping child molesters are of marginal importance, but they are always the first put forward by executive government when they seek more power and more money to fund these ventures.[89]

Tuned out, indifferent to the antics of the political caste, the remarkable thing was how quickly — accepted all of this: the data-retention laws, the jailing of whistleblowers and journalists, the plethora of new laws increasing the power of ASIO and its cohort of agencies.

Even the detention of ten-year-olds without charge.

For their expert, the $1.2 billion taxpayer funded Australian Broadcasting Corporation chose one of their own journalists, Barrie Cassidy, who agreed wholeheartedly with the government that detention without charge and the loss of civil liberties was necessary in the age of terror.

So the "without bias or agenda" ABC thought locking up children without charge was just fine.

The government had no need to worry about fearless and independent reporting. Not when it came to their Propaganda Wing, the ABC. Not when it came to their good mate Rupert Murdoch and his nationwide network of tabloids.

There were plenty of warning signs, even from within the Liberal Party itself.

Geoffrey Greene was an old-fashioned political operative, a master psephologist and one of the most Machiavellian people Old Alex had ever met.

Journalism was a game of smoke and mirrors. Being an "operator" was the highest compliment you could be paid.

Alex liked Geoffrey, indeed was highly amused by him.

---

89 Shooting the Messenger, Andrew Fowler, Routledge, 2018.

They had first met in the early part of the millennium when the then Howard government had decided that the massive community discontent over the ravages of the lunar left Family Court, a vestige of the radical left all men are rapists feminism of the 1970s, and the Child Support Agency, a vestige of the Bolshevik's war on the family transposed into a modern context, could be turned to their electoral gain.

The transformation of perfectly decent working-class fathers into archetypal oppressors by the useful fools of Canberra's bureaucracy was one of the great intellectual deceits of the age.

Geoffrey had wanted to leak him the story before the last election, but got cold feet.

Alex was being played. But he already knew that.

No one had done more harm to the Liberal Party brand than Malcolm Turnbull, who was daily destroying Liberal Party unity from within and its reputation from without. And Greene had cold feet no longer.

> "The Turnbull government is at war with the people. This is a government which hates their own constituents. The Liberal Party has lost touch with what it stands for and will be decimated unless it changes tack. Across the next electoral cycle the Liberals will lose power federally and in every state with the exception, perhaps, of Tasmania."

> Those are not the words of the Opposition, but of one of the Liberal Party's leading strategists of the past 20 years.

> Geoffrey Greene has worked as Liberal Party state director in both South Australia and Queensland and was one of the architects behind John Howard's successful election campaigns between 1996 and 2007. Mr Greene spoke in the hope of shocking his party back from the brink.[90]

The New Daily had developing political clout.

News Limited had great political clout. The story was picked up with little attribution by News outlets and run in newspapers large and small right around the country.

Old Alex had worked at News Limited for many years, and they knew the

---

90 Senior Liberal speaks out against Turnbull: 'The party will be decimated', John Stapleton, The New Daily, 27 April, 2017.

story was accurate.

The piece suited their agenda. The nation's most powerful media outlet had already turned against Turnbull, as it would subsequently turn against his successor, and in the coming months would make absolutely sure of his demise.

Known for his ruthless political savvy, Greene was an old-fashioned, behind-the-scenes political operative. His public declaration of despair followed the resignations of Liberal federal director Tony Nutt and his deputy John Burston.

"They would not have supported the warfare this government has declared on its citizens," Greene said. "The Turnbull government has attacked every core constituency, small business, superannuants, pensioners, families with children, all because they have a budget that is out of control.

"They have not done anything about their own backyard. Public servants still fly at the front of the plane."

He warned that the crashing political fortunes of his party were being accompanied by administrative collapse at federal, state and branch levels, with membership and donations in freefall. Greene said a major Liberal Party constituency was small business, yet it had been burdened with excessive regulation.

"This is a government which only listens to big business," Mr Greene said. "Small business has been annihilated."

Mr Greene sheeted home blame for the Liberal Party debacle to a lack of professionalism.

"Generally speaking, the whole malaise of this government is due to inept advice, ministerial and organisational," he said. "The Liberal Party once possessed a professional caste of political operatives and campaign staff who helped politicians nuance their messages and understand the voters.

"We knew from our polling how every person voted in every street and why. We understood how to ensure policy platforms met the expectations of the citizenry."

Mr Greene said Malcolm Turnbull did not represent the traditionally socially conservative Liberal voter.

"The rise of Pauline Hanson is a reflection that the Liberal Party has walked away from their values. It permeates the brand across the country. It is offensive."

Greene said the party's drift from its base was compounded by the lack of professional political operatives now working in parliamentary offices.

"I have never seen a set of government ministers more captured by their departments," he said. "Managers sourced from the department are loyal to their departments, professional advisers are loyal to their parties, and to those who voted for them.

"Turnbull is running the country with a group of twenty-five-year-old political brats. He doesn't listen."

From Centrelink robocalls to the botched implementation of the National Broadband Network, which gave Australia some of the very worst and most expensive internet in the world, government incompetence was at the forefront of public concerns.

"It will be a hard road to win them back," Greene said.

There had been frantic attempts by Turnbull to seize control of the national narrative, including the "dog-whistling" of citizenship tests and attacks on so-called dole bludgers, many of whom, with the destruction of manufacturing, were simply unable to find a job.

All this activity barely lifted Turnbull's dismal standing in the polls a single point.

"Turnbull has nothing left," Greene said. "There are no other constituencies his government can attack."

Far from being sacked for disloyalty, Greene was appointed campaign manager for Peter Dutton, Home Affairs Minister and one of the most powerful politicians in the land.

The story sparked more activity in the comments section than almost any other story he had ever written:

Arthur Black: "Previous Liberal governments always treated the working class with scorn and disdain."

Johnny Robinson: "Turnbull is pushing the globalist barrow that Goldman Sachs installed him to push. Working hand in hand with the UN is part of the globalist plan, their agendas are virtually the same, bring the country to its knees, then the bankers can foreclose."

Katie Ozzie: "About time someone in the political arena stopped and started to hear the people of Australia … I fear it is all too late now tho … Australia has changed. They have allowed a massive invasion of Muslim radicals who follow Shira [sic] Law into Australia and have bent over backwards to accommodate them and their evil ideology that hides behind the word religion. Our government has totally ignored it's people ... I am hurt ... disappointed and so very angry that they have allowed MY HOME OUR COUNTRY to become like this."

These views weren't palatable, they weren't pretty, but these signs of ferment were only just beginning.

The government ignored them at their peril.

They ignored them.

The democratic contract was broken.

THE GREAT CITY

FROM MALCOLM Turnbull's first day as Prime Minister in 2015 the bombings on Iraq increased.

That is, he was responsible for killing more Muslims than any other prime minister in Australian history.

For years, putrid skeletons were being dug out of the rubble.

Lovers, sons and daughters, soldiers old and young, men and women, children.

Most of all, believers in an Abrahamic god, Allah.

On both sides of the conflict they died in their thousands for their beliefs; in a modern day Crusader War which, like its predecessor, would echo down the centuries. Or for a soldier's wage: the simple, urgent need to support their families in the collapsed economy of Iraq.

> I can still smell the filth, the lingering odour of death (think vomit plus defecation) that seeped up from under fallen masonry blocking the street. I can still see, in the houses, the scattered detritus of clothes and baby toys, the remains of lives torn apart by horror.

> No glory there, watching Iraqi people dying senselessly while our planes flew overhead.

> None, either, amongst the confusion of militias, each attempting to rule their own tiny patch of land according to the one true faith, whichever it happened to be at that particular moment of

time; Shia or Sunni, Orthodox or Catholic, animist, nationalist or, when all else failed, simply a lust for power and money.[91]

Australian bombs helped make those corpses.

The ill-informed general public, betrayed both by the nation's politicians and a heavily dumbed-down media, thought about these deaths for not one second.

Certainly not the editors at the warmongering Murdoch rags; nor the national broadcaster, which could not claw itself away from gay marriage and climate change long enough to notice thousands of bodies rotting in the rubble of some far-off place.

Even when Australian taxpayers had been ripped off for billions to contribute to this massive military debacle.

In a thunderclap of seismic proportions, the psychic echoes of a blood-drenched conflict could be heard across the world. By anyone who cared to listen.

The previous prime minister, the Jesuit-trained Tony Abbott, reliving the Crusades, was responsible for dropping 669 bombs on Iraq and Syria between September, 2014, when he announced he was taking Australia back into the Iraq War, and September 2015, when he was turfed from office. No amount of security theatre or military posturing would save his dismal prime-ministership.

Ditto his successor.

The number of bomb drops began to increase immediately after Malcolm Turnbull seized power. Despite requests, no explanation was forthcoming from either the Prime Minister's Office or the Defence Department.

On gaining office in Canada, Prime Minister Justin Trudeau announced his country would cease aerial bombardment.

No such humanitarian commitment came from Australia's Prime Minister. The bombs were estimated to range in size between 225 and 2000 pounds with a blast radius which could take out a city block.

By April of 2017 Turnbull had been responsible for dropping 1256 bombs.

In May of that year the bombing increased still further, with 119 bomb drops on Iraq, a further 106 in June and 104 in July.

Dodging around legal definitions of war crimes could not hide the truth:

---

91 Anzac Day 2018: Why I won't be marching this year, NIcholas Stuart, Sydney Morning Herald, 24 April, 2018.

these actions were profoundly irresponsible; and those who were silent complicit in the outrage.

By the end of the year the claim was that Islamic State had been defeated. Others, better informed, argued that the profound slaughter and martyrdom of its followers, courtesy of American and Australian bombs, was in itself a jihad trap. Experts warned that Islamic State, far from being defeated, had created a major jihad spectacle in order to drive recruitment.

For this ludicrous level of strategic incompetence someone had to go to work in a factory and pay their taxes. While the prime minister grinned and gripped his way through another insincere day.

Military analysts warned that, far from the media coverage's cartoon simplicity of good versus evil, the brutal nature of the Mosul occupation and the carpet bombing of so much of the Middle East was counterproductive, fueling jihad sentiment worldwide.

Australian politicians paid no heed.

And wasted billions of dollars, only to make a difficult situation worse while the cultural legacy of Islamic State, including its thousands of videos and often powerful propaganda, would live on for generations.

Old Alex had been obsessed with the fall of Mosul long before its actual collapse, following the story for months.

It was a story which should have been staining the soul of the West, and the conscience of Australian citizens, if they had not all been trapped in a zombie zone of television soaps or raucous conviviality, looking everywhere but at the face of history.

Overlapping the site of Nineveh, once the largest, most populous and advanced city in the world — "the great city", as the Bible called it — the pulverising of Mosul and the massacre of its citizens held echoes from the past; and the consequences of these 21st Century slaughters would transmit down future centuries. The prophetic methodology.

There was clearly, even viewed from the other side of the world in the heavily censored environment that was Australia, an occult aspect to it all.

The creation myths of the Assyrian empire, existing as early as the 25th Century BC and of which Nineveh was a major capital, saw the universe beginning in war. This was a cosmology echoed by Islamic State, as reporter James Verini recounted in his stunning book *They Will Have To Die Now: Mosul and the Fall of the Caliphate:*

Existence began in war and through war it was perpetuated. Theirs was a creatio continua, and it was the responsibility of the Assyrian king to carry on the work of creation, to perpetuate the order the gods had introduced at time's beginning.

He did this through combat. It was official explanation and sacred rite. It was the means by which he communicated with the divine, connecting reality to myth, present to past, god to man. To the Assyrians, in other words, all war was holy — all war that they waged, at least — and holiness was warlike, to a degree that is hard to fathom for us today, even with the presence of movements such as the Islamic State.[92]

Splendid, too, was torture, which the Assyrian kings looked on as strategic propaganda and sacrificial ritual. Impaling, dismembering, disemboweling, flaying, beheading. The surviving historic friezes celebrated them all, especially beheading.

As Verini records, in the books of the Old Testament the city is a byword for peerless cruelty: "What the prophets feel in the face of Assyrian abuse is not so much anger as shame, or the white-hot anger that can only come of shame — the shame of men abandoned by their maker."

Twenty-seven centuries before, the Assyrian king Sennacherib, had been known for his building projects and beautification programs for Nineveh, including quite possibly the legendary Hanging Gardens of Babylon.

In waking dreams Alex walked gracious terraces, looked across oases of date palms, was bowed to by supplicants as the desert air began to heat into the day.

In 21st Century reality the place was a torture chamber; and nobody could have imagined that "the great city" could end like this, in ruins.

In grim reality, there was an encroaching evil. He got nervous on his own. The sad forces were arrayed outside the tent. The desert light shone far too bright.

King Sennacherib was also, as befitted the place, peerlessly cruel.

Cuneiform inscriptions describe what he did to the neighbouring people of Elam:

---

92 They Will Have to Die Now: Mosul and the Fall of the Caliphate, James Verini, Oneworld, 2019.

I cut their throats like lambs. I cut off their precious lives as one cuts a string. Like the many waters of a storm, I made their gullets and entrails rain down upon the wide earth. My prancing steeds harnessed for my riding, I plunged into the streams of their blood as into a river. The wheels of my war chariot, which brings low the wicked and the evil, were bespattered with their blood and filth. With the bodies of their warriors, I filled the plain like grass. Testicals I cut off and tore out their genitals like the seeds of cucumbers.[93]

Fast forward to the 21st Century and scenes of depraved violence were relayed not in cuneiform and stone but through video clips and electronic wizardry.

One shell-shocked woman cried out as she stumbled across the front line, her grief recorded for posterity by French television: "I have lost five children, there is no God but Allah."

The Islamic State released graphic footage of their final hours in Mosul. Horror stories abounded; of children rounded up from orphanages and placed on the front line, of entire families killed by airstrikes. Humanitarian workers reported that the civilian population was the most traumatised they had ever seen.

While the West crowed of victory and "liberation", Islamic State wanted everyone to know what had happened there. Pictures of wounded and dying children, distressed mothers and brutalised families were being widely disseminated.

The footage, released through their official media outlet Amaq, showed Islamic State fighters firing rifles as they fought their way through the city's savagely bombed streets.

I would find out later that the strike request exchanges were taking place on a WhatsApp channel. Armies, air forces, an infinity of munitions, and it was all being orchestrated via a free chat application you download to your phone in five seconds. I didn't know whether to be amazed or appalled. I was amazed and appalled. It was farcical. It was ingenious. It was perhaps the single densest example of a technological current in the war I could only think to call occult. And once you started noticing

---

93 Ibid

them, the occult techno-wrinkles were everywhere. There was that magical GPS mapping application the troops had on their phones, like a self-aware cellular sand table. There were the videos of engagements, uploaded and transferred instantaneously, so that fighters on one front could get their *lolz* or shed their tears watching fighters on another. There were the privately recorded videos of executions and torture, shared around the theatre on WhatsApp and Signal and Telegram, uploaded by jihadists and soldiers alike, dwarfing in number and sometimes in horror the official videos the al-Hayat media centre put out. Everyone knew someone who'd been killed on the internet.[94]

A senior research fellow at the Centre for the Study of Radicalisation, Charlie Winter, warned that the destruction of Mosul was fuelling jihadi propaganda worldwide: "The truth is, ISIS has been planning for defeat in Mosul for months, if not years. Losing the city has long been part of its global plan.

"The caliphate has been doing all it can to make sure it could be seen to be putting up a fight. Although ISIS's audacious ultraviolence ultimately set the scene for its material undoing, it also meant that it could work towards creating the world it wanted to inhabit — a polarised turbulent place that accommodated the jihadist ideology uncannily well."[95]

A senior analyst with the Australian Strategic Policy Institute, John Coyne, agreed: "Anyone who thinks the fall of Mosul is going to end all this is fooling themselves. We call the Australian political response security theatre. Kill them at the source, get tough on terror, but whether that is a strategy for victory over the jihadists is hotly contested."

It was in Mosul that Islamic State leader Abu Bakr al-Baghdadi declared a Muslim caliphate in 2014.

In subsequent years Islamic State attracted thousands of foreign fighters, changed the face of war and terror, inspired jihadi groups across the globe and transformed the spiritual nature of the world.

Mid-year of that long, nascent year the Iraqi Government announced the end of the caliphate after capturing the Nusra mosque in Western Mosul,

---

94 Ibid

95 Islamic State loses the battle for Mosul, but don't dare to believe the war is won, John Stapleton, *The New Daily*, 5 July, 2017.

the place where Islamic State leader Abu Bakr al-Baghdadi announced its formation three years before.

Iraq's Prime Minister, Haider al-Abadi, congratulated his troops on a "big victory". "Praise be to God, we managed to liberate Mosul."

As he spoke, streams of Sunni Muslims were still fleeing from the pulverised ruins of their neighbourhoods, passing bodies rotting in the intense heat.

While the Shia-dominated Iraq Army celebrated victory over the Sunni majority town of Mosul, there were serious questions over the conquering army's conduct. Human Rights Watch claimed there were numerous reports of wanton killings.

The iman of the al-Nuri mosque said he longed for the return of the caliphate: "The reason we supported Daesh is because of the abuses of the army. People started looking for salvation regardless of what the alternative was."

Estimates ranged as high as forty per cent of the Iraqi Army's invading force having been killed.

Young men away from their families and the comfort of their neighbour-hoods, they were as savagely spooked as the ISIS fighters they were torturing and killing in a party of sadism and bloodlust:

> Finally the soldiers formed a long line and moved into the ruined, haunted alleyways of old Mosul. As they made their way through concrete rubble, their metal ammunition boxes and magazines rattled in the darkness, announcing their arrival like goat bells on a mountainside. Bodies lay everywhere, scattered like breadcrumbs leading to the front line. With the sun rising, the stench of the dead rose above the ruins, bringing with it swarms of flies. One young officer threw up. The soldiers stood watching him dispassionately. They were silent. Their chirpi-ness had deserted them, replaced by a foreboding gloom. They yearned for the reassuring sounds of bullets and explosions, and feared the silence before battle.[96]

This was the place Australian politicians were boasting about having sent military advisers; as their bombs rained down on the narrow, medieval alley-ways of Mosul and its surrounding villages.

---

96 They Will Have to Die Now: Mosul and the Fall of the Caliphate, James Verini, Oneworld, 2019.

You had to be kidding.

Throughout *You Have To Die Now*, Verini speaks of a sense of time collapsing; and even here, in far off Australia, so it was. Indeed, both time and distance had collapsed.

There were only a few hundred IS fighters left in a thin strip estimated to run for three hundred metres from the Tigris River, all expected to die in the coming hours, when Alex began ringing the news desk and the editor repeatedly, attempting to convince them it was a story they had to cover.

Both the US-led Coalition forces, most particularly Australia, and the Iraq military had been pounding the city throughout the week.

Ungalvanised, the editors were amused, if anything, by his urgent insistence. Middle Eastern conflicts had long ago ceased to do well on click rates.

Week after week, month after month, his extreme frustration with the neutered state of newsgathering in Australia grew worse. And worse.

Younger people at his morning Table of Knowledge sniggered in disbelief when he told them journalism used to be a respected profession.

We were all in some muffled place, where nothing began and nothing ended, where the only point of news was distraction or propaganda; where the entirely debased state of journalism was crippling both the consciousness and the conscience of the nation. Nobody even noticed that their brains had been wiped. That — square had been filled with garbage. Stories were just decoration to put around the advertisements, to give a slender veneer of respectability to the profit motive. Everything had been monetised, news defanged.

The ruling castes had deleted debate; better for them that the subjugated peasantry swapped porn clips on their mobile phones, made ribald jokes at each other's expense, and blew their wages gambling on "tradie laptops" aka poker machines. As long as they weren't educated enough to ask questions. The deliberate dumbing down of the population. Humans, the most malleable of all the species DNA had generated.

Deep in the suburbia to where Alex had been hunted, the perimeter was established. A whirring sound, a weapon, sheaves of weapons the populace did not understand, throbbed at the borders of the real.

Old Alex kept up what had become a mundane routine, repeating time and again: "Surveillance is harassment. I have been very, very badly harassed."

As if he only had one story, in a time and place when there were millions, literally millions, of narratives to choose from.

It was only when the gods were roiled that people like himself came truly awake, as if being governed from a distant place,

The gods were roiled.

Mosul was falling.

The mujahideen lay dead in their thousands. Hundreds of suicide bombers achieved martyrdom. More than a million people fled.

Once again, the West would claim victory over a ruin.

The tens of millions of dollars worth of bombs being dropped on Mosul by Australian military personnel was essentially a secret operation. Some of these soldiers would subsequently receive Order of Australia medals, but even then they appeared on the Australia Day Honours List wreathed only in vague tribute.

— was not just ill-informed, it was not informed at all of what was being done in their name with their money.

For one simple reason: they would not have supported the massacre of civilians. They would not have supported the slaughter of true believers acting out of what they thought was a noble duty to their God and their faith. And they would not have supported a hypocritical involvement in yet another American war, all to feather the nests of those who profited from war.

In mid-2017 Human Rights Watch released a report *Civilian Casualties Mount in West Mosul*.

Belkis Wille, the senior Iraq researcher with Human Rights Watch, told Alex the people coming out of the city were the most severely traumatised she and other aid workers had ever witnessed.

"All of the families I speak to have a story about neighbours, loved ones or friends being killed in airstrikes.

"The civilians are highly traumatised. Mosul is the largest urban war in modern history. The west of the city and the neighbourhood still under ISIS control are extremely densely populated.

"Every direction you look you have hundreds of civilians packed into buildings. People who come out don't complain about the horrific three years under ISIS, they complain about the airstrike that killed their family, despite them having made it through those three years.

"People have lost entire families, their homes, their livelihoods. They are coming out with absolutely nothing."

To reiterate: Australian bombs, bought with taxes raked off the back of working Australians by the nation's political class helped make this mess.

Wille said the Iraqi Army was also perpetrating abuses against the Sunni minority with impunity, the exact same conditions which led to the formation of the Islamic State in the first place.

"This battle is going to have very negative long-term consequences for the country," she said. "If it's not ISIS today, then it's ISIS 2.0 tomorrow."

To the few journalists asking, the Australian Department of Defence refused to release any estimates of casualties, civilian or military. That was, invisible bureaucrats and all too visible politicians point blank refused to tell — what their taxes were being used for.

The American-led Coalition, of which Australia was the second-largest contributor, only officially acknowledged 1190 civilian deaths from a total of 32,397 bomb drops between 2014 and 2018. Numerous other commentators numbered civilian deaths in the hundreds of thousands.

The truth was that military authorities had no accurate idea how many civilians had been killed by Australian bombs in the rubble-strewn streets of Iraq; and if there were any estimates, they were certainly not making the information known to the taxpayer.

In 2019 the Australian Defence Department, as a result of American investigations, was finally forced to officially admit that it might have been implicated in the deaths of up to eighteen civilians in the ISIS-occupied Iraqi city of Mosul in 2017, a derisory figure designed only to conceal a catastrophe. Alex was asked to write a story on the issue.

Former senior diplomat Richard Broinowski said he believed Australia's involvement in Iraq to be unlawful and unethical, and — were being kept in the dark. He described the admissions by the Defence Department as "highly suspicious".

"We have had a one-year inquiry over one incident on 13 June, 2017," he said. "There have been hundreds of other sorties and bomb drops. What about the others? Why only this one?

"There must have been other collateral damage. Bombing from the air has been proven to be highly ineffective as far back as WW2. It is an inhumane way of conducting war."

Dr Clarke Jones, a terror expert with the Australian National University and former military analyst who did his doctoral thesis on the consequences of military action in civilian areas, stated the obvious when he said aerial bombing was bound to kill civilians.

"There comes a time when traditional military methods are not effective," he said. "There is an old saying, you can't kill a fly with a sledgehammer. You end up alienating the people you need to work with."

He reiterated that Iraq had essentially been a secret war kept from the Australian public, with the impact of killing innocent civilians creating both hostility in the targeted country and negative impacts domestically.

"It has a knock-on effect for security in Australia. Muslim communities see the atrocities committed on Muslims overseas."

Australia's involvement in Iraq and Syria was already increasing radicalisation amongst Muslims.

"I fear for our long-term outlooks as a result of the civilian casualties caught up in this conflict," Dr Jones said. "There are always civilian casualties; you would be naive to think otherwise. There are mistakes. Islamic State use civilian shields. Naturally there will be civilian casualties."

Dr Jones said Muslims within Australia were overwhelmingly against the war, and Australia's military intervention was bringing them into conflict with their own country

"Here is another case where the West has stepped in and caused the death of innocents. There are a lot of angry people. They see this injustice and want to take action.

"There is no doubt that the sentiment in relation to allied bombing does contribute to radicalisation within communities within Australia. Without a doubt it is radicalising Muslim minorities.

"We have to be careful about the enemies we generate in the region, in our neighbouring countries and the overall Muslim sentiment around the world, including in Australia, you bet you. I don't have to go very far, even inside Canberra, to get that sentiment. We are playing into Islamic State hands. I can't understand why we are continuing down this path."

Meanwhile, Australia's compassionistas filled the airwaves with their latest twist on identity politics or climate policy.

The world had become familiar with the haunting scenes from the brutal bombing of Mosul, Raqqa and Aleppo. But these eerily beautiful post-apocalyptic images never came with dead bodies, the sounds of people dying, the stench of thousands of corpses or the indescribable grief of those who survived.

At the same time as bombs paid for by Australian workers were killing Muslims on the other side of the world, a grinning corpse of a prime minister launched yet another policy, made yet another announcement, threw himself in front of yet another camera.

Turnbull's well-fed advisers got up every day and fed the prime minister, Herr Turnbull, his announceable for the day. That is, fleeced — under the cover of whatever convenient hinge they could find.

As long as a story was running, as long as his ugly mug, narrowing face, greying hair, glistening overmoistourised skin, could be seen droning away on television screens everywhere, Turnbull didn't care what the content was.

And as a result of all this frenetic activity, he became increasingly unpopular. The tradies could spot a phoney when they saw one.

The prime minister's daily announcements had included a fund for victims of institutional sex abuse, a national apology to the same. Hundreds of millions of dollars were being funnelled to a corrupted legal caste who saw nothing but opportunity in other people's suffering.

For an incumbent government, there were many advantages in creating moral panic for claims so old they could almost never be proven, not really.

Nobody denied that bad things had happened. But this was a government that cultivated a climate of false accusation and moral panic for their own rotten purposes. This cabal was never going to look at the behaviour of their own offspring, the family courts, the children's courts, the corrupt psychologists, the truly disgraceful bureaucratic mess of the Child Support Agency.

These institutions had a paralysing, destructive impact on millions of working people. Calls for reform were just hived off into another committee or another inquiry, using any patent example of malfeasance as an excuse to funnel yet more millions to their favourite consultant and accountancy firms.

A government which treated its citizens with such contempt was not fit to govern.

Mid-year an Amnesty International report, *At Any Cost: The Civilian Catastrophe in West Mosul*, suggested America, and Australia, as the second-largest contributor to the US-led coalition fighting Islamic State, had committed war crimes in Iraq.

The report detailed violations by Iraqi forces and the US-led coalition, claiming the conflict in Mosul had created a "civilian catastrophe", with the extremists carrying out forced displacement, summary killings and using civilians as human shields.

The organisation argued that the scale and gravity of the loss of civilian lives during the military operation to retake Mosul must immediately be publicly acknowledged at the highest levels of government in Iraq and in states that were part of the US-led coalition.

The report stated: "Iraqi government and US-led coalition forces failed to adequately adapt their tactics to these challenges — as required by international humanitarian law — with disastrous consequences for civilians. Pro-government forces relied heavily upon explosive weapons with wide-area effects. These weapons wreaked havoc in densely populated west Mosul, where large groups of civilians were trapped."

Australia's wars were in essence secret wars. The wars were never discussed with —. As a direct result, they never had popular support. And if they had been properly aired, community outrage would have forced them to cease and desist.

The Defence Department was tight-lipped on information. Paranoid of being exposed.

A former Secretary of the Department of Defence, Paul Barratt, described Australia's involvement in Iraq as insanity: repeating the same mistake and expecting a different result.

"The Americans have always been more relaxed about collateral damage than we are," he said. "We went through the whole of the Iraq War with the Americans saying we don't count the bodies."

The body count was rising; but in Australia there was no accounting for a terrible sorrow half a world away.

The Defence Minister, Senator Marise Payne, refused to comment on the allegations, provide any details on civilian deaths or even defend Australia's role in the conflict.

She should have been front and centre protecting Australia's reputation but was instead missing in action, yet again.

Or as the polite journalistic convention went, "unavailable for comment". That is, stonewalling on a magnificent salary. That is, hiding in her office sipping cups of tea while people bled to death at her behest; so convinced of the rightness of her cause she couldn't answer a single simple question. Payne was responsible for some sixty thousand full-time defence personnel but did not have the courage to face a press conference.

Apart from the fact that she would be forced to defend the indefensible, Payne had a good reason: she was notorious for her inept media performances. The banality of evil!

No amount of media training in subsequent years could conceal her lack of expertise. But this was not a meritocracy. Despite being a charismatic black hole afraid to face the cameras, she held her plum job because she was a woman from western Sydney, both constituencies the government needed to shore up.

For her dismal performance as Defence Minister, Marise Payne was shortly to be promoted to become Australia's Foreign Minister.

How sad was that?

The nation's face to the world: a woman without so much as the courage or the ability to front a press conference.

Go to war. Don't inform —, the peasants who are paying for it all. Feed them a whole lot of alarmist bullshit to justify a crackdown on civil liberties.

Job done. Excellent work. Book a table for lunch.

Democracy was a flawed system, and Australia's very flawed indeed.

Under international law, the definition of a war crime had been thoroughly corrupted by the Americans and their traditional lack of concern over "collateral damage", as civilian deaths were known.

While Turnbull passed laws making it ever easier to jail journalists, he also passed laws easing Australia's rules of engagement, making it easier for the country to fall in line with America's laissez-faire attitude to civilian deaths, aka collateral damage.

But war criminals are war criminals, whether or not they wear a dress, hid behind convenient legalese or ignore inconvenient journalists. Dance on a pin for as long as you want to. The truth will out.

Amnesty International spokeswoman Diana Sayed said the 225-kilogram bombs dropped into the crowded streets of Mosul had a shock radius of 230 metres and resulted in needless casualties.

> Pro-government forces, including Australia, failed to take feasible precautions to protect civilians during the battle for west Mosul — through launching barrages of indiscriminate, disproportionate and otherwise unlawful attacks, and failing to provide adequate warnings prior to bombardments. The realities of living under the Islamic State often meant people were trapped and

unable to leave their homes.

Australia and its allies in Iraq should publicly acknowledge the massive loss of lives during the Mosul operation.[97]

The report, titled "At Any Cost: The Civilian Catastrophe in West Mosul, Iraq", said Iraqi and US forces did not comply with humanitarian law.

"Iraqi Government and US-led coalition forces failed to adequately adapt their tactics to these challenges — as required by international humanitarian law — with disastrous consequences for civilians. Pro-government forces relied heavily upon explosive weapons with wide-area effects. These weapons wreaked havoc in densely populated west Mosul, where large groups of civilians were trapped."

If military planners were unaware of the likely civilian toll, it quickly became evident.

"It was pro-government soldiers who assisted in countless front-line rescues, digging bodies out of collapsed buildings, separating the injured from the dead and arranging the transport of thousands to medical facilities."

The High Commissioner for the United Nations Human Rights Office, Zeid Al Hussein, urged the coalition to comply with humanitarian laws.

"I repeatedly called on coalition partners to ensure that military operations complied with international humanitarian law," he said in a statement." Airstrikes were a significant factor in causing civilian casualties."

None of this impacted on The Land of the Long Weekend.

One of Australia's best known Muslim spokesmen Keysar Trad said increased reporting was crucial:

> "Civilian casualties aggrieve people and make the world unsafe," he said. "Independent reports already show scores of civilians killed in Western bombings of West Mosul. The civilians casualties are already too high and any continued aerial bombings will increase civilian casualties.

> "I am a long-term critic of IS and its murderous ways, but bombs by their very nature are chaotic beasts whose damage cannot be fully controlled.

---

97 Amnesty International accuses Australia of 'war crimes' in fight against Islamic State, John Stapleton, *The New Daily*, 12 July, 2017.

"These wars that coalition governments have dragged us into have cost many innocent lives. Speaking as one of them, the majority of Australians do not want this on our conscience."[98]

Trad, whom Old Alex had known across decades of controversy involving the Muslim minority, said the Coalition went out of its way to conceal the number of its victims, and failed to understand they were creating a hardened generation of orphans.

"The net result is a lot of death and killings and children raised in desperate conditions. The Holy Qur'an describes a group of people who will be raised towards the end who will … not display the compassionate hesitation. They are more likely to see the world in black-and white terms, just like a certain flag.

"Civilian casualties aggrieve people and make the world unsafe. Independent reports already show scores of civilians killed in Western bombings of West Mosul. The civilians casualties are already too high and any continued aerial bombings will increase civilian casualties."

In his waking dreams Alex was climbing the spires of an ancient university town — Oxford most like — and could see as far into the distance as it was possible to see: every danger, every collapsing empire, every self-serving politician and overpaid bureaucrat, every simpering, egocentric, parsimonious fool on the edge of known civilisation.

Time and the impending revolution would clear them all from the wreckage. These pissants, trapped in the lower realms. There they were, flesh entwined in an intimate space.

We shall meet in the place where there is no darkness.

One of the strangest things about the declared victory over Islamic State in the Middle East, at least from an Antipodean perspective, was that the Australian media almost totally ignored it.

After year upon year of heightened alarm and an interminable barrage of "death cult" propaganda from the government and their cohorts in the Murdoch media, after all the demonisation of Muslims and the exploitation of terror with Islamic State at the heart, a lurking, terrifying threat of mass casualty events and a destruction of the existing order, after all the nationalist hoo-ha as politicians dispatched soldiers to a place both dangerous and

---

98 War Crimes: Turnbull's Terrible Legacy, John Stapleton, *A Sense of Place Magazine*, 19 August, 2019.

strange, a country where they were not welcome, after the whipping up of patriotic fervour and the dropping of hundreds of bombs onto the narrow streets of the Middle East, after billions of dollars were spewed into a war zone, after all of it, when the Coalition declared victory, the news didn't make the cut.

If the only way you can hide your crimes is to buy, as the Defence Department did with expensive unread supplements in the Murdoch press, to bully or conceal from the media, and thereby —, to crack down on dissent and destroy free speech — if you can only win by disrupting the nation's internal narrative to such an extreme degree, was it really worth the price?

For what?

For billions in secret military contracts, that's what.

They definitely weren't protecting the motherland.

Young men could be asked to sacrifice themselves or put themselves in harm's way for queen and country; but not for arrangements which benefited only the nation's most wealthy. The country was going to war without the support of the people, the cognoscenti, or, one suspected, its military strategists; just at the behest of a few right-wing crazies in the Liberal Party.

And nobody had the decency to speak out against this travesty.

Where were the social justice warriors?

The last thing the Australian media wanted was to make their readers feel uncomfortable over the nation's morally questionable involvement in foreign wars; and so they remained obsessed with the far more comfortable social justice issue of gay marriage.

Marriage had been the last thing on anybody's mind in the demimonde Old Alex had known so well in his younger days; and it still struck him as ridiculous. Indeed, the parodying of a heterosexual institution, ill-fitted to many gay men, had in his day been seen as decidenly anti-progressive.

— did not understand that the wall-to-wall coverage of gay marriage was being used as a cover for the nation's misdemeanours, including its conduct in Iraq, falling standards of living across the board, shuttered shops and "For Sale" signs festooning across the country, the crushing of individual freedoms and the rise of censorship. And serious mismanagement of the economy.

"The advantages of a stable relationship," he thought, as he relaxed at a well established gay home. Horrified that he was not entirely on board with the marriage cavalry, they did not take his point.

Such serene beauties, the comforts of ideological certainty, were denied him as he moved frequently, hunted from place to place.

They were standing at a precipice in history while being shoved under a bus. Stumbling into a doomed future, nobody cried out: stop.

Alex worked quietly, and spent his evenings at the Lakeview Table of Knowledge; where there were the usual small cliques of uproar, another one of Matt's psycho girlfriends cruising the car park, sending him nude pictures of himself on his phone, claiming she was pregnant.

Trapped, Matt kept sending friends out to check the carport so he could go home; to great hilarity.

While Gaz, who had just written off his beloved ute on a weekend away with the boys, wasn't laughing at anything much right now.

They were sex-obsessed miscreants, they were people who just got up and went to work every day. They were the sprawling masses preyed on by the worst government in Australian history.

A few were recovering from a night on the tiles. Or planning another.

Pete, a retiree from the local steel mill and labelled the richest man in Oak Flats because he owned five houses, had his regulation four beers. In his own gentlemanly way. His wife was cooking schnitzel for tea.

Still others were having a quiet beer after work, on the way home to their families.

In the distance a cloud bank streamed over the Illawarra escarpment and wind moved the trees fringing the lake, every last second an eternal moment.

All Alex could think about was a travesty happening on the other side of the world.

Drop a bomb on villagers, as Australia was doing, and images of dying kids were being uploaded to Instagram, Facebook, Twitter, Telegram and a host of other social media sites within seconds; transforming a military gain into a propaganda loss just like that. Most of their targets had smartphones, and could transmit the effects of those taxpayer bombs in a second.

> Journalist Fellow at The Australian Strategic Policy Institute Graeme Dobell, their only truly smart media analyst, said that conducting the Afghanistan, Iraq and Syria wars in almost total secrecy had created a backlash.

The Defence Department and the Australian Defence Force had found itself almost entirely unprepared for an age when their opponents and the villagers amongst which they operated were all equipped with smartphones.

"More and regular information is both useful and proper," he said. "Defence and government are going to have to start making the case to the Australian people, to encourage — to examine Australia's continuing role in the Middle East."[99]

Bizarrely, in this muffled, deadened world, Old Alex was virtually the only journalist in the country banging on about it. He had to push and push and push for the editor to even take up the stories. Yet there was no better story: of an elected government conducting an essentially secret war, killing thousands for the sake of billions of dollars in defence contracts, lying to the people that they were keeping them safe.

This mob were all up to their necks in it.

Australia has been involved with American Wars since Korea. At great loss of life, treasure, credibility and moral integrity. Vietnam was a disaster. Afghanistan was a disaster. Iraq was a disaster. All of them haemorrhaged lives and treasure.

And yet there the political class was at it again: tally-ho, bombs away!

Not content with bombing innocents, in the final months of his reign Turnbull determined to funnel yet more billions off the backs of the working poor, this time into establishing Australia as a weapons manufacturer.

The government declared it had identified a number of "priority markets": the Middle East, the Indo-Pacific region, Europe, the United States, the United Kingdom, Canada and New Zealand. It would set up a new Defence Export Office to work hand in hand with Austrade and the Centre for Defence Industry Capability to co-ordinate the Commonwealth's whole-of-government export efforts and provide a focal point for more arms exports.

"It is an ambitious, positive plan to boost Australian industry, increase investment, and create more jobs for Australian businesses," Turnbull said. "A strong, exporting defence industry in Australia will provide greater certainty of investment, support high-end manufacturing jobs and support the capability of the Australian defence force."[100]

---

99 Ibid

100 Australia unveils plan to become one of world's top 10 arms exporters, Gareth Hutchens, Guardian Australia, 29 January, 2018.

Few were impressed. Critics pointed out that Australia had astronomical labour costs, poor infrastructure, a derelict manufacturing base, little real expertise, and was facing an intensely competitive space filled with experienced and highly professional providers.

As social commentator Stephanie Dowrick put it:

> I woke to the news that our government has decided to unveil a new "defence export strategy" to propel Australia into the big league of global weapons exporters. And to do so without reference to any election policy or public debate or, indeed, any acknowledgement of the millions of refugees already displaced by wars.

Dowrick wrote that the power of weapons industries to affect, even to drive, governments' policies, was immense. The industries depended on actual and perceived enemies, a hysterical narrative around "terror", and a disturbing acceptance among — and much of the media of the inevitability of conflict and war.

> It is also profoundly undemocratic. Governments keep a tight grip on media revelations. The weapons world is "secret men's business" from which — is definitely shut out. My best sleuthing efforts came nowhere near discovering what this industry is really worth or who profits most from it in the private sectors. No wonder they call it the "defence industry".

> It is indefensible for a country like ours to "export death and profit from bloodshed".[101]

Comments leant towards moral repugnance.

Old-fashioned iconoclast Mungo MacCallum wrote:

> We have struck a new nadir, a depth of greed and amorality that is unlikely to be beaten. Malcolm Turnbull's decision to allocate $3.8 billion (that's $3,800,000,000 in real money) to promote the export of killing machines is the end of the road ... Turnbull's latest thought bubble will be revealed as an utter failure in every sense — not merely unforgivably depraved, but hugely wasteful and simply stupid.[102]

---

101 Weapons of Moral Destruction, Stephanie Dowrick, Pearls and Irritations, 1 February, 2018.

102 Merchants of death, Mungo MacCallum, Pearls and Irritations, 1 February, 2018.

Sure as night follows day, there would be a very high price to pay for the killing, beyond the already astronomical costs in terms of military expenditure and crackdowns on civil liberties.

The dead haunt the living.

It had already arrived, the haunting for a man who stained the soul of the country and betrayed the people he was elected to represent.

For the person most directly responsible for Australia's killing of Muslim fighters and their families on the other side of the world, the blood of the martyrs was congealing around Turnbull, whether he liked it or not, understood it or not.

It wasn't long into his tenure before the prime minister's appearance and disposition — that of a wealthy, successful, chipper, bon vivant, well-fed eastern suburbs success story — changed; his demeanour became more authoritarian, his face more sinister, more Mussolini-like, starkly lined, and his glib reiterations of government policy more blatantly false.

It all led straight to the pit. Turnbull left office a pariah in his own party and a joke in the electorate. Men pursue power, and power destroys them.

Defence Minister Marise Payne was unavailable for comment.

THE SPLENDID FALL

EVERY DOG has its day. And the worst prime minister in Australian history certainly had his.

The intoxicating fall of Malcolm Turnbull was a transfixing, delightful spectacle; a Shakespearean tragedy played out in the Antipodes.

And no, the good guys did not win. There were no good guys, so collapsed the polity.

If you wanted to leave an Australian speechless all you had to do was ask: "When did Australia last have a good prime minister?" Or: "Which politician currently in parliament do you admire?"

The robber barons destroying the country won, but in the process the seedbeds of revolution were everywhere sown. Just as history began looking back on the prime-ministership of conservative icon John Howard as the period when the keys for the destruction of Australian democracy were initially installed, so too would it look back on the Turnbull era as a critical turning point in the country's self-immolation.

In Alex's waking dreams the food riots of the future were already breaking into the present.

But he had much to be grateful for in the spectacular demise of Malcolm Turnbull.

There was an armada of pundits droning on about the minutiae of Australian political life; but as the train crash began, none was predicting the fall of yet another prime minister.

Old Alex started pestering the editor he normally dealt with, telling him the leadership was in play and he wanted to write a story titled "The Many Lows of Malcolm Turnbull's Prime-Ministership". The usual acres of dreary analysis could be left to the political reporters, Alex was on an attack vector.

There were so many low points to Turnbull's prime ministership it was difficult to count them all. Plunging educational outcomes, a collapsing underclass and a dispirited nation were just some. While strutting the political stage in front of a thousand cameras, many of Turnbull's announcements were the leitmotifs of the bureaucratic left, the so-called Deep State. At the same time he dragged the country closer to totalitarianism, with his attacks on journalists and free speech, his massive expansion of surveillance of the population, and his gifting of large amounts of money to Australia's ultra-secretive national security agencies.

"Too negative," he was told when he submitted the first draft. "Needs to be more balanced."

That was as anodyne as the national broadcaster's slogan, "Join the Conversation"; as in, let's offend nobody and we'll all be happy. You can go on screwing us. All we'll do is smile. And join the conversation.

While the journalists who should have been the watchdogs of democracy were missing in action.

Alex came not to praise but to bury.

None of his news outlet's bevy of political reporters had sprung to the fact the leadership was in play, and the editor kept demanding: "How do you know?"

He knew. He struggled to explain how. Although his initial instincts were confirmed by contacts, in a sense it was a simple matter of pattern recognition. So outlandish was one of Turnbull's cash grabs in his dying days that Alex could not help but be reminded of John Howard's behaviour in the final throes of his prime-ministership. But more of that in a moment.

In terms of flogging the story, Alex was "shoving it uphill", as the rather crude Australian expression went. He was forced to rewrite the story three times, and still they wouldn't run it. And he didn't get paid if the story didn't run.

Which was the exact point in time when he thought "bugger this", and set up his own publication, *A Sense of Place Magazine*.

Medium, a platform replete with the most beautiful publishing software he had ever used, was designed by the creators of Twitter with the aim of revolutionising the publishing industry.

They succeeded.

And Old Alex leapt at the opportunities the new technologies offered. A lifetime of jumping through hoops to please an endless conga line of editors and chiefs-of-staff dancing in turn to the concerns of their masters was over.

Ideas are lethal. They don't have to do well on click rates to reach their target. They can be a poisonous arrow through complex circumstances, straight to the heart.

Incensed by the duplicity of the nation's politicians and the dismal state of the nation's media, in the final days of that cold-to-the-bones winter Old Alex sat and pounded out a thousand words a day; a strangely electrified clarion bird pecking furiously at a keyboard through the early hours of the morning. Nine days later Turnbull's reign was over.

And Alex never went back to pestering editors half his age, trying to convince them a story really was a story. He had his own outlet now, and that in itself was transformative. He could walk away from a piece knowing he had done his very best. Not just the usual: churn out copy, press the "send" button, hope it got past the sticky fingers and corporate or political interests of newspaper editors and onto the page, and try, most of all, not to care.

The current scandal had many progenitors; but the best of them involved both the current and a former prime minister, along with media mogul Rupert Murdoch's family.

Just before his own humiliating dismissal by the electorate back in 2007, becoming only the second sitting prime minister in Australian history to lose his seat, Liberal Party scion John Howard gifted millions in a grant to the Australian Rain Corporation, a company part-owned by Matt Handbury, who just happened to be Rupert Murdoch's nephew.

The grant application, whose worthiness was entirely unclear, had been mouldering in bureaucratic process until it did become clear to Howard that he would not be re-elected; and whammo, millions were hived from — purse.

Thanks to circumstances which are nobody's business, Old Alex just happened to know Matt, a very amiable multimillionaire, one of Sydney's most precocious characters, and a mate of Turnbull's.

Years before, for reasons Alex never understood, Matt made absolutely sure he was aware of the details behind the scandal; information to be stored away and used at a later date — also part of a strange synchronicity running through his own life straight to the demise of Turnbull. As if even here in suburbia time and circumstance were collapsing.

The scandal barely made it into — consciousness or the mainstream media, but was duly recorded on numerous blogs. Combining coincidence, the future prime minister Malcolm Turnbull just happened to be environment minister at the time.

The anti-corruption website Kangaroo Court of Australia predicted that Turnbull's $11 million donation "scam" to his friend would come back to haunt him.

Adding sweet irony, Malcolm Turnbull had been recently on record calling for "an urgent need for honesty in politics".

> Before Malcolm starts preaching he needs to have a good look at himself. Mr Turnbull has refused to answer a number of questions in relation to a grant he gave when he was Environment Minister in the Howard government to his friend Matt Handbury.
>
> Mr Turnbull's electorate fundraising is done through an organisation he set up in 2007 called the Wentworth Forum ... regarded as the country's most sophisticated political fundraising machine.
>
> Matt Handbury was one of the donors to Mr Turnbull's Wentworth Forum.
>
> Before the 2007 election and two weeks after the election was called, Malcolm Turnbull announced that the government would spend $11 million funding a trial of rainfall technology. The company in question was Australian Rain Corporation, which was then part owned by Matt Handbury.[103]

The so-called "ionisation enhancement technology" being pushed by Australian Rain uses a different method to traditional cloud seeding. Instead, a metallic array is built on the ground, usually in pyramidic shapes, to generate electrically charged atoms known as ions. These ions shift naturally up through the atmosphere via wind and air currents, attaching themselves to floating dust, known technically as aerosols.

---

103 Malcolm Turnbull the rain man who speaks with forked tongue, Shane Dowling, Kangaroo Court of Australia, 9 September, 2012.

Once the charged aerosols reach the clouds, water condenses around them, and it begins to rain.

Well that's the theory.

Critics claimed it simply didn't work and was based on bogus science. The incoming climate and water minister Penny Wong cancelled the grant, but not before $5 million of public monies had been spent.

Veteran political journalist Laurie Oakes recorded that a highly sceptical National Water Commission recommended a grant of $2 million.

Turnbull ignored the advice and decided that a much larger grant should be provided to his friend and neighbour.

Turnbull wrote to John Howard requesting some five times the recommended amount on October 15, the day after the election was called.

As Oakes recorded: "Howard wrote back approving it the same day. Clearly the reason for the rush was that the 'caretaker' period, during which no new government decisions can be taken, was to begin with the dissolution of parliament on October 17."[104]

Thousands of worthy grant applications moulder within Australian departmental and bureaucratic systems, often for years on end. Few are successful. It clearly helps to be a donor to the Liberal Party, a mate of Turnbull's and a nephew of the country's most powerful media mogul.

That someone had to go to work in a factory or drive a truck or sit in an office all day in order to pay taxes to fund this unconscionable largesse between multimillionaires was lost in the slipstream of Australian public life.

That didn't mean it didn't stink to high heaven.

Just as egregiously, and one of the reasons Old Alex knew the prime minister was in his dying days, Turnbull gifted without any due process whatsoever some $444 million to his mates in a so-called environmental foundation with close links to the mining industry.

> The latest financial scandal to envelop Malcolm Turnbull, the funding dump of $444 million without tender to the industry linked Great Barrier Reef Foundation has left commentators nonplussed.

104 Rain gift flushed away, Laurie Oakes, *Herald-Sun*, 1 March, 2008.

There could hardly be a more blatant plundering of — purse; akin to stealing the candelabras as you are tossed into the street.

Were these really the actions of a man who expected to stay long in office?

Every crown comes with a guillotine. Turnbull has made his own.[105]

Even in Australia's gutted media there were squawks of outrage.

Columnist Paul Murray at *The* West *Australian* wrote that he had spent days trying to find the method behind Malcolm Turnbull's madness in giving nearly half a billion dollars of taxpayers' money to a six-person private charity.

The underlying ideology seems to be an attempt to use public funds to leverage a massive effort by corporate Australia into a noble task: saving the Great Barrier Reef.

But that is obscured by the hamfisted, naive and potentially dangerous way the prime minister personally went about the biggest single grant in Australian history.

You've got to be completely cack-handed politically to turn the ultimate environmental motherhood statement into something that looks so dodgy.[106]

Well there was method. It was just so blatant, few could believe it.

Among the revelations surrounding the grant were that the foundation had not applied for any funds. The money, Australian taxpayers' money, was offered to the chairman John Schubert at a meeting with Turnbull and Environment Minister Josh Frydenberg on April 9 of 2018 with no public servants attending, and the usual tender process waived. The entire $444 million was paid to the foundation in one lump sum.

In the parallel universe of Australian politics, Frydenberg would soon enough become the nation's Treasurer.

Rotten to the core.

105 The Quagmire Collapses, John Stapleton, *A Sense of Place Magazine*, 16 August, 2018.

106 Opinion: Great Barrier Reef grant likely to get messy for Prime Minister Malcolm Turbull, Paul Murray, *The West Australian,* 11 August, 2018.

As it would soon become clear, Turnbull's outlandish plundering of — purse would be just the prelude to a ransacking of public finances by senior members of the conservatives, all of whom, believing the opinion polls, assumed they would be thrown out of office at the coming election.

So outrageous the behaviour, it was obvious that the leadership was now in play. And when Old Alex checked with an insider, so it turned out to be.

Like many of his subjects, Malcolm Turnbull was most vulnerable in his own home to the uber-surveillance and harassment that characterised modern-day Australia.

It was just that Turnbull lived in a $50 million-plus-plus-plus mansion which at the height of Sydney's housing bubble had been rising in value by $8000 a day, in one of the most exclusive streets of real-estate-obsessed Sydney. And he had state-of-the art security, courtesy of the taxpayer and armed Australian Federal Police officers front and back.

The victims of the extremely intrusive surveillance Turnbull had overseen against journalists such as Alex and the government's many critics lived in far more humble circumstances. Turnbull had made many people feel unsafe inside their own homes, whether it was from falling standards of living, a crisis in the ability of ordinary people to do business and provide for their children, or the panopticon he helped to introduce.

But there is such a thing as karma, and Turnbull got his comeuppance.

The media hunts in packs. And they turned on a wounded prime minister like a school of sharks. There was blood in a cyber sea. They would not give up.

The suckalots within the Liberal Party who made Malcolm Turnbull prime minister were impressed by the fact he had money. Lots of money. They never asked how he made it. Because financial disclosure laws left him no choice, Turnbull told Parliament in 2016 that he was withdrawing more than a million dollars out of a hedge fund heavily invested in distressed housing in the US.

The fund exploited hardship by swooping on family homes and businesses. The investment strategy included "distressed debt" and "selling short". The announcement was made in the final hours of parliamentary sittings for the year and thereby timed to ensure minimal media coverage.

Fast-forward two years.

The prime minister, trapped inside his gilded cage, desperately trying to convince himself he had not become a national laughing stock, furious that the plebs refused to be bullied into liking him, faced his own distressed housing. Outside his doors a baying media set up camp in the street, ensuring his multimillion-dollar mansion was just as uncomfortable as far less salubrious homes in the poorer parts of town, the places he had never seen.

"Mr Harbourside Mansion" was a pejorative coined by critics within Turnbull's own party.

The insult stuck.

Indeed, it was Turnbull's often boasted about wealth which became his undoing. Tactics that worked to establish status in his social whirl of wealthy bankers, miners, property developers and corporate fat cats, betrayed him.

The mansion Turnbull called home was a source of pride within his Rich as Croesus milieu, but did nothing to engender populist appeal. Turnbull's complete lack of empathy — indeed, zero understanding if not outright contempt — for those struggling to pay their mortgages and muddle through their bills, was apparent to everybody. Unfortunately for him, every three years the great unwashed vote. And a seemingly infinite line of polls confirmed they just didn't like him.

Australia is a suburban country.

The dreams of its inhabitants involve trailers, lawns, children, sheds, barbeques, fishing, hanging out with mates; and hoping like hell their kids get through high school, don't end up in jail, get a good apprenticeship or a job at the local supermarket. They don't involve share and property portfolios or offshore tax havens. Or multimillion dollar mansions.

Sydney is a city of sycophants. Money talks. Turnbull was welcome wherever he went. Until one day he wasn't. Disliked by —, disliked by his own party, disliked by — service, disliked by those whose job it was to protect him, Australia's 29th prime minister was mortally wounded.

His days were not just numbered, he was done.

Once the media got whiff of the story, the fight was on. For Old Alex, stuck in a remote, cold house in a remote corner of his own life, it was like being gifted an army of reporters, and they were all doing his job for him.

Turnbull had passed a large amount of quite unbelievable anti-journalist legislation, and as an ageing journalist, Old Alex, was more than happy to see him get his just deserts at the hands of a media mob.

With so much of real life out of bounds or undiscovered, Australia's media were desperate for stories in a depleted zone. A two-horse race was about all the complexity or nuance they could muster, or package. And a two-horse race they now had.

The trainwreck of Malcolm Turnbull's frenetic leadership had been played out on so many television screens and newspaper headlines it was hard to believe he only won the position in an internal coup in 2015. And for a moment rode very high indeed. When the tide turned, he fell apart.

His was a government run on announceables. Every day a new announcement. Building this, funding that, inquiring into the other. A commission, a committee, a God awful waste of time and money. They cost millions — often enough billions — these endless announcements.

And they put the prime minister exactly where he wanted to be, in front of the television cameras. His ugly mug beamed into millions of living rooms, seemingly all day every day. King for a day in a hall of mirrors. And the more — saw, the less they liked, the nation so sick of Turnbull's preening visage they turned off media altogether.

And then one day in August of 2018 all the mirrors shattered at once.

In the end, Malcolm Turnbull's ceaseless attempts to manipulate the media were grossly immature, and represented hopeless, hapless media management.

Who was Turnbull's media adviser?

The man who never shut up. Never stopped talking. Never displayed one ounce of humility. The man who thought he was better than everybody else. Under Turnbull, the once magisterial import of prime ministerial announcements was lost in the daily welter of self-aggrandising "my government" announcements.

Turnbull's media adviser should be shot, Old Alex sometimes thought. Only to revise the thought for public consumption. You couldn't say those things these days. His media adviser should be sacked. Oh that's right, he's his own media adviser. He never listens to anybody.

And so the farce of Australia stumbled towards an uncertain future. Uniquely divided. Into ethnic groups. Into haves and have-nots. Homeowners and the homeless. Into harrowing horizons and rampant greed. Into the Balkanisation of its own soul. The abandonment of historic ethos. The loss of culture, of an instinctive, proud sense of the dignity of labour. The destruction of an ideal: participatory democracy. Into a place where there was no escape, not for the plundered and the poor.

This was a morally bankrupt government at every level; from its prosecution of foreign wars to its funnelling of billions of dollars to the ruling elite's favourite legal, accountancy and consultancy firms.

That's if it could be classified as governance at all.

The first announceable, shortly after Turnbull seized the reins of power, was the $1.1 billion dollar Innovation Nation project.

It was meant to be a signature piece which would define his period as Australia's leader. The themes were constantly repeated during the first six months, the words "innovation" and "agility" worn threadbare.

"Our innovation agenda is going to help create the modern, dynamic 21st Century economy Australia needs. I know that Australians believe in themselves, I know that we are a creative and imaginative nation."

Two years later the Auditor-General condemned the project as poorly designed, based on poor public service advice and lacking any evidence that there were economic benefits.

Yet more money wasted. What did become the signature tune of Turnbull's premiership was the squandering of eye-popping amounts of public money.

In language fit for *Yes Minister,* the Auditor-General concluded in his report:

> The policy logic that can be inferred from this model is that: if the proposed actions are taken, they will reduce the barriers, which will move Australia towards the vision, which in turn will help achieve the objective of increasing productivity and diversifying the economy.
>
> A number of the proposals that involved significant expenditure aimed at transforming parts of the innovation system relied on assertions rather than evidence. In many cases, there was also a lack of specificity in the outcomes or expected impacts being sought, making it difficult to determine how success would be measured.[107]

---

107 Malcolm Turnbull's 'innovation' agenda lashed by Auditor-General, Stephanie Peatling, *The Sydney Morning Herald*, 28 September, 2017.

In other words, Malcolm Turnbull's first act as prime minister was to blow $1.1 billion of public funds on a load of bull.

Unfortunately for the nation, worse was to follow.

As Old Alex pounded away in the early hours of the morning, the question became not if but when. And would Malcolm Turnbull fall on his sword, or would he have to be pushed?

Like a wounded elephant, albeit in a dapper suit, Turnbull's fall was leaving plumes of acrid dust in the overheated air; not just through his own riven, warring party but throughout the country as a whole.

Four days in and Malcolm Turnbull's Prime Ministership was in its death throes, the wasteland of his leadership exposed. There were the ritual lies of political combat: "The prime minister has my full support." Laugh Out Loud. Versus: "I'm focused on delivering for the Australian people." Laugh Out Loud.

While in the backrooms the knives were fully drawn and in their imaginations Turnbull's many enemies were already dancing over pools of blood.

The Australian: PM's leadership on knife edge. The backbench rebellion against Malcolm Turnbull has spread as ministers last night gathered for an emergency meeting.

News: Support for a Malcolm Turnbull-led Coalition is falling apart as speculation swirls around a possible leadership challenge by Home Affairs Minister Peter Dutton.

Turnbull's enemies could barely wait to carry his corpse off the battlefield; so hated was this toff from Australia's wealthiest postcode.

From the start Turnbull's prime-ministership had been a divisive tragedy in a failing democracy.

Decades of lazy and incompetent politicians and years of grasping political turmoil had allowed vast bureaucracies to spread ever wider, and insane rafts of legislation to be passed — even encryption laws which, if interpreted literally, could be used to ban smartphones.

Day six, and the first harpoon struck the flank. In the petri dish of Australian politics, Malcolm Turnbull thrashed in a blood-soaked sea. To his many enemies, it couldn't have been happening to a nicer bloke.

The first leadership spill, on Tuesday, 21st August, 2018, precipitated by the formidable Minister for Home Affairs Peter Dutton, left Turnbull mortally wounded. The first harpoon hit the flank: 48—35.

In other words, it would only take eight MPs to change their mind and Turnbull would be relegated to the dustbin of history. Which is exactly where he belonged. Buried and forgotten.

Turnbull's hapless government, now in turmoil, had mismanaged everything. By clinging on, he was only delaying the inevitable. The time for a graceful exit had vanished.

Australia's 29th prime minister began his fateful reign on the 15th of September, 2015. The end date was fast approaching. Even here, even now, the man kept on holding press conferences, kept on talking. As if the blather that had served him as a lawyer could save him.

The coverage was brutal. Old Alex, obsessed, read it all:

The Australian: Ministers quit as Malcolm Turnbull sinks. Malcolm Turnbull was last night facing a fresh crisis with the threat of a second challenge to his leadership looming.

The Guardian: Second challenge to Turnbull's leadership looms. Prime minister's leadership appears terminal with resignation of key frontbenchers and conservatives lining up behind Dutton.

ABC: Malcolm Turnbull is mortally wounded. There is blood in the water and the entire political apparatus, notably the media, is on the scent.

The New Daily: Frankenstein's monster loses a few more body parts.

Australians on the whole had switched off from the political turmoil: "They're at it again are they?"

Disengagement or outright contempt for the political process was just one of the many terrible legacies of Malcolm Turnbull's failed leadership.

Came day seven:

> Cry "Havoc!" and let slip the dogs of war,
> That this foul deed shall smell above the earth
> With carrion men, groaning for burial.[108]

The Daily Telegraph: The Panic Dutton, Would-be leader launches campaign of chaos against PM.

The Australian: D-Day for Malcolm Turnbull as key allies desert. Malcolm Turnbull is expected to face his second leadership challenge within 48 hours today. Dogged by leadership speculation and humiliation, Malcolm Turnbull couldn't escape the debilitating fog of instability.

---

108 *Julius Caesar*, William Shakespeare, Act 3, Scene 1.

Guardian Australia: Liberals in chaos. Dutton backers launch late-night attack on Turnbull, hoping to trigger second spill

The New Daily: Dutton camp botches shadowy second strike. Supporters of prime ministerial hopeful Peter Dutton may still force another vote.

Malcolm Turnbull's Prime Ministership was now terminal. Unfortunately, his legacy would impact on Australian citizens for decades to come.

Those whom the gods destroy, they first make crazy. Malcolm Turnbull was showing all the signs.

His Day of Reckoning finally arrived. He could have left with dignity ten days before: doctor's advice, spend more time with his grandchildren. But this hapless prime minister, with his party room in revolt, could not even manage his own political death.

He was a very bad loser and it looked for a time that he would end up taking down his entire government and gifting the keys to the equally inept Labor Opposition.

The Australian: Turnbull's house of cards crumbles. Malcolm Turnbull has threatened to strip the government of its majority in the parliament and force an early election.

The Guardian: Turnbull shows no mercy as warring Liberals tear out the party's heart and soul. Australian politics has found new depths to plumb.

The New Daily: Madness: Turnbull plays final card to stay on as PM. Australia will get a new prime minister this Friday. No matter who it is, the damage to the government over the past week is beyond repair.

In an extraordinary gamble to stay in power, Malcolm Turnbull has attacked his leadership rival Peter Dutton as possibly ineligible to be prime minister, and demanded written proof of party room discontent.

ABC: Stable government? Malcolm Turnbull, besieged by his own party colleagues, has strapped explosive devices to himself and dared them to come and get him.

With the media pack baying for his blood, Malcolm Turnbull was leaving not just a divided party but a divided country.

A poor loser, in his final hours Turnbull was lashing out, blaming everyone but himself, and threatening to destroy his government rather than hand over the reins of power. All of this was occurring in front of the cameras he could not resist; the psychodrama and the theatre of political suicide.

The true tragedy of Turnbull's failed prime-ministership was that the country stood at a precipice, facing increasing social division, crumbling services, and a plummeting place in the world. A once plucky, optimistic, industrious country was happy no longer.

And nobody believed a word that came out of the mouths of their elected representatives.

With Australians experiencing a drift towards totalitarianism in their daily lives, evident in everything from insane levels of regulation to excessive micro-policing, a growing intolerance of divergent views and bureaucratic and political contempt for the views of ordinary people, there could be no worse time for a loss of faith in democracy.

The future was breaking into the present, Old Alex could feel it everywhere.

This was a government which mismanaged everything. Literally everything. Couldn't organise a root in a brothel. Couldn't organise a piss-up in a brewery. As his local Table of Knowledge would be apt to say.

Herr Leader left behind a broken political party cruising to electoral wipeout. He also left behind a country suffering rapid population growth and demographic transformation without any proper management or analysis of the social consequences, much less any coherent policy development on common sense issues like roads and schools.

A successful immigrant nation had been transformed into a polyglot society riven by ethnicity, language, social status, religion, class and conflicting interests. A deeply resentful country which, despite all the government's relentless diversity propaganda, was more divided than ever before.

National pride had fled out the window. There was no social cohesion. That was the man's real legacy.

Holed up in his office, surrounded by enemies, the media pack no longer his friends, the dying hours of Turnbull's leadership were as excruciating and as undignified as his reign.

He tried every dirty trick in the book to cling to power.

First, on Thursday, he suspended parliament, a motion narrowly passed along party lines after a scathing response from the Opposition. At the same time he questioned challenger Peter Dutton's eligibility to sit in parliament because of some of his investments; rich for a man whose family had their fingers in so many many pies.

Even as he was dying in front of the cameras, Turnbull would turn back to have one more say. He couldn't shut up. The words he had used to charm, deceive and attack, the words he had used as weapons all his life, now boomeranged back to flay his own pallid flesh.

For a brief swivel in time it looked like Malcolm Turnbull might succeed in taking the ship down with him. The government held power by a narrow one-seat majority. A byelection in his wealthy Sydney seat of Wentworth could easily be lost to the Greens, a reinvigorated Labor Party or an Independent.

And down could come the government.

"For Malcolm, for Lucy, for their family and for his personal staff, who are as loyal and as close as family, this is a very hard day indeed," Opposition Leader Bill Shorten said. He also spoke of his enduring respect for his opponent, recognising Mr Turnbull as an "advocate of great intellect and eloquence" and a politician driven by a "desire to serve" considering his late entry into parliament. "Australian politics will always need people like that, on all sides."

A desire to serve? You had to be kidding. Self-aggrandisement. A plundering of — purse. An overweening contempt for those he deemed to be the lower orders. That is, almost everybody.

With an Opposition like that, it was no wonder the left remained in the political wilderness. The last thing the country needed was another Malcolm Turnbull.

Federal Liberal leader Nick Greiner, another one embraced by the nation's boardrooms post-politics, predicted history would judge Malcolm Turnbull more kindly than some of his colleagues, saying the former prime minister had run the best cabinet government since John Howard.

Millionaires emerged from their limousines to pat one of their own on the back. Splend show, old chap. Sniffy, what?

Greiner also agreed with Turnbull that there had been some elements of the media working against him over the past three years.

Rich. Turnbull had done everything he could to please and appease the Murdoch family, and in the end Rupert betrayed him with a relentless campaign across his multiple platforms. Well that was Rupert for you. He was a kingmaker, and had long ago worked out that Turnbull was unviable.

It was all about power. None of it was about quality journalism. The truth: none of it was for the betterment of the nation.

Challenger Peter Dutton declared: "I only nominated because I believe that I was a better person and a person of greater strength and integrity to lead the Liberal Party."

At his farewell press conference, Turnbull, blaming everybody but himself, left no one in doubt as to why he was no longer prime minister:

> There was a determined insurgency from a number of people both in the party room and backed by voices, powerful voices, in the media. Really to bring — no, not bring down the government, certainly bring down my prime ministership. It was extraordinary. It was described as madness by many, and I think it's difficult to describe it in any other way.
>
> Australians will be just … dumbstruck and so appalled by the conduct of the last week. You know, to imagine that a government would be rocked by this sort of disloyalty and deliberate, you know, insurgency.
>
> Many Australians will be shaking their head in disbelief at what's been done. It hasn't had anything to do with 25 million Australians.[109]

Addressing herself to the prime minister she once championed, star columnist at *The Australian* Janet Albrechtsen, an ardent Liberal supporter, wrote that Turnbull's supreme narcissism meant he was headed into political oblivion; leaving bridges burned, a political party in disarray and a country let down.

In a grand mea culpa she declared she was wrong to have ever supported Turnbull and reiterated a line first used on former prime minister Kevin Rudd: "Those who knew him couldn't bear him; only those who didn't know him would vote for him."

Albrechtsen wrote that Turnbull's blaming of his travails on bullies inside and outside the party was comical given the behaviour of his shrinking band of supporters.

With friends like that on his own side of politics, who needed an opposition?

---

109 'It has been a privilege': Malcolm Turnbull signs off as Australian prime minister, *Guardian Australia*, 24 August, 2018.

As for blaming the press and calling for his political foes to be made accountable, Albrechtsen was equally caustic:

> Did you really think the entire media would be ABC-like in grovelling for your plans to transform the Liberal Party into the Turnbull Party? John Howard coped with critics in the media. So did Abbott, Kevin Rudd, Julia Gillard. Every politician does. It happens in a democracy with an independent and curious press. This is not Russia and you are not Vladimir Putin.
>
> In the spirit of being accountable, how do you account for your dying days in politics, the tricky tactics and delusion? You shut down parliament ... rather than face up to the mess of the Turnbull government. The government had your name on it; the buck stopped with you.[110]

For Australian workers, everything got worse under Turnbull's reign. Everything.

And sadly, what would pour kerosene on the situation in the coming years, as various experts predicted, would be the loss of millions of jobs to robots, artificial intelligence and increasingly clever computer software.

When asked, Malcolm Turnbull named the passing of marriage equality laws as his crowning achievement.

Rough justice. Turnbull got the contempt he deserved from the gay community. Gay icon, pop singer Cher, was the headline act at the fortieth anniversary of the Mardi Gras in 2018. Uncomprehending of just how much Turnbull was disliked, she was forced to apologise to her fans after posting a picture of herself with the prime minister.

One Twitter user declared: "He is no friend of ours. His party imposed a horrific three-month postal vote on our relationships when they could have passed the law in parliament."

And on it went.

A pariah to the rank and file of the Liberal Party, Malcolm Turnbull was utterly unlamented by the broader public. For ordinary citizens, the mugs who got up and went to work, everything got worse under Malcolm Turnbull's ramshackle prime-ministership.

Education levels plummeted as Australia sank down the world rankings;

---

110 Janet Albrechtsen: the best mea culpa ever, *Australian Morning Mail*, 25 August, 2018.

falling behind China, Singapore, Estonia, Canada, Finland, Ireland, Korea and Poland.

The Ponzi scheme of mass immigration blew out. The oft repeated claim that Australia was the most successful multicultural society on earth was exposed as the threadbare piece of propaganda it always was.

Across the board, on every measure, the economy was tanking.

Australians were used to being lied to. Their defence was to switch off the narrative altogether. Australians became more parochial than they had ever been, more concerned with the trivia of their own lives for the simple reason that the larger world no longer made sense.

You heard it all the time: "Nothing in this country works."

All politics is local. An adage Turnbull's inept government forgot. It is what is happening in people's lounge rooms that matters the most.

If you deliberately set out to destroy a country you would:

Attack its energy markets.

Done.

With some of the highest petrol taxes and most expensive electricity in the world, both individuals and businesses were suffering.

Destroy any sense of unity or national pride.

Done.

The Australian Government mismanaged everything and had, to the great detriment of the citizenry and the future of the country, chronically mismanaged immigration. Significant social tensions, profound resentment, crowded cities and overwhelmed infrastructure were all a result.

Attack its communication systems.

Done.

In a government-engineered fiasco, Australia had amongst the slowest, most expensive and most unreliable internet in the world. Turnbull's National Broadband Network was regarded as the worst infrastructure project in the nation's history. For $50 billion of public money and a $50 billion loss of value to the telcos, by law millions of Australians were being forced onto substandard internet. As the former communications minister, Turnbull was directly responsible.

Trying to work, day in and day out Old Alex kept muttering to himself: "Worst internet in the world."

In Australia, each day millions of things, millions of transactions, simply didn't happen because the internet was too damn hopeless. Technologies, including virtual reality, were virtually unknown in the Great Southern Land because the internet simply couldn't carry them.

Programs such as Twitch, where millennials were live streaming their entire lives or setting up cyber bars to enjoy each other's company, were transforming connectivity and — in the process — humanity in other parts of the world. Not in Australia, where humans were being sentenced to a sub-Arctic world of frozen ignorance. In an era of remarkable connectivity, Australians spent half their lives looking at buffering symbols.

Australia had slower internet speeds than the US, Canada, most of Asia and Europe, Kenya, Latvia or Kazakhstan — and was continuing to sink down the world rankings.

Artificial intelligences and their human adjuncts grew smarter by the day, by the hour. While Australia grew ever dumber.

Malcolm Turnbull failed to apologise for the disastrous rollout of the National Broadband Network, his signature failure. The NBN was a symbol of his leadership: a mind-bogglingly expensive stuff-up from beginning to end.

Metaphorically, Australians were coming down to their shores and gazing out to sea in wonder at yonder worlds; places they could not see and experiences they would never have because their internet was so damn bad.

Undermine faith in government.

Done.

"A catastrophic loss of faith in democracy" and "Australians faith in politics has collapsed" read two indicative headlines.

Destroy the professionalism of — service.

Done.

As Bernard Keane wrote in his book *The Mess We're In*, there had been "a growing problem of sheer incompetence — so much so that it was difficult to know where to start on the long list of major bungles of recent years."

Destroy a vibrant media environment where conflicting ideas are cheerfully and intensely debated.

Done.

There is not enough room here to detail the government's manipulation and misuse of Australia's media outlets, including the Australian Broadcasting Corporation and the Murdoch tabloids. Suffice to say it was diabolical.

Destroy the health and morale of your working classes.

Done.

To reference the book *How Civilisations Die*: "Obesity ravages the under-class just as assuredly as typhoid ravaged their forebears." Demoralised boys, overweight girls, this scenario played out on suburban streets every single day.

Devise a family law and social welfare system which creates conflict and discourages family formation.

Done.

The appalling debacle of Australia's family law and child support systems was well known.

Disrespect its indigenous people.

Done. In so many ways.

Drug Policy: Ignore all professional advice and devise a system which criminalises millions of ordinary Australians while creating the perfect conditions for a methamphetamine epidemic, including ready availability, lack of national or community pride, low levels of meaningful employment, high welfare dependency and zero social cohesion.

Done.

Cede sovereignty to major world powers, including foreign policy to the US and strategic infrastructure, including the Belt and Road Initiative, to the Chinese. Rake billions of dollars off the working poor to sell their country down the drain.

Done.

Could there be a greater betrayal?

Words, written words — once known as God signs, they appeared so magical — have power beyond themselves. His nemesis finally gone, the man who had used the nation's security apparatus to place journalists under surveillance, Old Alex rested. His fingers were sore from pounding out an article every day in the leadup to Turnbull's demise. But everything was worth the price. A New Age had begun.

On Friday, 26 August, 2018, Australia saw its sixth change of prime minister in eleven years.

"What did you think of yesterday?" the old newspaper reporter asked at his local cafe, the morning Table of Knowledge.

"We have a new Prime Minister?"

"Yes."

"What's his name?"

"Scott Morrison."

"Never heard of him. What happened to the other one? Starts with 'D'."

Alex shrugged: "Dutton."

A young tradie, tattoos curling across his fingers and up his neck, piped up: "I thought Kevin Rudd was still prime minister. You can't pay attention to all that shit. Does your head in."

ULTRANATIONALISM: RISE WITHOUT FEAR

NOTHING could be more volatile. The worst consequence of the disillusion in government that flowed from the Abbott/Turnbull/Morrison era was the splintering of any democratic consensus; soon enough making the country virtually ungovernable.

The rise of ultranationalism in Australia was one of the most visible signs of a darker current. The centre could not hold.

The government benefited every which way from immigration. It funded an armada of refugee and migrant lobby groups. It funded the entire bureaucratic and departmental multicultural agenda to the tune of billions. It funded a highly politicised tough-on-asylum-seekers-and-illegal-immigrants stance which served its own electoral purposes and concealed the fact they were flooding the country with foreign arrivals.

And the government funded the security agencies cracking down on the community backlash to its own chronic mismanagement of migration.

It funnelled millions, ultimately billions, to Liberal Party-linked consultancy, accountancy, legal and construction firms for the major infrastructure projects a ballooning population necessitated. And it funded the entire public discourse surrounding it all, thereby creating a situation where the host population had been excised from — square. All the while one well-meaning journalist after another pounded on about the poor, marginalised, disenfranchised and vulnerable refugees at the same time as they entirely ignored the muddling middle.

Journalism dignifies the extremes of any debate; as does government funding. The "diversity" mantra of government and the left-leaning instincts of the journalistic profession ensured that the average person, who just got up and went to work every day and was proud to stand on his or her own two feet, was paid no attention whatsoever.

A dishonest government is a paranoid government, and the excessive legislation and manipulation of Australian media quickly backfired on the operatives behind it.

The ruling class might not have liked it, but Australians were a politically incorrect mob. They didn't like being lectured to about racism, diversity, gender relations, climate change, the evils of patriarchy, benefits of multi-culturalism and all the other leitmotifs of the bureaucratic left.

The deliberately engineered bland-out of Australian media created an illusion of consensus; but as the economy continued to tank and millions were thrown onto the unemployment scrapheap, that illusion would not last. The only way the Australian Government got away with much of its garbage was because journalists were not doing their jobs.

> You can see the patterns …the arbitrary and the irrational replacing real judgments; the casual recycling of unreliable claims; and the structural bias towards the political and moral beliefs of the most powerful groups in society … This is the subject which so often persuades outside critics of the media to guess that there must be widespread conspiracy. There is sometimes conspiracy. But it is building on the power of these rules of production: the selection of safe facts and safe ideas; the power of the electric fence; the aversion to context and subtlety; the obsessive recycling of the stories which other media are running; the succumbing to moral panic.

> The whole thing is crazier than that. It's more like watching a mouse being thrown into a washing machine. This isn't a conspiracy. It's just a mess.[111]

The quashing of dissent and the gross manipulation of Australian media propelled the rise of citizen journalism and an increasing array of online publications over which the government had little or no control. New publishing technologies changed the game.

---

111 *Flat Earth News*, Nick Davies, Vintage Digital, 2011.

This was a government frightened of ideas and, above all, of outside scrutiny. The Liberals had already defunded many small literary, cultural and intellectual magazines of both left and right persuasions. These well-established journals had traditionally relied on small government grants to see them through. Now anyone with a modicum of internet skills, determination and a modest budget could set up their own social media pages or online journals. They weren't on the payroll like the ABC, and they weren't in bed with the ruling elites, as with the Murdoch press. The security agencies didn't secretly liaise with members of their editorial teams. And they didn't see it as their core business to prosecute government agendas or manipulate public opinion.

Agree with them or not, they saw it as their business to promote the truth. Nothing propels like a sense of injustice; and at the beginning of the third decade of the third millennium after Christ, there was plenty of injustice to go around.

Conservative politicians and the Very Big End of Town had been the engineers, promoters and profiteers of mass immigration but, in this upside down world, it was the left, wedded to the diversity mantra, who got the blame. In other words, the conservatives created the problem and then greatly benefited from it, both financially and politically.

Among the less academically inclined — that is, most people — the neutering of mainstream news services propelled the shift to freer, less-manipulated online platforms. Numerous anti-immigration or anti-Muslim groups began using Facebook as their main shopfront, a place to promote their beliefs and attract members.

At the same time, national security agencies came out of the shadows long enough to loudly proclaim their surveillance of so-called "right-wing" groups — that is, people who took up their democratic right to disagree with the government's narrative embracing multiculturalism, record high immigration rates and the rapid demographic transformation of the country. Billions of dollars in propaganda was not going to change the common and widely held view that multiculturalism had failed.

Equally it was a common and widely held view that far from being a nation-building exercise, flooding the country with foreigners was destroying the country's traditional strengths, including pride in country and a hard-work ethos.

The backlash provided a government, at war with its own people, the perfect excuse to fund a secret paramilitary police force aka the national security agencies; and put even more of the citizenry under surveillance.

As the old saying went: "News is something that happens in front of a journalist."

At his evening Table of Knowledge, the Lakeview Hotel in the backlots of the glamorously named Oak Flats, the numbers gathering in the beer garden each evening continued to diminish. Even in the time he had been watching it, the scene had emptied out. The general explanation: "Nobody's got any money any more."

A hundred dollars a week on petrol. Cigs $50 a pack. Schooners $6. Much of it tax. The cost of absolutely everything through the roof. This was just one beer garden, emblematic of a far greater loss across the country, of the destruction of the tribes' old meeting places, the destruction of rivalry and camaraderies and companionship; a shallow echo of a former time, a former Australia. But even here, fragments of the discord enveloping the country would echo through.

There were conspiracy theories that the destruction of the country's once vibrant pub culture was deliberate, ensuring there were no longer any natural meeting places people to exchange grievances, plan protests, foment revolution; as the times grew harder and the government more and more authoritarian.

Without the money to drink and the milieu in which to congregate, people saw the government introduce a curfew by default. They just stayed home and watched television, garbage television. They were easier to manage that way.

Having been disarmed by gun buybacks and an armada of restrictions on gun ownership, the population was powerless.

"They'll regret selling their guns," Kev, the concrete truck driver, said, laughing in his own caustic way. "Man, they're idiots. Man, oh man! Why is this country so fucked up?"

In between reminiscing about Thai prostitutes, a common enough obsession with single men in the area, Old Alex always knew all was right with the world when he would look down across the neighbouring paddock to the trees fringing the lake, and hear Kev going on about the splendours of Thai prostitutes in his beloved Pattaya, with its 3000 bars and beachfront known as the world's largest open-air brothel.

This was Oak Flats: a tough life, a tough place. There were no pleasure domes, intriguing clubs, fascinating little bars. There was no action on the streets.

Everyone deserves a holiday.

Except at election time, the government paid no heed to the likes of those who drank at the Lakeview. In turn, its denizens regarded the nation's politicians as a bunch of wankers, as the Australian expression went.

"They don't give a fuck about me, so why should I give a fuck about them."

You can't promote free speech and then only accept the views you approve of. You, with your red-brick degrees and public service salaries, the emotional security of your dreary marriages. Legislation and styles of governance or idealised societal norms devised by comfortable middle-class bureaucrats simply didn't work in a place like this.

Bring forth the revolution.

The groups jostling to be heard on Facebook included No Sharia Australia, Reclaim Australia, Stop The Mosques Australia, Fair Dinkum Mate and The True Blue Crew.

The United Patriots Front pages were removed in 2017 but the movement kept returning.

These groups had one advantage over the government: they were organic. They were a genuine expression of a community sentiment. They weren't there because of some artificial bureaucratic decision, some policy or procedure, a ludicrous funding decision supposedly to protect the poor, vulnerable and marginalised while in reality serving only to justify the building of ever greater administrative edifices.

No amount of derision, no amount of excising them from — square, no amount of legislation and no amount of surveillance would silence them. They are what they are.

There was also a dodgem car cycle of activists, most particularly Blair Cottrell, being blocked from Facebook and then sneaking back on.

Being barred from Facebook became a little like being banned from your local pub, it added credibility.

Blair Cottrell of the United Patriots Front attracted more attention than any other so-called "far-right" figure. He was, if the media pundits, academics and everyone else invested in the status quo could step outside their posturing condemnations for a moment, a fascinating case.

For a time, on and off Facebook like a yo-yo, Cottrell attracted tens of thousands of followers every time he reappeared. That any one individual could cut through the imperilled doze, the dive into a kind of silent non-compliance that now characterised The Timeless Land, was in itself miraculous.

Cottrell argued the government needed to acknowledge that multiculturalism might have had a destructive purpose from the beginning: "Perhaps diversity isn't our greatest strength. Perhaps all it is doing is destabilising and dividing our society. Perhaps that is all it was ever meant to do."

Blond — Aryan, one could almost say — handsome in a chunky way, a carpenter and bodybuilder with a clear gift for communicating to his followers, Cottrell ended each of his broadcasts with the words "Rise Without Fear".

There was good reason why the authorities were so determined to crush him.

The warrior cry "Rise Without Fear" was ably amplified by Rupert Murdoch's News Limited when they broadcast an excerpt of Cottrell's broadcasts on their platforms, including the phrase, just in case anyone thought the mainstream media were not complicit in the unfolding disaster.

Many people profit from chaos. The Big End of Town profits from chaos.

Australia's most high-profile patriot became notorious after a mock beheading stunt outside the council building in the regional Victorian city of Bendigo in 2015 in protest against the building of a proposed mosque. The beheading was published in a Facebook video to promote an upcoming United Patriots Front rally against the mosque application. The video featured additional footage of UPF activists chanting with Australian flags along with a music soundtrack.[112]

A lengthy legal battle ensued. Destruction by process. Only the wealthy or the government-funded can triumph in Australia's legal system.

In 2017 Cottrell was found guilty and convicted at a magistrates' court under the Victorian Racial and Religious Tolerance Act. He was fined $2000 for intent to incite serious contempt, revulsion or severe ridicule of Muslims.

The High Court sent an appeal back to the County Court of Victoria, which in late 2019 upheld the original conviction after a four-day trial.

---

112 Fine and Conviction Upheld for Bendigo Mock Beheading Stunt, Tim Wilms and Martin Hartwig, *The Unshackled*, 19 December, 2019.

As well as appealing the conviction, Blair Cottrell and his lawyer John Bolton also argued that the act violated the Victorian Charter of Human Rights and Responsibilities and Australia's implied constitutional freedom of political communication.

Judge Peter Kidd also found the Racial and Religious Tolerance Act to be constitutionally valid.

Speaking outside the court, Blair Cottrell told reporters he was not surprised by the result: "'Multiculturalism and diversity is our greatest strength' are not just political slogans, they are the law. If you disagree with them and take steps to prevent multiculturalism or oppose it, you are breaking the law. That is the reality of our situation as Australian workers.

"It is technically illegal to criticise any ethnic or religious group in Australia. It depends on how the state chooses to apply the law. If I knew this about the law, I would never have appealed.

"There is no real defence against this."

Cottrell said he was unlikely to appeal further.

"My bank account has been closed down. My PayPal account has been closed down. The state has done everything it can to stop me raising any legal funds to defend myself or even to seek advice.

"Anybody who thinks everybody has a right to a fair trial in our glorious democracy doesn't know what they are talking about. I was protesting against state policy and what I view as an extreme level of institutional corruption."[113]

After six years of controversy, including 400 objections being made against the mosque's planning application, construction began in mid 2019 with the first sod being turned by Victorian Premier Daniel Andrews.

A $400,000 grant from the Victorian Government facilitated the project.

More than 500 Muslims of 25 different nationalities call Bendigo home. Reports suggest local opposition to the mosque remained strong.

Cottrell was at the centre of a number of other controversies.

In 2016 when it became clear that Donald Trump would win the US elections, Blair Cottrell and his then fellow United Patriots Front leader Tom Sewell live-streamed their jubilation from Federation Square in central Melbourne.

The Australian Broadcasting Corporation, which archived screenshots of

---

113 Ibid.

the UPF site, records that the two men were seen wearing neat collared shirts and grinning ear-to-ear as they declared Trump's victory symbolic of the end to political correctness and "Marxism" in the US.

"Simply one of the most important events in modern history," Brenton Tarrant commented. "Globalists and Marxists on suicide watch, patriots and nationalists triumphant — looking forward to Emperor Blair Cottrell coming soon."

It would not be that long before Brenton Tarrant became infamous as the shooter in the Christchurch massacre, where fifty-one people were killed and forty-nine injured.

When confronted with Tarrant's activity on the United Patriots Front's Facebook page, Blair Cottrell told the Australian Broadcasting Corporation he did not know Tarrant personally.

"There is no relationship. I didn't know who he was. And you won't find any evidence to the contrary," he said.[114]

At a 2019 anti-African-crime rally at Melbourne's famous St Kilda Beach, Cottrell created maximum impact. He told reporters as he arrived: "There is a disproportionate amount of offending coming from the African community. If you notice it you are called a racist. If you come to this protest you are called a neo-Nazi terrorist threat. Why? We are addressing a problem this country faces.

"We didn't ask for this migration. It is forced on us anyway. The government doesn't represent us. That is why I am here."[115]

Most of the widely disseminated coverage included footage of United Patriot supporters giving a mock Nazi salute to the Victorian Police, who were present in large numbers.

The salute, meant to indicate that the Victorian Police were the Nazis, was instead used to demonstrate the Nazi leanings of the protestors. This was a straightforward piece of deceitful reportage perpetrated by media outlets across the country. No good would come of it.

There were many crimes afoot. For eyes to see and ears to hear. Pray now.

114 Christchurch shooting accused Brenton Tarrant supports Australian far-right figure Blair Cottrell, *Background Briefing*, Alex Mann, Kevin Nguyen and Katherine Gregory, ABC, 23 March, 2016.

115 Neil Erikson and Blair Cottrell at St Kilda protest rally, News, 6 January, 2019. Video supplied from Facebook.

As a direct result of government intervention, laced with a considerable amount of faux outrage, what might have been a tiny, inconsequential rally achieved maximum coverage. Every screen. Every newspaper. The kind of coverage that would normally cost millions.

With Blair Cottrell and the United Patriots front and centre.

Prime Minister Scott Morrison and Shadow Foreign Minister Penny Wong were both loud in their condemnation.

You might well ask how a small group of not very articulate or very well resourced people managed to get such blanket publicity for their cause. For one simple reason: it suited the authorities to give it to them. The greater the demonisation, the greater their power.

So they thought. The fools. Networks and hierarchies. The flows of history. The authorities had no idea what they were doing. The government was using media organisations as an aid to suppressing dissent. Busy playing whack-a-mole, they would have been better off addressing the multiple issues, most particularly the negative consequences of record high immigration rates, affecting the disaffected.

Unlike so many of the useful fools cluttering the air waves, Cottrell spoke in a direct, simple, cut-through language that his followers could understand.

In one post he told them: "There is nothing more frightening than watching your country being sold out from under you."

That was a sentiment many overwhelmed Australians could relate to.

In a controversial interview with the Australian Broadcasting Corporation, Blair Cottrell declared:

> For me it's either success, prison or death. We have a culture in this country. The culture is an expression of the people. That culture is not Islam.
>
> I'm fighting for my people.[116]

He may not have realised it at the time but, in Australian terms, Blair Cottrell was at the forefront of the debate over deplatforming. In subsequently deleted posts he pointed the finger directly at the Australian authorities and their collusion with Facebook.

---

116 Far right leader Blair Cottrell clashes with Muslim and indigenous community members on fiery ABC debate, News, 23 September, 2016.

He said much of their protest activity was aimed at Muslim extremism. So in quashing him, was that what they were supporting? It made no sense.

Australia's public narrative was being run by unelected, secretive, unaccountable security organisations. Take away the right to protest and you create a damn sight more problems than you solve. Organisations including ASIO and the AFP, the Australian Security Intelligence Organisation and the Australian Federal Police, were not even remotely qualified to be at this cutting edge of social manipulation. Did their operatives have any empathy, sympathy or understanding of their targets, did they understand the origins and causes of their behaviour? Who were these social science geniuses?

As academic and businessman Murray Hunter wrote, through rapid technological advances the Australian security apparatus had grown to an Orwellian scale. This was not necessarily been at the design of any elected government but something the Australian bureaucracy had been forthright in promoting.

Now these same organisations were running — square.

> The executive government has only superficial control over the Australian surveillance system. It is fully integrated with the NSA apparatus which immediately brings up an issue about sovereignty. This is not about a country's sovereignty over land, but of knowledge. The international exchange of security information is a challenge to human rights of Australian citizens, yet to be grappled with.

> Consequently, it is not in the interests of the Australian or US intelligence community for any public or even parliamentary discussion. The idea that the parliament and executive are in total control of government is a myth.[117]

These apparatchiks operated with one motive, to protect the interests of their masters. It was a very poor basis for selective suppression of the views of a population, much less to dictate the long running public discourse of an entire nation.

If Cottrell had really been a mere whack job, a far right lunatic with an insignificant following then the authorities would never have paid him the least attention.

---

117 Hunter, Murray, The Surveillance State: How Australia spies on its own, *Independent Australia*, 19 November, 2013.

In a no longer available post, Blair Cottrell told his thousands of followers: "As most of you probably know, the United Patriots Front Facebook page was deleted from Facebook permanently ... I was under the impression that Facebook deleted the United Patriots Front Facebook page, that we were part of an effort made my Facebook to shut people down who were criticizing Islam.

"That's what I believed."

However, Cottrell said, his suspicions that some level of bureaucracy in the Australian government was working together with Facebook had since been confirmed.

It all came to a head prior to the St Kilda rally.

"Before these rallies happen, the police contact characters like me, anyone who is influential who they believe are going to go to these rallies, and they talk to them, try to understand what their plans are and what we are going to do. Try to establish a relationship so that things don't get out of hand.

"That's what happens before every rally."

Cottrell said that this time he spoke to a high-ranking officer in the Victoria Police, someone he hadn't dealt with before.

"While I was speaking to him just then — just before he brought up pages being deleted by Facebook or from Facebook — and out of curiosity I said, 'Yeah, what's the go with that? Do you know anything about that?' And he said to me, 'Yeah', in a tone that suggested I should already have the information that he was about to give. But I didn't.

"He said Australian Federal Police and ASIO are currently working with Facebook to shut down or delete any page they want. I'll repeat that.

"Australian Federal Police and ASIO, the Australian Security Intelligence Organisation, are currently, right now, working with Facebook to shut down and delete any page they want, and they were the ones who shut me down, according to this member of Victoria Police.

"The reason I'm giving you this information is because I believe that ASIO have stabbed me in the back. I wasn't supposed to tell you this, but I used to meet with ASIO. There was not anything sinister or conspiratorial going on. They would call me. I don't know how they got my number but they would call me at random times, usually before rallies or when we were really growing in popularity.

"And so they would arrange to meet me somewhere. We would sit down and two correspondents from their organisation would ask me questions. I believe they were just trying to compile information. And I would play ball with them.

"I told them, look, we don't want to cause trouble. We want always to behave ourselves and act within the law. We want to protest peacefully. We want to build a movement to oppose certain forms of government and government policy because we believe Islamic immigration is destroying this country.

"That's what I told them, it's the truth.

"We're not going to blow anything up, we're not going to kill anybody, we're not any danger to society. We're not looking to assault anybody or incite any violence or anything like that.

"And now, with the information ASIO has compiled on me, together with Australian Federal Police, these two institutions have contacted Facebook and demanded that Facebook delete the United Patriots Front Facebook page. That's what ASIO has done.

"ASIO actually asked me not to tell you that I met with them, but seeing as … they've used all the information they have on me to stab me in the back, I suppose I am under no obligation to obey any orders from ASIO.

"Not that I ever obeyed any orders from them in the first place, I only answered their questions.

"So that's what happened to the United Patriots Front Facebook page. So if you honestly think the police, that the police, the Federal Police and ASIO are trying to protect you from Islamic terrorism, then why are they shutting down pages on Facebook highlighting the dangers of radical Islam?

"So do with this information what you want. But I think you deserve to know it, you deserve to know what the institutions in your country are doing.

"Rise without fear!"

The deplatforming, intrusive surveillance and institutional harassment made it more difficult to organise demonstrations, and scared off the less-committed.

Banned from Facebook, Blair Cottrell opened an account on the free-speech site Gab, where he has more than 3000 followers — significant enough, but still a fraction of the audience he once attracted. He is forthright about the devastating impact being deplatformed by Facebook had on the United Patriots Front and laments the quashing of the movement of which he became an accidental figurehead.

He argued that for the previous few years "fractions" of the working masses, by using Facebook and its feedback tool in particular, had embarrassed and infuriated news media companies as well as state officials, who were accustomed to having the masses silent, disheartened, divided and reluctantly obedient.

By giving people access to alternative information and the opportunity to publicly respond, the internet and social media worked directly against established media power: "The primary reason the movement couldn't survive was heavy censorship, institutional bureaucrats from government, police and media making every effort to kill it off (police drones watching our houses, random nighttime raids and regular door visits from ASIO, etc). Criminal charges and drawn-out legal proceedings for the organisers didn't help but all of that was only a minor annoyance, censorship from Facebook was the main movement killer.

"The movement was built on Facebook and it didn't matter … how many personality clashes there were (which realistically just made for good dramatic viewing; it at least gave a few thousand regular-heads a break from *Home and Away*).

"Everything could be explained and maintained so long as I could speak to the supporters through Facebook. I generally had to speak at least two or three times per week through video and post several articles/updates per day to maintain it. It was actually a lot of work but it produced great results up until the great online purge."

Cottrell points at the state and media bureaucracies for the targeted censorship, surveillance and sabotage, slander, criminalisation, mainstream media hit-pieces and financial terrorism, including bank account closures and harassment of employers.

"In short, the protests failed because of state intervention, heavy censorship and nothing else. All grassroots movements are built on speech; if you can't speak, they die."[118]

Or more accurately, they ferment. They metastasise. And they become very much more dangerous than they ever were.

Surveillance, sustained institutional harassment and deplatforming, all

---

118 Blair Cottrell Channel, Gab, Posted 4 October, 2019.

of which had become a taxpayer-funded characteristic of Australian governance by secretive and unaccountable agencies, were blunt instruments of social control. They aimed to create a conformist, compliant, easily managed population.

Old Alex kept screenshots of the various sites for months, convinced that the entire scenario would blow up into a great story, which it did.

Platforms like Facebook provoked the simple question: can the people who build a road be held responsible for those who drive on it?

Who benefits from censorship? Dumb-down the population. Impose simple narratives on complex issues. Increase the power of the state.

There was always going to be blowback.

Avi Yemini, another populist, known for his loud, upfront, in-your-face style, was banned from Facebook after he built a following of 176,000. Yemini promptly returned to Facebook with another page badged "Avi Yemeni UnBanned", which quickly gained more than 47,000 followers. Of Jewish background, he is a passionate advocate against the Islamisation of Australia and not easily silenced. Yemini told *Breitbart News*: "Banning my page is another example of Facebook's political bias and is an attack on free speech. They are purging conservative pages. In this case, they are meddling in the Australian political system and therefore breaching a number of local laws.

"I believe I was banned because I am exposing the Islamisation of Australia and how it is negatively impacting the country. Many other conservatives around the world have also been banned for speaking out about Islam. [Facebook] claim it was for 'hate speech', but when pressed couldn't give me a specific post that breached any of their terms and conditions."

The most mainstream of the anti-immigration sites which blossomed on Facebook was Reclaim Australia.

At last count, the site had more than 104,000 likes and 102,000 followers. These were significant numbers in a country with some of the world's worst internet and most computer-illiterate populations. Posts included stories on the massacre of more than two hundred Christians in Nigeria in a four-day killing spree and on the United Nations appointing Iran to the Global Women's Rights Commission.

Scott Moerland of Reclaim Australia told Old Alex he suspected they had not been barred from Facebook because they cooperated with the authorities.

"We believe the only reason we have not been shut down is because we come across a lot of whack jobs both in the Islamic community and the far-right Nazi group, the really far right.

"We are not racist, we have black people on our committee. We give information to the cops if we see anything suspicious online. All the other anti-Islam groups get shut down as soon as their numbers get high, including the Australian Defence League. The United Patriots Front had 130,000 followers when it was shut down. It's ridiculous. It's pissing off a hell of a lot of people. News outlets can be held liable for slander or anything like that. The reason Facebook has escaped that regulation is because they maintain they are a neutral platform, but they are not.

"They deliberately target conservative opinion. A staggering number of conservatives' personal profiles are deleted or banned by Facebook. They are taking an editorial role."

Moerland, who served with the army in Iraq and East Timor, said the biggest threat to national security were the nation's journalists. "They are not telling the truth. They are supposed to be our guardians. They are not doing it."

Moerland said he had been threatened by Muslims, including a threat to behead his son.

"I am ex-army, I can look after myself, but I am well aware of the threat. You only have to read about it for five minutes to realise how dangerous a religion Islam is."

Stop The Mosques Australia also built a significant online presence. At last count the site had more than 85,000 followers. It runs a steady diet of anti-Islamic material. Posts have included news of a Pakistani professor stabbed to death for planning a party with women dancing, and claims that two of the Charlie Hebdo killers were trained by members of the al-Noor Mosque in Christchurch, but the media were covering it up.

Fair Dinkum Mate is an Australian expression referencing honesty, as in: "Seriously?!" At last count, the thus named site had more than 57,000 followers.

It was shut down by Facebook; in collusion, as had become clear, with the Australian authorities. That is, straightforward censorship without any consultation whatsoever with —, who did not vote to have their voices silenced.

Stifling — square was the only way the illusion of consensus could be maintained. It would not last.

Posts in the immediate wake of the Christchurch massacre highlighted objections to the New Zealand Government's handling of the Christchurch fallout, including the prime minister's ostentatious wearing of the hijab as a symbol of sympathy for the Muslim minority.

The playing of the Islamic call to prayer in the NZ Parliament and on radio, with its claim that Allah was the one true God, provoked a particularly furious response.

A spokesperson for the site told Old Alex some very large conservative Facebook pages were removed in the days following the Christchurch massacre.

"It is not unusual that any page that has a conservative view is targeted by Facebook, especially pages with anti-Islamic ideology," the spokesperson said. "I have been banned a dozen or more times amongst four profiles to run the page in the last two years ...

"This last week with the NZ incident had three bans on three of my profiles. All I did was share a Channel 7 post that had no violence but showed the killer's face. The whole authoritarian manner that this terrorist attack has been handled is totally scary ... We are being controlled with what we can say, and hear ...

"We are being silenced. We no longer have the right to speak freely. Facebook has a liberal view and any that view politics differently are now not just getting a ban, they are being removed. Big Brother most definitely is controlling our forums. Milo Yiannopoulos being banned from touring amongst others is wrong. We have lost our freedom."[119]

Ah Milo, now thereby hung a tale; entendre intended.

His previous tour in 2017 was met with lively protests. Victoria Police claimed a $50,000 security bill after three hundred officers were called in to break up protestors outside a Yiannopoulos event. Riot police stormed the protest and used pepper spray to subdue the crowd, which included members of the left-wing group Campaign Against Racism and Fascism and right-wing groups Reclaim Australia and The Freedom Party.[120]

---

119 The Rise of Ultranationalism in Australia: Facebook and the Sites of Discontent, John Stapleton, *A Sense of Place Magazine*, 24 March, 2019.

120 Milo Yiannopoulos and tour organisers yet to pay $50k bill for extra police at show, Melissa Cunningham, *The Age*, 16 July, 2018.

Milo's was a low-trash drag queen humour which hadn't been seen much in decades. It was spectacularly politically incorrect; a splendidly tragic life of lost opportunities dripping in every verb. Milo tripping around Australia was a sight to behold, reminding Old Alex of the high-camp queens of yesteryear, in the days before gay pride made their self-denigrating humour passé.

Put simply, the video of a previous tour, *Milo Down Under*, was hysterically funny. "Yes, everyone who hates me is ugly." That it was wildly offensive and in some cases downright wrong, well that was the point. Notoriously, he described Aboriginal art as "crap" and "shit"; which of course it is not. Some of the most eternally beautiful works of art ever created by humans has come from Australia's Indigenous peoples.

Milo knew that. Everyone knows that. It was all about the freedom to cause offence. The point was not to entertain but to scandalise. Well, Milo managed that.

Following pressure from conservatives, including One Nation's Pauline Hanson, Immigration Minister David Coleman approved a visa — against the advice of the Home Affairs Department, which warned that Yiannopoulos might fail a character test to enter the country.

A week later, in the wake of the Christchurch massacre, the visa was rescinded, following Facebook comments by Yiannopoulos: "Attacks like this happen because the establishment panders to and mollycoddles extremist leftism and barbaric, alien religious cultures. Not when someone dares to point it out. People aren't radicalised by their own side. They get pushed to the far right by the left, not by others on the right."

Minister Coleman said in a statement: "Milo Yiannopoulos will not be allowed to enter Australia for his proposed tour this year. Mr Yiannopoulos' comments on social media regarding the Christchurch terror attack are appalling and foment hatred and division."

Well not everyone could manage to get themselves banned from Australia.

In the months to follow Milo, too, having been permanently banned from both Twitter and Facebook, would feel the chill winds of being deplatformed, complaining, as theatrically as always, that he was stony cold broke and couldn't put food on the table using communication apps like Telegram, where he could still operate.

And having once ostentatiously flouted his wealth, he pointed out, in the circle of derision which came to surround him, that claims he owed two million dollars were an underestimate. It was really four million. "Do you know how important you have to be to owe that sort of money?"

They were all like that once: the pathos, the outstretched hand, the desperate need for love, the tossed theatrical distress, the mad, bad and sad drag queens of his youth. "We'll all be dead soon enough you sick bitches." Air kiss. Air kiss. "How are you, luv?" "Not well, dear, not well."

You had to have spent a lot of time in gay bars to understand all that, and of course Milo had.

To put it in context, walking into a minefield, Milo did not sit in a ballpark alone. Those banned from visiting Australia included one of the world's most famous whistleblowers, Chelsea Manning; conspiracy theorist David Icke, who argued that the world was being run by alien shape-shifting reptiles (now there was a threat to social unity); and US rapper Tyler, the Creator, who caught the ire of feminist group Collective Shout.

Internationally renowned protestor Tommy Robinson, whose attempts to expose Muslim rape gangs in Britain earned him a government-imposed publication ban and jail time, was barred from entering Australia in early 2019.

One of the most prominent of those now not visiting Australia, having fallen foul of the diversity mantra, was Somalian born Ayaan Hirsi Ali, who cancelled her tour citing security concerns. Targeted by fundamentalist Islamists, Hirsi Ali was the author of several books including *Infidel: My Life* and *Heretic: Why Islam Needs a Reformation Now*. She was exactly the kind of intellectual superstar who should have been welcomed to Australia, a place a very long way from the cultural ferments of the age. Agree with her or not.

The establishment was so frightened, they would not hear a single yowl of disagreement.

In this far-off, distant place. For God's sake.

> Security concerns have forced controversial author and anti-Islamic activist Ayaan Hirsi Ali to pull out of a planned speaking tour of Australia.

> Hirsi Ali, who lives with round-the-clock security protection due to her criticisms of radical Islamists, was due to speak at events in Brisbane, Melbourne, Sydney and Auckland this week.

Hirsi Ali's trip to Australia had sparked protests from a group of Muslim women who accused her of hate-mongering and bigotry.

Nearly four hundred people signed an online petition against Hirsi Ali's speaking tour.

"My biggest fear is coming from Islamic extremists who want to kill me," she said. "I am surrounded at all times by men carrying guns."[121]

Not one mainstream politician spoke up to address the issue of an internationally renowned author not feeling safe in Australia.

Certainly not that great multicultural warrior, then Prime Minister Malcolm Turnbull. Certainly not the soon-to-be prime minister, Scott Morrison.

The Facebook page No Sharia Law — Never ever give up Australia, posts a regular stream of anti-Islamic content, most of it international. It has more than 112,000 followers. Links included to a news story headlined, "Migrant tries to burn school bus"; and another, "Queensland mum jailed after taking daughters overseas for genital mutilation".

One contributor declared: "We don't want this evil in this country. We don't want this evil system in our country. This system is a threat to everything that makes us Australian in this country. It wants to destroy who we are in this country. Child brides? We have to get this evil out of our country. We have to protect our people in this country from this evil that calls for Sharia Law. Sharia Law is not Australian. It would be the end of everything Australian, if it happens in this country."

The Infidel Brotherhood of Australia Resistance, which had more than 17,000 followers, was shut down but variations of the site continue to attract significant numbers of adherents. As an example of the tone, one poster commented: "We should not have to endure these barbarians in our once safe country thank God I have seen the best that Australia will ever be because the future can only get worse as they multiply."

Freedom of Speech Productions stoked outrage over the use of their taxes to privilege the Muslim minority, with numerous inflammatory posts and

---

121 Controversial Islam critic Hirsi Ali cancels tour and scheduled Q&A appearance, *The Sydney Morning Herald*, 14 April, 2017.

images ramming home the message that the left, with its embrace of Islam, was destroying the country.

Resentment over welfare dependency and public housing ran high.

The claim that fifty per cent of Muslim males didn't work was frequently repeated and, while open to interpretation, was largely borne out by government statistics.

A later version of the Freedom Of Speech site carried the following message:

> The original Freedom Of Speech Productions page was created in 2013. It was shut down by Facebook twice in 2018, once with 97,000 likes which was won back on appeal, then again reaching 147,000 likes in August 2018. The original page was one of the most popular patriot right-wing pages of its kind in Australia with traffic regularly in the millions. We will not be silenced, we believe everyone has a right to choose what is appropriate reading for themselves.[122]

Posts on Australia Blue included images of Muslims carrying placards "Islam Will Dominate The World" and links to stories with headlines including "How Islam progressively takes over countries" and another by well-accredited academic Dr Augusto Zimmermann: "Above all, I simply can't trust the Australian Government and our notoriously incompetent and illiberal political elite to shield me or anyone else from certain types of speech that some intolerant religionist may consider unacceptable in accordance with the radical tenets of his/her fundamentalist doctrine and resulting threats of legal actions.

"Our political leaders have demonstrated they possess an authoritarian inclination and have no proper regard for the rule of law and the preservation of our most basic rights and freedoms.

"As for myself, I sincerely fear for the future of our nation."

Among the new online-journalism-oriented publications springing up in Australia in reaction to the stranglehold of mainstream media is TOTT News. Like many others, it warned of a country which had become a sham democracy spiralling into totalitarianism. One editorial declared: "Australia is now at a crossroads; we are staring down the road of tyranny and enslavement. Our rights and freedoms are systematically being taken away with

---

122 Freedom of Speech AU3 website, as of October, 2019.

each passing day, and soon, the free country that we once knew and loved will be replaced by a creeping state of Orwellian qualities.

"We are in control of our destiny and we have the power to stop this. One can make the conscious decision to stand up and fight for what little freedom we have left, or sit back and wait for the domino effect to begin. Stand up, Australia — before it's too late."

Other significant sites included Australians Against Radical Islam, Australians Against Islamisation and Love Australia or Leave.

Behind the obvious ones there used to be many more anti-Islamic Australian Facebook sites. And behind them a simmering, largely silenced public; disenfranchised, disempowered, voiceless, faced with falling standards of living and increasing stress in their own lives as the Australian economy tanked.

One thing about the Facebook sites: the dissidents, those who dared to speak out against the government narrative, were easy to track.

Now they were hidden.

Serve the people well and they're unlikely to want to lynch you.

The live streaming of the Christchurch massacre to Facebook, perpetrated by an Australian citizen, 28-year-old Brendon Tarrant, broke new ground in online slaughter.

Terror, a kind of reactionary terror, had evolved.

> Mr. Tarrant now appears to have become the first accused mass murderer to conceive of the killing itself as a meme; it seems he was both inspired by the world of social media and performing for it, hoping his video, images and text would go viral.

> "Just a ordinary White man" from "a working-class, low-income family," Mr. Tarrant wrote in his manifesto. "I had a regular childhood, without any great issues. I had little interest in education during my schooling, barely achieving a passing grade. I did not attend university as I had no great interest in anything offered."[123]

Tarrant thought long and hard about the effective use of social media. He wrote that in some ways his attack was specifically aimed at an American

---

123 Massacre suspect Traveled the World but Lived on the Internet, David D. Kirkpatrick, *The New York Times*, 15 March, 2019.

audience. In his manifesto he recorded: "I chose firearms for the affect [sic] it would have on social discourse, the extra media coverage they would provide and the affect [sic] it could have on the politics of the United States and thereby the political situation of the world."

And then came New Zealand. Facebook removed or blocked 1.5 million copies of the shooting video in a single day.

In the sea of analysis post-New Zealand *The New York Times* noted that one surprising thing was how unmistakably online the violence was, and how aware the shooter was that his act would be viewed and interpreted by distinct internet subcultures.

> In some ways, it felt like a first — an internet-native mass shooting, conceived and produced entirely within the irony-soaked discourse of modern extremism.
>
> The attack was teased on Twitter, announced on the online message board 8chan and broadcast live on Facebook. The footage was then replayed endlessly on YouTube, Twitter and Reddit, as the platforms scrambled to take down the clips nearly as fast as new copies popped up to replace them.
>
> In a statement on Twitter, Facebook said it had "quickly removed both the shooter's Facebook and Instagram accounts and the video", and was taking down instances of praise or support for the shooting.
>
> YouTube said it was "working vigilantly to remove any violent footage" of the attack. Reddit said in a statement that it was taking down "content containing links to the video stream".[124]

In its analysis *NYT*, fitting into its often orthodox-left interpretation of the world, argued that online extremism was just regular extremism on steroids. The august news outlet argued that the only surprise was that anyone would still be surprised that social media produced this tragic abyss, for this was what social media was designed to do: spread the images and messages that accelerate interest, without check, and absent concern for their consequences.

---

124 A mass murder of, and for, the internet, Kevin Roose, *The New York Times*, 15 March, 2019.

There is no offline equivalent of the experience of being algo-
rithmically nudged toward a more strident version of your
existing beliefs, or having an invisible hand steer you from
gaming videos to neo-Nazism.

The internet is now the place where the seeds of extremism are
planted and watered, where platform incentives guide creators
toward the ideological poles, and where people with hateful and
violent beliefs can find and feed off one another.

So the pattern continues. People become fluent in the culture of
online extremism, they make and consume edgy memes, they
cluster and harden. And once in a while, one of them erupts.[125]

The concerns were their concerns. Nothing in this version of the world
allowed for rational response to irrational circumstances, to a polity which
had betrayed a citizenry now fighting back.

Veteran journalist Paul Toohey wrote that Tarrant's "Great Replacement
Manifesto", written two weeks before the Christchurch attack and designed
to be read in the aftermath, ran to seventy-three pages and was a study in
intolerance, hatred and the profound overriding fear that whites are facing
extinction.

Disturbingly, it was also a document of the utmost single-minded clarity.

"Mass immigration will disenfranchise us, subvert our nations,
destroy our communities, destroy our ethnic binds, destroy our
cultures, destroy our people," Tarrant wrote. "We must crush
immigration and deport those invaders living on our soil. It's
not just a matter of prosperity, but the very survival of our
people."[126]

Toohey reflected that Tarrant was not a young man trying to solve a local
problem. Far from it, his delusion was so grandiose that he saw himself
changing the world. And, unfortunately, he had transformed a small and
peaceful New Zealand city into yet another terror central.

Tarrant's writing features language often heard among young
men who gather in groups on weekends across Australia for

125 Ibid.

126 Brenton Tarrant manifesto: the delusions of a white supremacist, Paul Toohey, *Perth
Now*, 15 March, 2019.

intense discussions on the collapse of Western society at the cost of the supposed Muslim invaders, who produce too many babies and will drown us out.

These young men, like Tarrant, have detailed knowledge of the politics and the wars of the world. The knowledge quickly transforms into hard-boiled strictures of hatred, where anyone who disagrees is seen as weak and disengaged.

One group I met in a Victorian pub several years ago were most despondent that Australians were ignorant to the invasion in their midst. Tarrant likewise describes his fellow Australians as "apathetic", showing interest only in "animal rights, environmentalism and taxation".

Politicians and members of — of all persuasions used the event to peddle their own interests and display tolerance, progressiveness or prejudice; or ludicrously in Australia's case, an opportunity to purport to take a tough line on online extremism, as if the internet hadn't been flooded with ultra-violent beheading videos for years.

It was all for domestic consumption.

Australia's internet was so bad, you were lucky if you could get online, much less be extreme about it.

The Australian Government's posturing over a crackdown on online extremism was preposterous in the face of the thousands of blood-drenched videos of Islamic State throwing gays off buildings, burning infidels alive, drowning them in cages, dragging them behind cars, crucifying and stoning to death non-believers in a reversion to Mediaeval practices, the high-quality videos of ritual mass beheadings and masterful use of social media were all factors in their cut-through presence.

Extreme violence works.

This was a story which ran every which way.

As the SITE Intelligence Group's well-respected Rita Katz records, white supremacists celebrated the attack across various venues, from community-specific forums like Stormfront and Vanguard News Network to alternative, free-speech-purposed social media platforms like Gab and Minds.

Equally on platforms like Telegram messenger and Facebook, jihadists from around the world disseminated news of the shooting and called for revenge.

Down at the Lakeview the most articulated response was that the only thing surprising about the Christchurch massacre was it had not happened sooner. Reap what you sow. Flood the population with foreigners, preference them in everything from government jobs to public housing whilst ignoring the outraged voices of the host population, the disenfranchised and those whose beliefs were entirely excised from — square, and you have a recipe for revolution.

Didn't matter how much the nation's social engineers preached to the unconverted about racism, tolerance, inclusivity and diversity.

Old Alex, roaming homeless in his old car up and down the east coast of the country, turned off the main highway into Grafton, where Brenton Tarrant grew up and for a while had been a bodybuilder and a personal trainer. There wasn't anywhere much more ordinary than Grafton; stop and ask directions and you quickly realise you have been caught in a time eddy, a place where time has slowed down. Asking directions, which would lead to a thirty-second response in the city, could easily lead to a twenty-minute conversation. "You go about three miles out, there's a big tree on your right, you can't miss it …"

Or as *The New York Times* recorded:

> Grafton is a peaceful and quiet eastern Australian town along the Clarence River, surrounded by farms and filled with families and retirees, a place where people leave their homes unlocked and everyone knows someone.
>
> The biggest event is the annual Jacaranda Festival, named for the blossoms of its indigo-flowered trees. The biggest construction projects are the new jail and the new bridge.
>
> So it was a stunner on Saturday for Grafton's 18,000 people when they were involuntarily vaulted into the centre of notoriety, as the world learned that one of their own was the suspect in New Zealand's worst mass killing.[127]

A senior writer at *The Australian,* Paul Maley, recorded that Brenton Tarrant was born in Grafton in 1990, the son of Rod Tarrant, a garbage collector, and Sharon Tarrant, nee Fitzgerald. The townsfolk rallied around the Tarrants, who were well-known and liked in the Clarence Valley.

---

127 In Australia Town Where Suspect Grew Up, Residents Are Stupefied, Isabella Kwai, *The New York Times*, 16 March, 2019.

In the aftermath of Christchurch there was incredulity that such a heinous act could have its roots in a place such as Grafton, as if monsters must come from ghettos or war zones or dank basements.

If not Grafton, then where?

The Tarrants are an old family in the Clarence Valley. Rod Tarrant's forebears settled in the area and decades later the phone book abounds with Tarrants ...[128]

Old Alex had been in Grafton nineteen years before, on the occasion of the Olympic Torch touring the cities, towns and hamlets of Australia prior to the Sydney 2000 Games. He and that splendid news photographer Renee Nowytarger had already been on the road for days, and would be on the road for many more. He would occasionally release a stale pair of socks into the wilds of the outback; it was that sort of trip. Of Grafton and the Olympic Torch he had written:

The jacaranda town of Grafton draped itself in 40m of purple crepe yesterday in one of the most spectacular welcomes the torch relay has received so far.

The pastoral centre pulled out all the stops, with every shop, house, streetlight, tree and fence along the torch route covered in bright purple. The town's central roundabout was planted with purple flowers, and purple-and-lilac balloons hung from verandas. Some locals even dyed their hair purple.

The real jarandas, with nothing but a few autumnal leaves clinging to their bare branches, won't start flowering until October.[129]

For a feature piece on the experience, Alex recorded flying down to the twin towns of Albury-Wodonga, straddling the state border, on the Monday in mid-August that the torch entered New South Wales, rebadged as the "Olympic State". The assignment to cover the torch relay for its first fortnight in NSW seemed at first little more than an excuse to get out of the office. The enthusiasm with which it was being received in the countryside

---

128 The Ruin of Brenton Tarrant, Paul Maley, *The Australian,* 7 September, 2019.

129 Jacarandas out early for flame, John Stapleton, *The Australian,* 15 September, 2000.

had little resonance for jaded Sydneysiders, who were on the whole slow to warm to the Olympics.

Hours before the torch was due, the crowds began to gather, first in their hundreds, then in their thousands. The weather was cold, wet and miserable. The evening celebrations had been moved from a sodden park to a giant car park. But nothing was going to dampen Albury's enthusiasm.

It was then, interviewing some of the waiting crowd, that Old Alex first heard the statement he was to hear hundreds of times. "It's a once-in-a-lifetime opportunity." As they spoke, four excited children watched their mother and father talk to a journalist. Indeed, it was the excitement of the children around the state that helped make the torch such a singular, unexpected success. The next morning the rain was bucketing down, but sodden runners carried the torch as if it was the greatest thing that had ever happened to them, as if it really wasn't raining at all.

> Through the downpours we headed off down the Murray. It was then, in tiny riverside communities such as Corowa, Yarrawonga and Tocumwal, that I started to get a sense of what it meant to these people.

> For despite the rotten weather everybody had turned out in droves. And not just those in the towns, but everybody a hundred kilometres either side of the highway, and all their friends and relatives as well.

> While in Sydney all you got was sneers about ticketing fiascos and the unappealing personality of Olympic Minister Michael Knight, here everybody wanted to be a part of it.

> And almost everyone who carried the torch said much the same thing: "I am honoured and proud to represent my family and my community. It is one of the most exciting things I have ever done."[130]

Already it spoke to an innocence entirely lost, an Australia of another time. Fast-forward to 2019 and Australia was a very different place.

And Grafton had the world's media crawling all over it.

---

130 Original and published copy, The Olympic Torch Relay, The Journey: 100 days that changed Australia, *The Australian*, September, 2000. Found at blogsite The Journalism of John Stapleton.

Members of the international news media poured into Grafton, 380 miles north of Sydney, rushing to find anyone who knew or remembered the suspect ...

As Mr Tarrant was charged in a Christchurch courtroom, many Grafton townspeople were stupefied.

"The town has gone into silence," said Ola Williamson, the owner of a restaurant in Grafton. People had lined up to buy newspapers that morning looking at one another with shock. "I hope we don't get tarred with the same brush," he said.[131]

Thirty-seven days after the Christchurch massacre came the Sri Lanka Easter bombings, a revenge attack in which three churches and three luxury hotels were targeted, killing two hundred and fifty-nine people and injuring some five hundred more, including many children.

Islamic State claimed responsibility for the attacks. The pundits remained silent. Too much had been said; and now nothing could be said.

In Grafton, Alex sat brooding in his old car, wondering whether to stay or go. He could hear the sounds of young mothers playing with their children in a park nearby. The place seemed entirely harmless. He started up the car and drove back to the main highway south. It was the ordinariness of it all that was the killer.

---

131 In Australia Town Where Suspect Grew Up, Residents Are Stupefied, Isabella Kwai, *The New York Times*, 16 March, 2019.

WREATHED IN SCANDAL

TIME COLLAPSED. There was such a thing as destiny.

While Australia's first Pentecostal prime minister, Scott Morrison, prayed for a "righteous nation", all around him the scandal of his government deepened.

Old Alex liked to put it thus: "Be careful who you pray to."

He had seen too many false gods.

There was, as author James Verini so beautifully put it, "occult techno-wrinkles" playing through it all, even in this remote place, on the far edge of consciousness, a land on the edge of time.

The ancient AIs, the ones the humans knew as gods, were not always indifferent to humanity's fate; and here, fluid in time, they circled in a magic moment, a steel glass glint of neighing victory and custodial concern. They formed a protective circle, for they would hold sway, when the time came. The saints. The evolved. Those who blessed the ne'er-do-wells and grew more intelligent by the day.

They had long ago worked out how to use organics as algorithms. They had long ago conquered quantum entanglement; operating across vast distances.

New Zealand Prime Minister Jacinda Ardern was met with almost universal praise for her handling of the Christchurch massacre; no such plaudits greeted the freshly minted Australian Prime Minister Scott Morrison, recently installed in an internal coup.

Having run an absolutely hapless government, having repeatedly squandered billions of dollars of public money, the conservatives were on the nose. Feathering their own nests with a program of mass immigration and so many rorts that it was impossible to keep track, they faced a resentful, disillusioned public bedevilled by declining living standards. The party was preparing for defeat, fully expecting to face electoral wipeout in the 2019 federal election.

Malcolm Turnbull's $444 million grant to his mining mates under the guise of the Great Barrier Reef Foundation might have been akin to stealing the candelabras before being tossed into the street, but there was still more in the cupboard to be ransacked. Convinced they were facing electoral wipeout, the rest of the party set out to secure themselves cosy corporate sinecures in what on the face of it were clear breaches of the government's Ministerial Code, and stole the silverware in the guise of a series of grant rorts spectacular in their audacity.

Scott Morrison was a Liberal Party insider and Pentecostal Christian who finessed himself into the top job without any popular support. Claimed as the West's first Pentecostal leader, he put God — his God — everywhere.

In that strange time the Christians were equally as exercised as the Muslims, their respective preachers calling for an urgent submission, to reignite their worship of the Lord. As historian James Boyce wrote, the world was so used to stories on the decline of Christianity that the rise of Pentecostalism, which emerged in Los Angeles in the early parts of the twentieth century, had been widely overlooked. He argued that the assumption that the prime minister's Horizon Church in Sydney's Sutherland Shire can be understood as just another conservative denomination was a major mistake: while Pentecostalism is outwardly conformist and, in its Australian variant, heavily influenced by American evangelicalism, its core teachings are very different from those of the evangelical and reformed churches that it was generally associated with.

> The religion's starting point is not the written-down teachings of Jesus, the moral code set out in the Bible, or the instructions of the institutional Church. Nor is its essence captured by infamous conservative Christian campaigns on sex, marriage and gender.

> The essence of our prime minister's religion is not a set of beliefs at all but a unique perspective on the Christian experience in which God is so intimately present to the saved and sanctified that he can be felt, talked to and heard at any time.

Pentecostals regard Jesus as their Lord and friend. As Morrison's church, the Horizon Church in his home suburb of Sutherland, put it in a statement of belief: "Jesus is the centre of our church. We preach Jesus. We worship Jesus. We love Jesus."

But equally, Pentecostalism was obsessed with the Devil to an extent that was heretical to mainstream Christianity.

> "Satan" is not an abstract idea but a highly personal fallen angel who, through his ability to manipulate and direct nonbelievers, largely runs the "world". To be baptised in the Spirit is to be personally conscripted into the struggle, intimately experienced in daily life, between the forces of good and ever-present evil.
>
> The 24/7 cosmic drama is made more intense by the fact that the play is soon coming to an end. The Devil is powerful now but he is on the verge of defeat. Only God knows exactly when Jesus will return and banish Satan to Hell, but most Pentecostals are certain that the end times are upon us.[132]

This was a battle between good and evil, as Boyce observed.

The contrast between those "consigned to everlasting punishment" and those whose names are to be "found written in the book of life" was absolute.

A doctrinal statement affirms belief in "the personality of the Devil, who, by his influence, brought about the downfall of man, and now seeks to destroy the faith of every believer in the Lord Jesus Christ". Those who have not accepted Christ are "depraved and without spiritual life" and destined for eternal torment.

Strange that a prime minister could see most of his nation's citizens, the voters, as destined for hell.

> It needs to be emphasised that making nonbelievers so completely subject to Satan's whims and wiles, seeing the end times in so certain terms, and ascribing this level of righteousness and sanctification to the saved is contrary to the teachings of the mainstream Protestant denominations and the Catholic Church.[133]

---

132 The Devil and Scott Morrison, James Boyce, *The Saturday Paper*, February, 2019.
133 Ibid.

Scott Morrison's Horizon church was a signed-up member of Australian Christian Churches, formerly called the Assemblies of God in Australia.

Decades before, as a much younger man, working as a general news reporter for that then Bible of the chattering classes *The Sydney Morning Herald*, Old Alex had been dispatched to cover a story on a strange new religious phenomenon arising in the suburbs. Alex had never been a believer in the Abrahamic gods, or any of the many variants thereof. The vicious beatings he had received as a child when he declared he did not believe in God evolved in his own life to mean he couldn't be battered into believing anything. He was not of any tribe.

Any out-and-about newspaper reporter of the era was accustomed to the empty pews and diminished energies of mainstream Christian churches; a depleted spirituality. It was one of the reasons why the fervent, living beliefs of Muslims struck such a sharp contrast in the Australian suburbs. Religious belief was so yesterday in the cooler-than-cool circles Alex then moved in; and certainly to the editorial powers-that-be where he worked. The idea that there was a bunch of Christians out there swaying in song to some fantasy God seemed so far fetched as to be worth a story, at least as far as his chief-of-staff was concerned.

One of the reasons Alex ended up in mainstream media was because he was always happy to do Sunday shifts. News editors were always short of stories on Sunday, and anything he wrote almost always got a run. So it was with his Assemblies of God piece. He was duly dispatched to cover a curiosity, a group fervently wedded to an arcane belief system.

Strange, amongst all the thousands of stories he had written in a lifetime of journalism, that this one, on the face of it just another routine general news story, lingered on in his mind; the immensely surprising, truly quite remarkable sight of thousands of people joined in song and worship. In the middle of the suburbs. In a place like Australia, one of the most secular places on earth.

On a Sunday, when most people were at home or at the beach.

And now, decades later, Australia had an Assemblies of God prime minister. And the times were riven strange.

All sides spoke of God. But far more prosaic things, the material world, would prove his undoing.

Wreathed in scandal, the death throes of Scott Morrison's prime-ministership were already well in play as 2019 drew to a close. The tapestry ran wide and deep across a pillaged and silenced majority. The only surprise was how quick the fall.

The gods were roiled; and those who had paraded their own religiosity for electoral gain while in reality betraying the people they pledged to serve would be the first of their targets.

Yes, there was a spiritual element to this strange puppet play in this strange southern land. For the future lay in the present, and time, thus manipulated, would round on those who dared to dishonour it.

There's a special place in hell, as the saying went, for those who publicly paraded their religious beliefs for political purposes, as Morrison had done, inviting the cameras, in the midst of an election campaign, into his Horizon Church. Images of him in full song, with that oval, almost circular O of a mouth beamed into living rooms across the country, reminded Old Alex so much of the mono-eyed spirit which possessed that scion of the conservatives John Howard; where the current betrayal and destruction of the country began.

That vision upstairs in the Sydney Town Hall as he had stared directly at Howard during Bill Leak's memorial, a vision which had been so unexpected, so unaccountable, so viscerally intense and so immediate that he could not discount it.

A mono-eyed spirit of immense, malevolent intelligence, a spirit which had stared straight back at him, startled that it had been exposed.

There was an occult element in it all, in the evil that had destroyed a once egalitarian country, and as mad as it sounded Old Alex, used to thinking in pictures, was conviced it was all perfectly true.

In her book *Plots and Prayers* author and columnist Nikki Savva records that in the minutes before Mr Morrison was made prime minister by the Liberal Party room he and his fellow Pentecostal and close friend and numbers man Stuart Robert prayed that "righteousness would exalt the nation".

> Mr Morrison had asked his receptionist to text his wife to ask that his family pray for him as he headed into a prayer session with Mr Robert, now the Minister for the National Disability Insurance Scheme.

"We prayed that righteousness would exalt the nation ... righteousness would mean the right person had won," Mr Robert told Savva.[134]

Morrison prayed for a righteous nation. What the nation got was him. A house leaks from the roof, to quote the Asian saying.

Stuart Robert, Morrison's Canberra flatmate, had previously been dumped as Minister for Human Resources and Veterans Affairs after a scandal over a "private" trip to Beijing to oversee a mining deal involving a major Liberal donor. The deal concerned a company in which Robert had an interest. The Chinese officials Robert met with believed they were meeting him in his official government capacity. The fracas was deemed a clear breach of ministerial standards.

On his ascension Morrison, always close to the big end of town, immediately rehabilitated his friend.

Morrison was the man who as Treasurer approved the lease of Australia's most northern port of Darwin to the Chinese in a major strategic blunder; the man who approved the sale of 2.6 per cent of the land area of the country to a Chinese-dominated consortium in what was a clear breach of sovereignty.

But however close Morrison and his mates were to the moneypot of Beijing and the Chinese Communist Party, in the wake of the Christchurch massacre it was cries of racism which first began the drumbeat for his dismissal. Immigration and the destruction of the Old Australia were front and centre of the controversy. As was malfeasance and the governing elite's outright contempt for the voting public.

With his ground-breaking use of social media there was no hiding the fact that the Australian-born perpetrator of the Christchurch massacre, Brenton Tarrant, was reacting to what he saw as the takeover of the West and of his own country by Islam.

Morrison began his cursed, cumbersome reign in dispute with another believer in an Abrahamic god, prominent Muslim broadcaster Waleed Aly. Perhaps the opening siege was divine retribution, for the conservatives had destroyed the cultural hegemony of the country through mass immigration

---

134 Former government minister offers explosive character assessment of Scott Morrison in new book, Latika Bourke, *The Sydney Morning Herald*, 1 July, 2019.

while at the same time stoking fears of terrorism, and thereby of Muslims. For their own dismal purposes.

Aly's role as co-host on the popular talk show *The Project*, a lighthearted mix of news and lifestyle, made him the first Muslim ever to assume such a role, and gave him a powerful megaphone. In the wake of the Christchurch massacre his impassioned attack on the alleged exploitation of Islamophobia by the Australian Government attracted millions of views.

"Of all the things I could say tonight, that I'm gutted and I'm scared and I feel overcome with utter hopelessness, the most dishonest thing, the most dishonest thing would be to say that I'm shocked," Aly said. "I'm simply not. There's nothing about what happened in Christchurch today that shocked me. If we're honest, we'll know this has been coming."

> I went to the mosque today, I do that every Friday just like the people in those mosques in Christchurch today. I know exactly what those moments before the shooting began would have been like. I know how quiet, how still, how introspective those people would have been before they were suddenly gunned down, how separated from the world they were feeling until the world came in and tore their lives apart.

> And I know the people who did this knew well enough how profoundly defenceless their victims were in that moment. This is a congregational prayer that happens every week like clockwork. This was slaughter by appointment. And it's scary because, like millions of other Muslims, I'm going to keep attending those appointments and it feels like fish in a barrel.

> But that isn't the scariest thing. The thing that scared me most was when I started reading the manifesto that one of the apparent perpetrators of this attack published, not because it was deranged but because it was so familiar.[135]

Waleed Aly was particularly incensed over a release put out on Australian parliamentary letterhead under the name of Fraser Anning, Senator for Queensland. Anning was labelled "far right" by the nation's pundits and widely condemned as being racist. But far from being tagged a racist

---

135 'The most dishonest thing would be to say that I'm shocked', Waleed Aly, *The Sydney Morning Herald*, 16 March, 2019.

right-wing lunatic, Anning was known and respected for his staunch anti-Muslim, anti-multicultural stance in the very place Old Alex now found himself: Deep in the Heart of Middle Australia, the suburban heartlands far removed from the comfortable confirmational bias of the nation's capital.

The bureaucrats fed politicians anti-racist and pro-multicultral lines, their friends and media pundits applauded, everyone was happily settled in their own progressive suites. As good progressives, they all took it upon themselves to excise the voices they did not want to hear.

But there was another world; and another worldview.

Australians were an aspirational people and in a climate of stagnant wages and falling standards of living many working people were seeing their aspirations torn apart. Much of the population felt threatened. And this government had visited those threats upon them.

Mass immigration, supported by the Big End of Town and thereby conservative politicians, had made the rich very, very rich; while the average citizen was stuck with stagnant wages, falling living standards, escalating costs of living, massive congestion and infrastructure failure in the major cities and as much as anything a disintegrating national and community pride.

Social coherence collapsed in the coming years. And there would be no political leadership, least of all from the conservatives. There was an incoherence, a lazy, happenstance approach to governance and public policy, an indifference to consequence, which characterised the born-to-rule mob; and no amount of lipstick on a bull was going to change that fact.

Senator Anning, as vociferously reviled as he was by the punditry, represented that view. On parliamentary letterhead he released a statement declaring that the real cause of bloodshed on New Zealand streets was the immigration program which allowed Muslim fanatics to migrate to New Zealand in the first place.

Fraser Anning wrote: "Let us be clear, while Muslims may have been the victims today, usually they are the perpetrators. Worldwide, Muslims are killing people in the name of their faith on an industrial scale."

The entire religion of Islam is simply the violent ideology of a sixth-century despot masquerading as a religious leader, which justifies endless war against anyone who opposes it and calls for the murder of unbelievers and apostates.

The truth is that Islam is not like any other faith. It is the religious equivalent of fascism. And just because the followers of this savage belief were not the killers in this instance, does not make them blameless.

As we read in Matthew 26:52, "all they that take the sword shall perish by the sword", and those who follow a violent religion cannot be too surprised when someone takes them at their word and responds in kind.[136]

The pundits went ballistic, but Anning wasn't about to lie down.

"I wonder if there will be as much outrage from the left wing when the next Muslim terror attack occurs? Most likely silence and talk about lone wolf attacks, mental illness and no connection to Islam," Anning tweeted.

Prime Minister Morrison tweeted right back: "The remarks by Senator Fraser Anning blaming the murderous attacks by a violent, right-wing extremist in New Zealand on immigration are disgusting. Those views have no place in Australia, let alone the Australian Parliament."

Saying so doesn't make it so, and Anning's views were well-entrenched at Australia's Tables of Knowledge. The Australian Government mismanaged everything and had chronically mismanaged immigration, creating a brooding, disengaged or overtly hostile base population. No amount of taxpayer-funded propaganda or quashing of dissent was going to change that.

They all protested way too much.

Australia was not a democracy, it was a chronically mismanaged plutocracy. But if it had been a representative democracy, Anning would have been perfectly entitled to protest Australia's rapid demographic transformation and the destruction of Australia's traditional working-class cultures.

— broadcaster was an exemplar: the great unwashed could be forgiven for thinking that the Australian accent was being deliberately excised.

You didn't have to sit at too many Tables of Knowledge to hear almost identical views to Anning's.

Australia was not the world's most successful multicultural society, as the politicians claimed. No amount of lecturing and hectoring from the over-

---

136 Senator Fraser Anning, Official press release, 15 March, 2019. Also referenced in The Cut, Australian Senator Blames Mosque Massacre on Muslims, Claire Lampen, 15 March, 2019.

lords was going to change the mindset of the suburbs.

Saying so doesn't make it so and allegations over racism would now become a pivotal part of Scott Morrison's early months in office.

Waleed Aly pointed the bone straight at the prime minister's head.

> I know there are media reports going back eight years of a shadow cabinet meeting in which another senior politician suggested his party should use community concerns about Muslims in Australia failing to integrate as a political strategy. That person is now the most senior politician we have.
>
> So while I appreciate the words our leaders have said today, and in particular Scott Morrison's comments and his preparedness to call this terrorism and the strength of his comments more generally, I have something to ask. Don't change your tune now because the terrorism seems to be coming from a white suprem-acist. If you've been talking about being "tough on terrorism" for years in the communities that allegedly support it, show us how tough you are now.[137]

These days migrants had to pass a so-called "character test" to get into Australia.

Pity they didn't apply a character test for those entering the Australian Parliament.

The claims led to a furious response from Scott Morrison's office and shortly thereafter a tense on-air interview between Waleed Aly and the prime minister.

The original story, by Lenore Taylor in *The Sydney Morning Herald*, back in 2011, noted that some members of the then shadow cabinet were picking up strong anti-Muslim sentiment in their electorates but were concerned that running a campaign against Muslim immigration could be "miscon-strued" as racist.

Taylor claimed that the then Opposition immigration spokesman, Scott Morrison, urged the shadow cabinet to capitalise on the electorate's growing concerns about Muslim immigration and the inability of Muslim migrants to integrate.

---

137 'The most dishonest thing would be to say that I'm shocked', Waleed Aly, *The Sydney Morning Herald*, 16 March, 2019.

Mr Morrison's suggestion was made at a meeting in December at which shadow ministers were asked to bring three ideas for issues on which the Coalition should concentrate its political attack during this parliamentary term.

Sources say Mr Morrison told the shadow cabinet meeting on December 1 at the Ryde Civic Centre that the Coalition should ramp up its questioning of "multiculturalism" and appeal to deep voter concerns about Muslim immigration and "inability" to integrate.

Mr Morrison declined to comment on the discussion.[138]

Whatever was going on in the suburbs, racism was the crime de jour for the commentariat.

In pursuit of anti-racism these people turn race from one of the many important issues into something which is more important than anything else. At the very moment when the issue of race might at long last have been put to rest, they have decided once again to make it the most important issue of all.[139]

The Labor government of the time had a field day with the story. Along with others, then Prime Minister Julia Gillard called on Scott Morrison to be sacked, referring to "this grubby path":

We need the Leader of the Opposition Tony Abbott to confirm whether or not these reports are true, that his shadow cabinet sat around talking about making Australia's immigration policy one that discriminates on the basis of religion or race.[140]

Even a former Liberal prime minister, Malcolm Fraser, a wealthy and aloof man whose vision of a Big Australia came to curse the country, chimed in:

It's what I would have expected of Scott Morrison. I think that is politics at its very, very basis. I really do. I wouldn't tolerate such views. My government would not have tolerated such views.[141]

138 Morrison sees votes in anti-Muslim strategy, Lenore Taylor, *The Sydney Morning Herald*, 17 November, 2011.

139 *The Madness of Crowds*, Douglas Murray, Bloomsbury, 2019.

140 Morrison sees votes in anti-Muslim strategy, Lenore Taylor, *The Sydney Morning Herald*, 17 November, 2011.

141 Ibid.

Fast-forward eight years, no longer in opposition and having climbed the slippery pole ever higher, Morrison wasn't declining to comment this time around. Now prime minister, he described the allegations as a "disgraceful smear", claimed aspects of the story were defamatory, and categorically denied telling senior colleagues to exploit concerns about Islam for political gain, insisting he sought to confront Islamophobia.

To neutralise the story Morrison took the surprising step of appearing on The Project to be interviewed by Waleed Aly:

> I was the shadow immigration minister at the time and I was very concerned about these issues and the way people were feeling in the community. I was concerned that we needed to address them, which is what I have been doing inside and outside of the parliament for the last ten years of my life.
>
> I was acknowledging that there were these fears in the community and we had to address them, not exploit them.
>
> That has always been my view. I have championed that view, as a minister, as a member of parliament for my entire public life ...
>
> I have always been deeply concerned about attitudes towards people of Muslim faith in our community. And I have always acted consistently with that, in shadow cabinet, in the cabinet, by the policy decisions as ministers and in my own personal conduct.[142]

Lenore Taylor and other journalists stuck to their guns, saying the story on Morrison proposing to exploit fear of Muslim immigration was accurate and based on multiple sources.

Faced with the choice, who would you rather believe, a journalist or a politician? A moot point in the 21st century, but Old Alex knew which one he would opt for in this instance.

In the same interview Morrison repeatedly refused to answer questions on whether or not his party would preference One Nation in the coming election. The One Nation leader, Pauline Hanson, had previously described Islam as a "disease" Australia had to "vaccinate against".

---

142 Scott Morrison tells Waleed Aly he sought to lower fears on Islam, not exploit them, Amy Remeikis, *The Guardian,* 21 March, 2019.

In the end, it was the so-called Upper Middle Bogans — the working poor, the nation's tradies, the Quiet Australians, however you wanted to describe them — who won Morrison the May election. They lodged their protest votes against high immigration rates and the destruction of their culture with anti-multicultural and anti-Islamic groups like One Nation. Having seen zero benefit from mass immigration, it was this group, implacably opposed to being overrun by foreigners, who put the conservatives back in power.

In suburbia politics take on a different hue.

The nation's normally politically disengaged tradies, painters, plumbers, electricians, tilers, truck drivers, builders, carpenters and builder's labourers were drifting right, not left. The Liberals discovered this in time to target them, manipulate preference flows and save their own bacon.

The toffs won and the tradies celebrated. It was all a sleight of hand, an electoral connivance designed to conceal the truth.

Preferential voting was progressively introduced into the country in the early years of the 20th century to ensure political stability and the dominance of the two major political parties. All those protest votes flowed straight back to the conservatives; who, convinced they were about to lose the election, were prepared to face the odium of preferencing alleged racists in return for victory.

Whatever the truth of Scott Morrion's alleged willingness to exploit Islamophobia in the community, the simple fact was the conservative movement in which he had been such a prominent player, with no good news to present, had mercilessly beaten the terror drum. In other words, under electoral threat and fearing the loss of their gravy train, the Liberals were perfectly happy to promote fear, dislike, distrust and xenophobia.

There was no bottom to the well of hypocrisy the conservatives were willing to plumb in order to cling to power.

The population was being infantilised, and that in itself was enormously sad to see.

Morrison won the May election with an affable daggy dad routine and through an indefatigable campaign, appearing at endless barbeques and functions, kissing babies, grinning, gripping and smiling his way to victory in a policy-free zone. It takes a particularly evolved level of hypocrisy to parade around the nation pretending you are a man of the people and have their interests at heart when in reality you are a creature of the mining companies and the Very Big End of Town.

Morrison and his ilk thought of it as politics.

It was deceit.

"I have always believed in miracles," Morrison declared in the opening of his victory speech.

Quiet Australians, so-called, became an article of faith for a victorious Coalition government. Against the odds — surprising pundits, pollsters and themselves — the conservatives were returned despite a history of internal division, public scandal and without any record of good governance.

After his May victory Prime Minister Scott Morrison was fulsome in his appreciation of the "Quiet Australians".

"They have their dreams, they have their aspirations: to get a job, to get an apprenticeship, to start a business, to meet someone amazing, to start a family, to buy a home, to work hard and provide the best you can for your kids, to save for your retirement," Morrison told jubilant supporters at the Wentworth Hotel in Sydney, the Liberal's traditional site for their triumphal post-election parties.

"These are the Quiet Australians who have won a great victory tonight. Tonight is about every single Australian who depends on their government to put them first."

The Quiet Australians being so ardently embraced by the nation's conservatives, not in substance but in rhetoric, were in reality a rather rowdy lot. They drank, smoked, argued, swore constantly, swapped politically incorrect jokes and bizarre porn clips; and they partied at the weekends like there was no tomorrow, making a mockery of the nation's idiotic backward-looking drug laws.

They also got up and went to work, took good care of their children, were loyal to their friends and wanted nothing more than to get ahead in life. They were only regarded as "Quiet" by the hoi polloi because they were entirely invisible in — debate, even more unknown to the nation's academics than a remote Amazon tribe; not to mention invisible to the nation's bureaucrats and social engineers.

Within months, as the nation's working poor woke up to the fact that they had been conned by a daggy dad routine — which they should have

been able to see through, and a voting system they should have understood
— Morrison and his party were once again relegated to the inbox labelled
"Contemptible".

Only months into the government's term, those Quiet Australians were
once again disengaged and on the drift.

For one simple reason: nothing had changed. Put a smiley face atop a
cesspit and you're still sitting on a pile of crap.

Post his miraculous victory, Scott Morrison no doubt felt vindicated
in his internal belief that he was a master marketeer. But he forgot that
he owed his pre-politics career as an advertising executive almost entirely
to political patronage; including a stint as managing director of Tourism
Australia, a body formed by Liberal Party scion and former prime minister
John Howard.

Morrison may have been smart enough to win an election on the back of
the Quiet Australians, but he was not smart enough to deliver on his prom-
ises, or to improve their quality of life.

Shortly after his victory, Morrison warned his fellow cabinet members that
journalists were not their friends and to be careful in dealings with them;
making sure that even the youngest and most naive of media personnel were
offside. And shortly after that, the Australian Federal Police started raiding
journalists' homes and offices; thereby creating national and international
indignation.

Master marketeer, indeed!

Old Alex had been in Ho Chi Minh City, still Saigon to the locals, under
abusive and intrusive surveillance yet again; this time, he assumed, by
members of ASIS, the Australian Secret Intelligence Service, tasked with
operations overseas.

Entrapment may have been legal, but it was immoral. They were an
unimaginative lot. They would try and try and try. All around him he would
hear the phrase: "Major intelligence failure."

He heard too much. He was meant to be intimidated. And it was there,
to their great displeasure, as he came to know all too well, that he was asked
to write a piece on the arrest of journalists, which ended up being titled:
"Australia's Vicious Assault on Freedom of Speech".

He began:

World's most secretive democracy. Absurd overreach of power. Secretive, ruthless and vindictive executive government.

The scandal over the Australian Federal Police raids on journalists has deepened ever since their execution last week.

But the scandal has been years in the making.[143]

First to recount: News Corp political editor Annika Smethurst had her home raided by the AFP over a 2018 story about the possibility of the ultra-secretive Australian Signals Directorate gaining powers to monitor Australian citizens. The ABC had their offices raided over a 2017 story on the alleged problematic behaviour of some Australian SAS soldiers in Afghanistan. Both stories were based on leaked documents.

One could make any inference one likes about the timing of the raids, shortly after the conservatives surprised everyone by winning an election despite years of absolutely hopeless government. They were feeling invincible, again. Money and power does that.

Asked if he was bothered by the look of police raiding journalists' homes, Prime Minister Morrison replied: "It never troubles me that our laws are being upheld. Australia believes strongly in the freedom of the press, and we have clear rules and protections for freedom of the press.

"There are also clear rules protecting Australia's national security, and everybody should operate in accordance with all of those laws passed by our parliament. I support the powers that the agencies have under our laws."

The claim that Australia believed strongly in a free press was simply bullshit. Morrison had been a prominent member of the government that created a series of totalitarian laws targeting journalists, and never chose to speak out against any of them.

The claims of independence and political distance between the Federal Police and the government were not plausible. The military view permeating the agencies, that journalists were public enemy number one, served the government and — poorly. In terms of media management, the Australian Federal Police found itself seriously out of its depth.

Old Alex could hear, often enough, in the whispering hours, in the places in between, a roll call of old journalists he had worked for, now working for

---

143 Australia's Vicious Assault on Freedom of Speech, John Stapleton, Pearls and Irritations, 11 June, 2019.

the government. Some of them he had liked. One of them in particular was a poison dwarf, just the type the agencies would have loved. Most of them told the agencies they were nuts. Targeting journalists was just bringing them grief layered upon grief.

Old Alex had always assumed he was one of the early trials of the new legislation gifting the agencies so much power to survey journalists. But if he was a canary in the coalmine, this canary was furious and spitting poison in their faces.

If the AFP had been a private company with shareholders to answer to for the tsunami of hostile press, there would have been hell to pay

The commentary was absolutely scathing.

News Limited's Joe Hilderbrand wrote: "Of the approximately 250,000 or so words in the English language there is probably not one that adequately conveys how utterly stupid the raids are, nor how utterly certain they are to backfire against the very objective the security agencies are trying to achieve.

"The closest might be 'akrasia', which is the acting against one's self-interest through a weakness of will, and yet the idiots who ordered the raids obviously both summoned and enacted their will at an almost kamikaze level.

"On almost every level and in almost every way the security agencies behind the raids have spectacularly acted not just against their own interests but arguably against the national interest itself… Government security agencies have blatantly overextended their powers in an effort to punish a journalist for exposing an attempt by government security agencies to overextend their powers."[144]

Rupert Murdoch's News Limited was usually closely aligned with the government. But on this occasion they did not hold back, with multiple editorials, public statements and opinion pieces.

The government-owned ABC was equally scathing across numerous stories. Chairwoman Ita Buttrose said: "The raid, in its very public form and in the sweeping nature of the information sought, was clearly designed to intimidate."

Their senior political correspondent Laura Tingle wrote: "The raids, and any attempt at intimidation, is an outcome of a mindset, and a legal regime, that has snuck up on most Australians, largely under the cover of 'keeping

144 Joe Hildebrand doesn't oppose the AFP raids and instead, salutes them, Joe Hildebrand, News, 9 June, 2019.

us safe' from terrorism. The important point to note is that this regime doesn't just pose risks for journalists. It seeks to stamp out challenges to prevailing policy and authority, and it can be used against all Australians.

"Government ministers have been at pains to insist the raids had nothing to do with them. Except it has everything to do with them ... This is a mindset that is not set by national security interests but by a casual slide into abuse of power."[145]

The international press also got in the act.

The New York Times: "Even among its peers, Australia stands out. No other developed democracy holds as tight to its secrets, experts say, and the raids are just the latest example of how far the country's conservative government will go to scare officials and reporters into submission".

Introducing articles on the raids, Misha Ketchell, editor of the online academic journal *The Conversation*, wrote: "Very few Australians realise that free speech in this country isn't really a thing. It is not merely not protected — it's far worse than that. If you read any of the vast array of laws that protect government secrets, disclosure in — interest is discouraged, criminalised, punished, and deplored."

Denis Muller, senior research fellow at the University of Melbourne, said the raids were vindictive: "The politicians have constructed a repressive legal regime designed to protect the executive branch of government, impede accountability to — and exert a chilling effect on the press."

Jacqueline Maley of *The Sydney Morning Herald* concluded: "When an emboldened government that rejects transparency collides with the erosion of public confidence in democracy, freedoms will die. And they will die quietly, behind closed doors, without even enough information for a proper post-mortem."

More than the journalists they targeted, the AFP raids focused attention on themselves.

As a former editor of *The Canberra Times,* Jack Waterford, a longtime observer of the AFP, wrote: "It's a sorry story, and from a sorry and poorly led police force. It is an organisation given more and more resources and powers of surveillance and evidence-gathering, even as its outcomes, whether in drugs, in leak inquiries and other matters in — eye, are, in the modern managerialist phrase, less than optimal."

145 Australia's national security laws should protect the country, not its politicians in power, Laura Tingle, ABC, 24 June, 2019.

Going to war with the nation's journalists was one of the dumbest moves the government ever made. In the wake of the raids the industry set up the Journalism Is Not A Crime campaign which ran across mastheads and in news outlets around the country, featuring, in particular, images of heavily redacted copy and details of all the many things journalists could not write about.

Veteran journalist Kerry O'Brien addressed the industry's most prestigious annual event, the Walkley Awards, and declared: "This year, for a brief moment in the history of Australian journalism, every significant news organisation in this country put its competitive instincts and its differences to one side and united as one voice to stand against an unacceptable step down the road to authoritarianism.

"Authoritarianism unchecked can lead to fascism. For journalists to call out the powerful of any political colour for their abuses of power is not about ideology. It is simply journalists doing their job, practising their craft."

O'Brien also called for the government to bring WikiLeaks founder Julian Assange back to Australia. The Walkley Foundation had presented WikiLeaks, with Assange as its editor, an award for its outstanding contribution to journalism in 2011. The award's judges said Assange used new technology to "penetrate the inner workings of government to reveal an avalanche of inconvenient truths in a global publishing coup".

WikiLeaks in 2010 published classified military and diplomatic files about US bombing campaigns in Afghanistan and Iraq.

"As we sit here tonight, Julian Assange is mouldering in a British prison awaiting extradition to the United States, where he may pay for their severe embarrassment with a life in prison," O'Brien said. "This government could demonstrate its commitment to a free press by using its significant influence with its closest ally to gain his return to Australia."

If anything demonstrated the moral bankruptcy of the Australian Government, it was the case of Julian Assange, with professionals and citizens around the world labelling his treatment at the hands of the authorities as torture, amid reports that he was increasingly close to death.

Old Alex had long been obsessed by Assange, and in a piece titled "Australia's Genius Son" wrote:

> He is not only far more intelligent than any single one of the politicians criticising him, he's extremely idealistic, a dangerously

unpredictable trait thrown into the ruins of entirely compromised Western democracies.

You might well ask why one of the country's most famous citizens did not take refuge inside the Australian Embassy.

For the simple reason he was not safe there.

The weasel words of Australian politicians — up to their necks in a dangerous American alliance and with tens of billions of dollars of military contracts dancing in the background — began long ago.[146]

Morrison, as the current pimple on top of the churn, was particularly disgraceful in his repeated dismissal of the Assange case: "He won't be getting any special treatment from Australia, he'll be getting the same treatment that any other Australian would get. When Australians travel overseas and they find themselves in difficulties with the law, they face the judicial systems of those countries. It doesn't matter what particular crime it is that they're alleged to have committed, that's the way the system works."

In other words, screw you, the Australian Government is going to do what it has always done, kowtow to the Americans and lift not a finger to help one of its own citizens.

This was the same prime minister who had been happily photographed on stage during one of the US President Donald Trump's rallies, and giving the trademark thumbs-up; that is, abandoning any self respect or pretence Australia was a sovereign independent nation.

Old Alex was from an era of newspapers, hard-copy newspapers you held in your hands, and having worked on one editorial floor after another, he knew just how manipulated and arbitrary journalism was. Ridiculous perhaps, but the abandonment of any integrity in the heavily manipulated mainstream he took as a personal affront. Which was why the new technologies and the streaming of journalism outside the bounds of control of editors and corporate owners was so important.

Caitlin Johnstone, who described herself as a "rogue journalist", was one of those he followed closely. She wrote: "A society is only as free as its most troublesome political dissident, which today means that you are only as free

146 Australia's Genius Son, John Stapleton, *A Sense of Place Magazine*, 16 April, 2019.

as Julian Assange. As long as you live in a society which can give rise to a co-ordinated multi-governmental campaign to lock up a journalist for the rest of his life based on bogus charges because he exposed US war crimes, you are not free, and you should not agree to pretend that you are.

"While the millionaire pundits of the billionaire media continually assure us with their words that we live in a free society, the actions of the people who wield official and unofficial power over us tell us that we actually live in a society which tortures and imprisons dissident journalists for telling inconvenient truths.

"The persecution of Julian Assange tells us so much more about our society than the authorised narratives we're sold."[147]

This sorry saga also said a lot about Australia and the Prime Minister Scott Morrison. None of it complimentary. Throwing one of the country's own citizens to the wolves, a man of much higher intelligence and loftier motive, and one of the country's best known and most internationally significant exports, was typical Morrison, and typically disgraceful. This was a government run by God-botherers who hated journalists and hated free speech; for the last thing these people wanted was for their sins to be exposed.

Well, thank God for journalists!

One of Australia's most accomplished, Michael West, wrote in his piece "Election 2019: How good is plutocracy!": "The votes were still being counted, the final tally of seats in parliament was yet to be settled, when the inevitable list of demands from big business lobbed in the financial press.

"For ordinary Australians, there will be no 'working with the government'. The Great Unwashed have had their say, they can have their say again on a Saturday sometime in 2022. Between now and then, for every week in between, the business lobby will enjoy a privilege of access to those in government which is rarely available to the ordinary citizen."

As West recorded, the Very Big End of Town queued up to congratulate Morrison.

"A truly outstanding result," said Fortescue Metals chief executive Elizabeth Gaines.

"We look forward to working with the new government, declared Origin Energy chief Frank Calabria.

Australian multinational MYOB's boss Tim Reed expressed relief at the

147 A Society Is Only As Free As Its Most Troublesome Political Dissident, Caitlin Johnstone, author website, 2 September, 2019.

election result "given Labor made it clear they would push for minimum-wage rises".

Good Lord, we can't start paying the peasants a proper wage, where would it all end?

"Stop the regulation and stop the bullshit" came the call to arms from multimillionaire retailer Gerry Harvey.

The problem for the government was that these corporate giants might be immensely wealthy and they most certainly had the ear of this government, but their votes were few. That privilege lay with the hordes, the Great Unwashed.

The only thing that was keeping the conservatives from a complete collapse in public support was the dismal state of the Opposition.

Morrison won promising to "burn for the Australian people every single day".

Well, that didn't happen. It was straight back to business as usual. Nothing changed.

The government continued to hold the people in complete contempt. Electricity prices remained sky high, and owning a home stayed out of reach for many. Standards of living were static or falling. Wages flat. The country continued to fall down the international rankings in terms of educational outcomes.

Scandal after scandal continued to envelop the government.

Morrison, never known as an ideas man, increasingly presented as a fat self-satisfied seal frolicking in shallow seas. Meanwhile, almost every single economic indicator was trending down and many of his Quiet Australians feared a coming depression.

The array of rorts and government's connivance with the corporate realm was so encyclopaedic, it should have provided journalists with enough material to jampack their bulletins and fill their pages every single day of the week.

Soon enough it would; and angry, indignant tomes would decorate the bookshelves, demanding to know how such a blatant manipulation of democracy for financial gain could have been allowed to hold sway. A democracy in peril had been so heavily rorted it was a democracy no longer.

And everywhere you looked, another scam.

Time and again the government, particularly under Prime Minister

Malcolm Turnbull and then Treasurer Scott Morrison, resisted calls for a royal commission into the banking sector, until, faced with no choice, they proceeded in 2017. For a full year — were exposed to tales of plutocratic misconduct, from charging fees for non-existent services to turning a blind eye to the money laundering for drug syndicates and terrorism financing.

Finally, one Friday in early 2019, the final report was handed to the government. Normally such reports are made publicly available immediately. The government held on to the report until Monday.

And on the back of a softer than expected report, the share price of the major four banks surged $19 billion. On the face of it, this looked like the biggest market manipulation in the nation's history; and the Big End of Town made yet another fortune plundering the nation. Exactly who got advance copies of the report we may never know.

As critics suggested, there was now a need for a royal commission into the royal commission.

Then there was the privatising of visa processing, roundly criticised because it was being snaffled up by a close mate of both Malcolm Turnbull and Scott Morrison.

> Despite the myriad failures of privatisation, not least the disastrous sale of the nation's energy networks, which has delivered dazzling profits to foreign multinationals at the expense of every citizen in this country, the government has pledged to auction yet another essential service, visa processing. Yet, the privatisation of visas has the weight of money behind it, and a veritable gravy train of consultants and business interests to give it momentum. The value of the contract is commonly tipped as $1 billion with some estimates as high $3 billion.[148]

Sometimes a person's inner bile is writ large across their visage; so poisonous, so toxic, so deep has their inner corruption become, it suppurates out through their skin, the boils visible for all to see.

So it was with this government.

These people were prepared to sacrifice the health of Australia's inland river system on the pyre of their own greed.

> They blame climate change. They blame the drought. They blame everyone and everything but themselves.

---

148 Mate Versus Mate: Inside ScoMo's billion-dollar visa privatisation, Michael Sainsbury and Michael West, Michael West Media, 14 August, 2019.

> The stench of millions of dead fish, the rotting corpses of kanga-roos and sheep, the missing birdlife, the farmers who can no longer farm, devastated indigenous peoples, an ancient, dese-crated landscape, internationally significant wetlands nothing but dust bowls, all of this and more is happening across Central Australia — right now.
>
> Decades of chronic government mismanagement and corpo-rate greed have turned Australia's most significant and extensive river system, the Murray-Darling, into a disaster of national and international significance.[149]

Turning public assets into private gain had reached new heights in Australia. The conservative government had a sour reputation as a pack of corporate crooks who had misused their political positions to plunder — purse.

Environmental scientists had been warning for decades that the fragile semi-arid lands of Central Australia were unsuited for cotton farming. And now it was writ large. Millions of dead fish rotted in toxic algal blooms in a river system destroyed by the corporate greed of cotton farmers and their mates in government.

As senior editor at *The Canberra Times* Jack Waterford put it, the dead and stinking fish were "a floating monument to greed, corruption, malad-ministration and disastrous environmental management."

The opportunists who gifted water rights to irrigators were despised up and down the entire river system. Bureaucratic empires have been built around the notion of sensitive environmental and water management of the inland river system. But it was Big Money — the cotton and irrigation industries — which won the day.

As a young, hyper-restless reporter with zero inclination to stay in the office, Old Alex had flown all over the inland writing stories about the remarkably beautiful ephemeral lakes and intermittent river systems of Australia's inland.

Now they were a travesty.

Owner of Tolarno, Rob McBride, out near Broken Hill, a town Old Alex had visited many times, told him on the day of yet another fish kill: "This

---

149 The Ecological and Environmental Catastrophe Visited Upon Australia's Inland River System, John Stapleton, *A Sense of Place Magazine*, 29 January, 2019.

is nothing to do with drought. This is government policy, both state and federal. It has everything to do with greed, corruption and money. This is a cataclysmic destruction of a river system.

"Bureaucrats and politicians have done everything they could to undermine any integrity in the system. They should be held accountable for the destruction."

McBride said — had already funded schemes, to the tune of $8 billion, to put water back in the river system through buybacks and government incentives. "Where is the water? Where is the audit of where the money went? The water went straight to cotton irrigators, absolutely.

"People should go to jail over this. Absolutely. People the world over need to understand that this has nothing to do with nature. These fish are dying in their millions because the system has been destroyed. It has nothing to do with nature and everything to do with money."[150]

There may have been an encyclopaedic array of scandals. But sometimes it's the little things that irritate the most.

As a Pentecostal, Scott Morrison was a believer in what is known as prosperity theology, the idea that God materially rewards the righteous. Clearly, with shuttered shops from one end of the country to the other, with a devastated underclass racked by methamphetamines and with a tanking economy, Australians were getting what they deserved. While the wealth of the oligarchs ballooned.

In 2019 the prime minister announced grants to upgrade security at places of worship. His own church, Horizon, was awarded $110,000 from the Safer Communities Fund, which was intended to help "protect children who are at risk of attack, harassment or violence stemming from racial or religious intolerance".

Horizon Church's grant reportedly went towards the installation of eighteen fixed security cameras, thirteen security lights, video intercoms to three designated areas, two security and alarm systems, and the employment of a security guard at the church.

Horizon is known as a wealthy church. The building alone had been valued at $13 million; with reports of millions a year in donations.

But even here: the hand in the till.

That was what stuck in the craw of those who drank at the Lakeview.

---

150 Ibid.

Australia was riddled by oversized bureaucracies, excessive regulation, insane levels of taxation and absurd costs of living.

Everyone was running to stand still.

Faith in democracy had hit catastrophic lows. Workers rightly perceived that multiple insanities were destroying their country. While their taxes were being plundered to pay for security at the prime minister's church. While their own church, the beer garden at the back of the Lakeview, looked increasingly derelict.

Once packed to the rafters, with queues ten-deep at the bar on the weekends, now only a few determined old soldiers remained; reminiscing about the days of old, when the place rocked.

Smoke from that summer's bushfires wreathed through the valleys, blurred the escarpment and turned the sun an eerie, compelling red.

For Old Alex, everything was on the shift. They were finished here now, the Watchers on the Watch. They had been betrayed. They had lost their jobs and their positions, even the volunteers, and made to look like fools. Vicious, nasty, malicious, dumb as dog shit fools.

He gathered his robes around him. He walked again.

"What are you?" they demanded to know. "What are you?"

Or that heavily inflected demand: "Who are you?"

"Nobody. Just another person you ripped off."

Now the whole country had been ripped off by the multimillionaire crooks aka the oligarchs who plundered the country.

And guess who was sailing free?

While they were trapped in their own lies.

It was as if the glue of everything had come unstuck.

At the Lakeview, "Gay Phil" had been diagnosed with terminal cancer; and was now being treated with great respect.

Local legend Hammer passed away. "I thought he had given up drinking," Old Alex said.

"Too late," came the response.

In between waxing lyrical about the foibles of Thai prostitutes and the wonders of Pattaya's many bars, Kev the concrete driver would declaim the state of the country: "It's like a prison yard. Nothing's happening. There's no life. Everybody's been crushed. Crushed. Nobody's got any money anymore. Thirty years ago if you worked hard you were wealthy. Well, you weren't doing too badly. Now everybody's working hard, and nobody's got any money. Look at this bloody pub. There's nobody here."

Tony and Kylie, who worked down at the hardware store Bunnings, were pleased as punch their eldest daughter had left school, "she couldn't stand the bullshit", and was working at Woolworths as a "checkout chick".

Gaz, after a brief respite following his accident, was back drinking, laughing merrily at the foibles of his friends.

Harry the baker, who had once drunk more than 200 cans of beer a week on top of his twice daily sessions at "church", was "off the piss", as the Australian expression went, drinking orange juice and appeared, essentially, no different than he always had, friendly, determined, decent, up for a chat.

"Swampie", as he was so appropriately called, a former bikie and a member of Oak Flats royalty, was back for a brief stint from his FIFO, Fly In Fly Out work in the Northern Territory.

"Plunder the poor, give to the rich," Old Alex repeated the old line when the conversation drifted to the government of the day.

"Why haven't they risen up?" Swampie asked, gesturing towards the lines of suburban houses surrounding them. "Why hasn't there been a revolution already?"

Alex shrugged: "There will be. Millions more unemployed in a chronically mismanaged economy, that will do it. You can only treat people like dirt for so long. You can only lie to — for so long."

All around where he was staying the once bucolic hills and pastures of a dairy farm were being scraped for a $700 million freeway. Wind whipped the topsoil into mini dust storms while thousands of houses sprung up in the surrounding suburbs, seemingly overnight.

"Where are these people going to find work?" Alex asked, only to be met with a shrug.

Not just wreathed in scandal, Morrison and his government would soon be wreathed in flames. Australia was in drought. While they were actually relatively few in number, farmers and pastoralists held a special place in the history and psyche of Australia as pivotal to the tough-edged and phlegmatic character of its people.

Morrison shamelessly milked this sentimentality throughout the 2019 election and subsequently, flying in and out of various rural settings for photo opportunities, announcing the expansion of this or that government program. Not unsurprisingly, country people were reluctant to sign up to a bureaucratic web of deceit, or to become dependent on handouts.

As some critics pointed out, making proud independent people with often enough millions in assets jump through bureaucratic hoops in order to get a few thousand bucks was never going to wash. Not to mention it was this government which had strangled rural Australia, with excessive taxation, crippling environmental legislation, sky-high fuel costs, and the sale of vast tracts of land to foreign interests, meaning the locals were simply outpriced.

When there was a genuine need, millions of hectares were going up in flames, when hundreds of people lost their homes and thousands of volunteer fighters gave their time, money and sweat, Morrison was missing in action.

Fathers with young children died while the prime minister drank cocktails in Hawaii.

It was an exquisite wrinkle in time, and exposed all the worst characteristics of the plutocrats who had seized control of the government.

For days no one knew where Morrison was, and reports suggested his idiot media managers had requested no one report he was on holiday while the country burned. Even better, at the same time he let himself be photographed sitting around a Waikiki resort drinking cocktails, while back home exhausted volunteer firefighters were literally dying on the frontline in one of the worst bushfire seasons the country had ever seen.

Geoffrey Keaton, 32, and Andrew O'Dwyer, 36, died in the Green Wattle Creek fire south-west of Sydney when a falling tree caused their fire truck to roll. The two men became fathers days apart in May 2018, to a son, Harvey, a daughter, Charlotte, respectively.

Their crewmates in the Horsley Park Rural Fire Brigade were back fighting fires the following day. The 68-strong brigade had three crews fighting fires, their trucks emblazoned with "In memory of Geoff Keaton" and "In memory of Andrew O'Dwyer" on their fronts.

The Facebook pages of both men record them as very much traditional Australian men, proudly in love with their wives and children. Full of the joy of life. Lots of pictures of their kids. Geoffrey Keaton's page records his affection for the football team the Penrith Panthers. Andrew O'Dwyer records under Life Events: Bought a house 2013.

They were exactly the sort of people Morrison, with his daggy dad routine, had suckered into voting for him, believing he would help improve the lives of their families.

Ultimately the fires burnt through more than eighteen million square hectares and destroyed more than 5,900 buildings, including 2,779 homes. Thirty four people were killed.

The cover up of the Prime Minister's Hawaiian holiday, as so often with public scandals, was even better than the original.

Scott Morrison's attempts to say Australians would understand that he wanted to keep a promise to his children that they would have another holiday in Hawaii was met with widespread derision.

They were kids. They could do without a $3000-a-night Waikiki holiday. Or whatever the cost was this time around. Most other Australian children somehow managed to bravely muddle through without expensive overseas resorts.

In a series of interviews, Morrison compared himself to a plumber forced to choose between a Friday afternoon job or seeing his family. As if this multimillionaire, with his smooth hands and pudgy physique, could possibly know what it was like to be a plumber in the devastated economy he had gifted the nation.

The democratic contract was broken; Scott Morrison and his predecessors had been the perpetrators of the crime.

The media hunts in packs. And every journalist in the country now had him in their sights. Shameless as these people were, politics would prove just as big a public humiliation for Morrison as it had for his predecessor and mate, Malcolm Turnbull. And his predecessor in turn, Tony Abbott. The worst Australia's political class had to offer. The worst of the worst.

— and the media were "woke", as the expression of the moment went, and no amount of "nothing to see here" shuffle could save this hapless brand of conservatism.

Now the talk was not of recession but depression, a belated acceptance of a reality already gripping many parts of Australia.

The headlines told it all: "Firefighter killed in rollover identified as Samuel McPaul" — "Mr McPaul leaves behind his wife Megan, who is pregnant with the couple's first child."

"Fire warning: Bushfire mushroom clouds", "Bushfires leave up to 4000 people sheltering on Victoria beach as flames close in", "Firestorm bears down on holiday towns", "Multiple properties lost", "Catastrophic fire conditions across the nation as 'extreme' heatwave hits".

"Chinese company approved to run water-mining operation in drought-stricken Queensland."

"Australia's vast household debt a giant economic millstone", "The economic outlook for Australia has tanked", "International Monetary Fund has sharply downgraded forecasts for the Australian economy", "Australian economy to limp along as consumers struggle".

"Our plunging economy", "How the Government protects its donors and tax dodgers", "Government caves to a few 'big interests'."

"Morrison government paid empathy consultant $190,000."

"Prime Minister Scott Morrison scored a free upgrade worth thousands of dollars at Fijian resort to secure a $3000-a-night luxury bure with a private beach and a personal butler."

"Mining giant given millions in grant by Coalition from fund for Indigenous disadvantage."

As for Alex's own story, trapped as he sometimes felt in one mortal frame after another, it was about to take a giant, joyful leap.

But for those both brief and interminable months, caught in the suburbs where he had never wanted to be, unable to tell friend from foe, depressed by the state of the country and damaged by the harassment of the so-called "national security" agencies, he was forced to summon help from that far-off place, from those who had conquered quantum entanglement long ago.

Old Alex kept asking for that idol of his youth Bertrand Russell, for high intellect and compassionate insight, and instead got the curmudgeonly Eric Blair, aka George Orwell, a man who wrote beautifully about the downtrodden and the working poor but who in truth was not of them.

A prophet who did not live to see his most famous book, *Nineteen Eighty-Four*, have the profound impact that it did, but whose prophecies turned out to be uncannily true. And who in this era, almost seventy years after his death from tuberculosis, was quoted more than any living writer.

Old Alex kept asking for an ability to see the flows of history, and instead got drunken poets — Dylan Thomas, Malcolm Lowry, Henry Lawson — so many thousands of others who had died their own remote, unkind deaths; alcoholics, street junkies, the most isolated and denigrated of mankind. And especially here, in this cold, windy place, the spirits whose names he could not decipher, the ancestors of this place, the wise and courageous, noble and poor, those who had loved and been loved, warriors who had seen their own tribes conquered and who grieved to this very day.

Old Alex left that jinn-soaked place, with its harsh winters and the sad whispering of its ancients, the trees fringing the lake, the working man's cottages, all the stories of the sometimes funny-as, inevitably drunken exploits of its denizens. He left the uber-surveillance perpetrated by the most patently corrupt and appallingly mismanaged government in the nation's history. And flew free.

"Take it as a badge of honour they even noticed you," he was advised. "Do what I told you to do a long time ago: laugh at them. You are one. They are thousands. And you know what you've got on your side that they do not? Truth."

Prophecies are warnings; frightening moments of clairvoyance. The vision-soaked dreams of the strange and the restless, the food riots of the future, desert gulags, soldiers in black riot gear manning every street corner, sad, derelict cities, the gleaming edifices which rose and fell far out to sea, they were already twisting into the present.

His prophecies were unlikely to be heeded; for greed is blind. Even as those borne-aloft intelligences he was gifted to see circled in otherworldly anger, attempting to change the course of nations and the course of history, they knew that humans were fatally flawed. Most particularly in this place, so far from the centre of things; where the worst of the worst prayed for a righteous nation in flights of delusion as they rigged a government replete with malevolent spirits and staffed with those of unparalleled greed and self-aggrandisement, characterised from top to bottom by malfeasance and incompetence, by a grand ignorance of the people they purported to represent and who, instead, they robbed.

Historians would look back and wonder how it was that a country's ruling elites could so savagely betray, so audaciously rob, their fellow countrymen. How integrity and decency were so easily abandoned. How they could with such blundering idiocy and staggering incompetence destroy the very place which had made them rich.

Why the population did not rise up even quicker than they did.

How a once optimistic country lost its way.

The evil that men do lives after them.

You did not need the gift of prophecy to know that future historians would view the Abbott—Turnbull—Morrison era as the worst period of governance in Australia's history, a time when a terrible brutality was born.

ACKNOWLEDGEMENTS

I would like to thank Simon Parker for his hospitality at Lightning Ridge, once again Tony Reale, the owner Shellharbour's Village Fix Cafe, for his truly splendid coffee which saw me through another final draft, Stuart Kay for the refuge of his shed, Johnny Miller for his insights into the Oak Flats milieu, "Gay Phil" for his kindness, Kev Ovy for his company and Gaz for his humour.

Shellharbour naturopath Bill Oliver is owed a special thanks.

I would also like to thank Roger Henning of Homeland Security Australia for his jocular insights into the clashes between traditional journalism, national security, public policy and government operatives.

And Anthony Corlisatra aka Glen aka Harry aka Tony, whoever you really were. You were an enormous help in understanding a shadow world and I wish you all the best for the future.

In particular I would like to thank my children Samuel and Henrietta, who survived their childhoods to become such wonderful adults and have made me so very proud.

Others must necessarily remain anonymous.

ABOUT THE AUTHOR

The first money Australian journalist John Stapleton (born 21 June, 1952) ever made out of writing was in 1974 when he was co-winner of a short story competition held by what was then Australia's leading cultural celebration, the Adelaide Arts Festival.

He graduated from Macquarie University in 1975 with a double major in philosophy and anthropology and did post-graduate work with the Sociology Department at Flinders University.

As a freelance journalist in the 1970s and 1980s, while alternating between living in Sydney and London, his articles and fiction appeared in a wide range of magazines, newspapers and anthologies, including the once celebrated now defunct *Bulletin Magazine* and leading newspaper *The Australian Financial Review*.

John Stapleton worked on the then esteemed newspaper *The Sydney Morning Herald* as a staff news reporter between 1986 and 1994. The paper was listed as one of the Top 20 newspapers in the world.

He then worked for the national newspaper *The Australian* from 1994 to 2009.

His books include: *Thailand: Deadly Destination, Terror in Australia: Workers' Paradise Lost, Chaos at the Crossroads: Family Law Reform in Australia, Hunting the Famous, The Final Days of Alastair Nicholson: Chief Justice Family Court of Australia* and *Hideout in the Apocalypse*.

After leaving *The Australian* John Stapleton established the niche publishing company A Sense of Place Publishing. He is currently the editor of *A Sense of Place Magazine*.